T0320950

CAPITALIST NETWORKS AND SOCIAL POWER
IN AUSTRALIA AND NEW ZEALAND

Corporate Social Responsibility Series

Series Editor:
Professor David Crowther, London Metropolitan University, UK

The series aims to provide high quality research books on all aspects of corporate social responsibility including: business ethics, corporate governance and accountability, globalization, civil protests, regulation, responsible marketing and social reporting.

The series is interdisciplinary in scope and global in application and is an essential forum for everyone with an interest in this area.

Also in the series

Making Ecopreneurs:
Developing Sustainable Entrepeneurship
Edited by Michael Schaper
0 7546 4491 X

Corporate Social Responsibility in the Mining Industries
Natalia Yakovleva
ISBN 0 7546 4268 2

Ethical Boundaries of Capitalism
Edited by Daniel Daianu and Radu Vranceanu
ISBN 0 7546 4395 6

Human Values in Management
Ananda Das Gupta
ISBN 0 7546 4275 5

Nonprofit Trusteeship in Different Contexts
Rikki Abzug and Jeffrey S. Simonoff
ISBN 0 7546 3016 1

Capitalist Networks
and Social Power in
Australia and New Zealand

GEORGINA MURRAY
School of Arts, Media and Culture, Griffith University, Brisbane, Australia

ASHGATE

Published by
Ashgate Publishing Limited
Gower House
Croft Road
Aldershot
Hampshire GU11 3HR
England

Ashgate Publishing Company
Suite 420
101 Cherry Street
Burlington, VT 05401-4405
USA

Ashgate website: http://www.ashgate.com

British Library Cataloguing in Publication Data
Murray, Georgina
    Capitalist networks and social power in Australia and New
    Zealand
    1.Elite (Social sciences) - Australia 2.Elite (Social
    sciences) - New Zealand 3.Power (Social sciences) -
    Australia 4.Power (Social sciences) - New Zealand
    5.Australia - Politics and government - 21st century
    6.Australia - Social conditions - Social conditions - 21st century 7.New
    Zealand - Politics and government - 21st century 8.New
    Zealand - Social conditions - 21st century
    I.Title
    305.5'234'0993

Library of Congress Cataloging-in-Publication Data
Murray, Georgina.
    Capitalist networks and social power in Australia and New Zealand / by Georgina
Murray.
        p. cm. -- (Corporate social responsibility series)
    Includes bibliographical references and index.
    ISBN-13: 978-0-7546-4708-9
    ISBN-10: 0-7546-4708-0
 1. Elite (Social sciences)--Australia. 2. Elite (Social sciences)--New Zealand. 3.
Executives--Australia. 4. Executives--New Zealand. 5. Power (Social sciences)--
Australia. 6. Power (Social sciences)--New Zealand. 7. Capitalism--Australia. 8.
Capitalism--New Zealand. I. Title.

    HN850.Z9E45 2006
    306.3'420993--dc22

                                                                    2006020639

ISBN-10: 0 7546 4708 0
ISBN-13: 978 0 7546 4708 9

Printed and bound in Great Britain by Antony Rowe Ltd, Chippenham, Wiltshire.

Contents

Figures and Tables

Acknowledgements

I would like to thank those who have read and commented on this work, or parts of this work, in its various incarnations. These include David Peetz, Christine Devine, Professor Frank Stilwell, Heather Peetz, Cecily Baker and Raymond Evans. You all made a great contribution. All of you helped to make it a much better piece of work than it would have been. Also, thanks go to those I worked with in Norway who were a constant source of ideas and stimulation: Sigmund Grønmo, John Scott and Ole Johnny Olsen. I would also like to thank the Centre for Work, Leisure and Community Research for its financial support, and in particular Elizabeth Ellis, Kay Bernicke and Professor Peter Brown. Others who have also helped and supported the book along the way are Meindert Fennema, Sue Jarvis, Beverley Jeppesen, Charles Crothers and Paul Turnbull. My thanks for inspirational teaching on this topic go to both David Bedggood and to James Devine. Thanks, too, for the love and friendship I received throughout the writing from Emma Left-Weatherley, Alaina Weatherley, Charlotte Weatherley, Lily Weatherley, Freya Weatherley, Scott Weatherley, Anna Haebich, Calum Hyslop, Vigdis Bjørkness, Nick Brander Peetz and most of all from David, whose love made 'focus' a real possibility.

Abbreviations

ABA	Australian Bankers Association
ABS	Australian Bureau of Statistics
AIM	Australian Institute of Management
ACC	Accident Compensation Corporation [NZ]
ACCC	Australian Competition and Consumer Commission
ACT	Australian Capital Territory
ACTU	Australian Council of Trade Unions
AICD	Australian Institute of Company Directors
AO	Officer of the Order of Australia
BCA	Business Council of Australia
CEDA	Committee for Economic Development of Australia
CEO	Chief Executive Officer
CEW	Chief Executive Women's network
CIS	Centre for Independent Studies
CTU	Council of Trade Unions
DPB	Domestic Purposes Benefit [NZ]
EAI	East Asian Institute
IPA	The Institute for Public Affairs
MD	Managing Director
MNC	Multi-national Corporation (home based)
MPS	Mont Pelerin Society
NE	Non Executive Director
NGO	Non-Government Organisation
NSW	New South Wales, an Australian State
NZBR	New Zealand Business Roundtable
OBE	Officer of the Order of the British Empire
OECD	Organisation for Economic Cooperation & Development
SA	South Australia
Tas.	Tasmania, formerly Van Dieman's Land, an Australian state
TI	Tasman Institute
TNC	Trans National Company (stateless)
UAP	United Australia Party
Vic.	Victoria, an Australian state
WA	Western Australia
WEF	World Economic Forum

For David, a brave and principled man.

Chapter 1

What Ruling Class?

Being rich isn't what it used to be. Once upon a time there was a very wealthy establishment with a tightly knit network that ruled Australia and New Zealand with help from the mother country. But those days of wealth and power are gone — anyone can become rich if they try hard enough or have the right breaks. No one feels any hostility towards the rich because everyone knows that they can be there too. There are no old networks of power to help them. These are gone. The new elite consist of left-leaning intellectuals and their sympathisers in the media, particularly the Australian ABC or the New Zealand NZBC. Or so we are led to believe.

Tony Abbott, an Australian Liberal government minister, encapsulated this perspective when he argued on the ABC that:

> The problem is that too many people in the commanding intellectual heights of our society have in recent times thought that because they were better educated and arguably better informed than the general public that they were therefore better people, and when it comes to basic value judgments there's no reason why a professor is going to be intrinsically better than a shopkeeper and I think that is the mistake that the 'elites' in inverted commas have tended to make.[1]

This book challenges this perspective. It also challenges the commonly expressed thought articulated by the former Liberal Premier of New South Wales, Robin William Askin (1965–1974), that 'we have no poor people ... nor any very rich people. Ours is a classless society'.[2] The intention is to find evidence of ruling classes in Australia and New Zealand based on wealth and power, not on political correctness. This book is based on interviews, analysis of annual company reports, and archival public records from primary and secondary sources. We will look at a picture drawn from multiple data sources and at changing networks in Australia and New Zealand from their time as colonies to their present fully integrated status as highly competitive capitalist economies operating within a global arena. We shall see a very exotic history of socially mobile networks, such as one in which one-third of the earliest wealthy in Australia were ex-convicts who had been transported to the new colony under the foulest imaginable conditions. We will form an impression of their world and contrast it with that of the present networks of wealth and power to see their unique but globally integrated interconnections within the New Zealand and Australian nation states.

We all want to know who really holds power over us. A 2004 Australian Electoral Study shows that Australians have a healthy scepticism about what we (the majority) have.[3] Seventy-two per cent of interviewees agreed 'Big business in this country has too much power' and 51 per cent thought 'income and wealth should be redistributed toward ordinary people'.[4]

This scepticism is notable since this country has what has been described as the most concentrated ownership of print media in the western world, where 'media monopolies are allowed to destroy diversity of opinion in a free society'.[5] This book aims to air information that seldom sees printed form, not only because there is no competition in a media dominated by too few players[6], but also because people need to be alerted to the scope of the who-rules-us jigsaw.[7]

In this introduction I acknowledge a rich overseas literature on the nature of the ruling class but I have also tried, where possible, to use Australian and New Zealand writers to describe what is happening within their nation states. For I feel that, like the Aboriginal dot painters, their thinking is often original, sometimes gifted and nearly always insightful to the nuances of their own landscape. This book looks at some of these ideas, interspersed with the classics, on who is, and what constitutes, the Australian and New Zealand ruling class. We will treat their ideas as competing, controversial and contested, to see whether it is possible to say, as a leading British academic says about the British, that 'we are ruled by a capitalist class whose economic dominance is sustained by the operations of the state and whose members are disproportionately represented in the power elite which rules the state apparatus'.[8]

The debates immediately following form the basis for the rest of the book, which will look at the evidence to support or refute ideas about class, networks and the reproduction of power.

What are Top Capitalist Networks?

There are lively debates about what constitutes the top capitalist networks. These centre on the nature of the ruling class or what others may call an 'over class'[9] comprising those who hold the greatest economic assets and subsequently political, cultural and social power in society. The problem is to understand how a few people can gain control of power within the Australian or New Zealand nation. However, we can extrapolate to some degree for any capitalist society. How is this so? It is because capitalism has some shared properties and can be described as a universal 'economic system of production, distribution and exchange based on economic power to distribute the wealth generated by productive labour'.[10] The modern state within which capitalism necessarily operates is one in which people's lives are organised around private ownership of property and where capital, as money or credit, is used to purchase goods or services. The capitalist classes are the owners of the marketised workplaces most of us work in. They control the amount of money we earn and the conditions in which we earn it, and this is central to their power and makes them the ruling class. This ruling class core is made up of a number of competing fractions that exploit workers' labour to make profit. This is exploitation because bosses will only ever pay workers the least possible they can to make them work, irrespective of the market value of what the worker creates. This simple outline introduces the complex argument of Karl Marx (1818–1883) who identifies the ruling class as the 'owners of capital and landowners, whose respective sources of income are profit and ground rent'.[11]

Power Comes from Capital

What Marx said about capitalism forms the basis of most debate on the nature of class, work and exploitation and subsequently how the ruling class organises. His words still offend the elites, as reported by Wheen in the *Observer*:

> A penniless asylum seeker in London was vilified across two pages of the *Daily Mail* last week. No surprises there perhaps except that the villain in question has been dead since 1883. 'Marx the Monster' was the *Mail*'s furious reaction to the news that thousands of Radio 4 listeners had chosen Marx as their favorite thinker'.[12]

Marx's version of capitalism is that capital starts from a process of expansion based on the circuit of production.[13] Someone with money (the boss) inherits, amasses and/or borrows money from the banks to buy commodities (raw material for production). In the subsequent circuit of production these commodities provide the raw material (like the bolt of cotton cloth to make a suit). Value is added to the commodity (the raw cotton is made into the suit) through the mix of labour power (that is, a person who sews the cloth) and use of machinery (in this case, a sewing machine). This value-added commodity (the suit) is sold, if possible, in the market. The seller (the factory owner or boss) of the product (the suit) must sell the product. If they encounter difficulty realising their money, they must undercut other competitive sellers or find a new market to sell their commodity at a profit. The profits from the sale of the commodity then go back into production; some will go into taxes to the state, or to their personal consumption, but most of the money for a competitive capitalist will go back into the circuit to invest in better machinery or expand production. The circuit is shown in Figure 1.1.

From this single circuit of capital we can extrapolate to look at single capitalists in one factory or at the dynamics underlying capitalist production within a community, town or country and even globally. We can divide capitalists operating within the circuit into fractions of capital — industrialists, pastoralists, financiers, wholesalers, retailers — emerging at different times in the circuit but also coming to prominence at different periods within business cycles. Marx's argument is that the circuit of production is the essence of capitalism and becomes the motivational force of globalisation. Capital only invests where it finds profits — it has no social, national or political commitment other than to profit.

Figure 1.1: Marx's Circuit of Capitalist Production

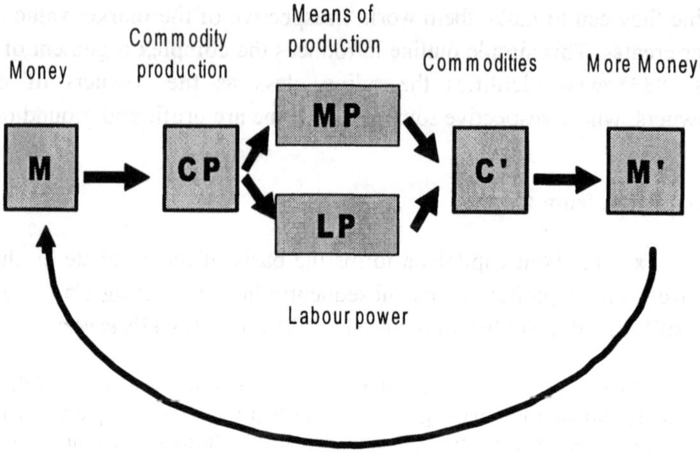

This is how one of the top 30 Australian directors describes the role of capital and the freedom of capitalists to invest where they like:

> Most governments that I have spoken to have no understanding of private capitalism. Now I have heard people say that you should feel privileged to be committed to invest in Australia. Really! The whole world is our oyster so what is so special about here? New Zealand is the same! Their attitude is we are permitting you to invest. So what! The whole world is on offer to us so what is so good about you? They think that they are the pearls in the oyster of the world. Australians in Canberra are remote from the real world. They don't understand why you invest. It isn't something that they have ever been involved in and they say, 'We have improved the conditions — so now you do your bit'. What do they mean — my turn? We don't have turns; we put our money out when we think that it's good for us. That's all we do. We don't look for any other reason — it's not a turn. Not when …Keating or Howard or other politicians say we have made all the conditions right, now it's up to you to go and do it, unless we can see the market we are not going to invest.[14]

Class relations emerge from Marx's simple equation (Figure 1.1) whereby one section of the population owns the means of production — the mines, the factories, the shops, the warehouses, the ships, the railways. On the other side are those men and women who own only their labour power that they sell for the highest wage. Exploitation exists because workers create objects for sale from which they will get back only the smallest value possible that the capitalist can get away with giving them. No matter what that profit is to the capitalist, workers will be paid only the least possible necessary to reproduce themselves and their families. That amount necessary for their reproduction is determined by the cost of consumer commodities, the likelihood that the worker will be lost to a higher wage-offering competitor and the bargaining power of workers, which is significantly enhanced if they form a collective (such as a union) and can demand living wages and higher working standards, pay and conditions.

Max Weber thought Karl Marx's model too economically determined. Whereas for Marx the starting point for understanding experience is the real world, Weber favoured an idealist position that reality was created by ideas.[15] Although he agreed that economic factors played a key role in our society, he went on to stress the power that ideas and influence had in creating a person's culture and life chances generally. Weber believed a multiplicity of factors affected an individual's class position. These concerned their relationship to the market (as an owner, rentier, employee etc), their access to educational opportunity and their different rewards associated with prestige and honour. But the essential difference between Marx's and Weber's models of class is that Weber's model operates primarily at the levels of distribution and exchange, whereas Marx's is located in production and its consequent exploitation.

This theory of exploitation makes Marx a particularly attractive theorist to a writer such as Erik Olin Wright, who maintains:

> Exploitation [is] a central, analytically powerful concept, both normatively and sociologically. Normatively, it matters not simply that some people have more assets than others, but that they use those assets to take advantage of vulnerability of others. Exploitation is the way we talk about this specific way of using ones resources. Sociologically, exploitation describes a particularly explosive form of interdependency between people, an interdependency in which one group (exploiters) simultaneously depend upon another (the exploited) for their own material well-being and impose harms on the well-being of the group on whom they depend. This defines a distinctive kind of social relation, which is not captured just by talking about unequal endowments of assets.[16]

This dichotomy of exploiter and exploited is challenged by those who argue that these categories are no longer relevant on the basis that current company share ownership is much more diverse than it was in Marx's day.

What is the Company?

Butterworths states that an Australian listed company is defined in more than one section of the *Corporations Act*. However, any company that is included in the official list of securities exchange in Australia or an external territory operates under the *Corporations Legislation Amendment Act* 2003.[17] A company is defined as an artificial legal person with a separate identity from its shareholders articulated in a 2002 judgment:

If a director or officer decides that the company should carry out an act that results in an infringement of the rights of a third party, the director is not necessarily rendered personally liable at the suit of the third party.[18]

For personal liability to be incurred, the directors must be 'recklessly indifferent as regards whether the company's act was unlawful and would cause harm', something difficult to prove because 'where the boundary lies ... cannot be stated with any precision'.[19] This distinction — a separate identity from members — gives the corporation its autonomy. The idea behind incorporation is that, as a company becomes a separate legal entity, it can buy property and assets and borrow with its limited shareholder liability. Liability relates only to the amount invested in the business through buying shares.

Incorporation of companies goes back to the medieval period when they were incorporated by royal charter and later by special acts of parliament.[20] Joel Bakan, in his history of the corporation, notes its rocky beginning in 1696 when the English commissioner for trade called it a 'wholly perverted' form.[21] This was an opinion shared by those in the English Parliament who banned the corporation in 1720. This banning followed the very dramatic collapse of the notorious South Seas Company. With the company collapse, large fortunes were lost, lives were ruined and an irate shareholder shot one of the directors — a Mr John Blunt. Parliament was assembled and the King recalled from the country to sort out the crisis. The result was the *Bubble Act* 1720 which made it a criminal offence to create a company 'presuming to be a corporate body' with the issuing of 'transferable stocks without legal authority'.[22] The *Bubble Act* was repealed in 1825 and legal incorporation again took place. The second act of reintegration of the corporation into modern British legislation was made by Liberal Prime Minister William Gladstone (1809–1898) when he introduced his *Joint Stock Companies Act* in 1844.[23]

Class is Dead: Long Live the Corporation

By the mid-twentieth century, writers were dismissing anti-capitalist/anti-corporation ideas as overly economically deterministic. They suggested that the old class lines had gone with the changing system from single or family company owners to a dispersed shareholder ownership structure with these new companies being controlled by civically responsive managers and directors.[24] A new class of socially aware technocrats meant (paradoxically) the end of economically determined class. This is a sociological tradition, premised on these ideas of technocratic elite leadership, and traceable back to the work of Henri Saint Simon (1760–1825). There were also strong ties with managerial pluralism. This philosophy held that diverse and competing interests, embedded in individuals throughout society, can be realised if we have the right personal attributes in a leadership role. Two of these early advocates of the theory were Adolf Berle and Gardiner Means. They suggested that as ownership was now divorced from control through the structure of the limited liability company, a new breed of managers was emerging — managers not driven by personal greed connected with company ownership but good corporate citizens.[25] This positive endorsement of the meritocracy of the market clearly comes from an economic liberal position, that is, one that advocates a 'free market' for labour and trade. These economic liberals push hard for the privatisation of state assets and social welfare and the deregulation of finance and some tariffs (excluding those that advantage their business).

James Burnham, who also subscribed to managerial pluralism, argued that Marx's analysis of capitalists and workers was now rooted in an obsolete set of outmoded social relations and this new multiple-corporate ownership structure effectively ends exploitation. This was a continuous postwar claim, and was addressed by neo-Marxists such as R.W. Connell.[26]

Owned and Controlled by Major Shareholders

An Australian critic of this 'class is dead' idea, Connell suggests that, although there is now an expanded base of capital from which major shareholders can raise money (the result of incorporation and the popularity of the limited liability company), this has not changed the very small numbers of people who derive their income from property ownership.[27] In Australia in 2000, small shareholders were 54 per cent of the shareholders listed with the Australian stock exchange, but of these small shareholders, 42 per cent had portfolios of $10,000 or less.[28] Dyer's Australian work shows in a 2003 survey that 86 per cent of shares were held by the wealthiest 10 per cent of families. This same 10 per cent of the wealthiest families owned 62 per cent of rental properties, 60 per cent of cash deposits and 50 per cent of business assets.[29] Andrew Dilnot's older study similarly showed that the number of people who derive their income from property ownership was very small in Australia. The top 20 per cent of Australians owned 72 per cent of all property and the bottom 50 per cent owned only 1.6 per cent of all property.[30] Regarding total wealth, the NATSEM study, undertaken approximately ten years later, showed that 10 per cent of the Australian population held 45 per cent of the wealth with the top 50 per cent holding 93 per cent of the total household wealth.[31] Dyer suggests that in 2003, 5 per cent of Australian households had 59 per cent of the country's wealth.[32] The Australian class project estimated the capitalist class size to be 1 per cent of the Australian population.[33]

Changing Left Criticism of Class

Rick Kuhn divided Australian left criticism of capital into historical themes.[34] The earliest written work, beginning in the 1840s and carrying through to the 1880s, expressed a hostility to land capital, particularly toward squatters. In the second period, 1880 to 1930, the enemies were defined in relation to the type of capital they held, focusing on banks, landlords and foreign financiers. The focus in the 1930–1960 period was rich families and monopolies controlling large-scale properties. In 1963, Ernie Campbell wrote a book, *Sixty Rich Families Who Own Australia*, in which he argued that key families dominated the Australian economy and have done so, in different sectors, since the beginning of Australian capitalism.[35] Other evidence of the concentration of business came from the work of Ted Wheelwright in 1953 and 1967 (with the help of his research assistant Judith Miskelly).[36] Wheelwright, interested in continuing his work begun in England on ownership and control of big companies, found in the early 1950s that the top 5 per cent of shareholders in Australia's biggest 102 companies owned 53 per cent of the shares.[37] By the late 1960s, the shareholders had diversified their ownership to the extent that 20 per cent of shareholders held 20 per cent of the shares in over the top 300 companies.

From the 1960s, a form of left nationalism arose that regarded multinational penetration into the local economy as the problem. Ashley Lavelle identifies a range of left-wing nationalist themes — for instance, the Australian state has been captured by multinationals that are crowding out domestic business interests and de-industrialising Australia by destroying manufacturing.[38] The example he uses to illustrate this is the writing of Wheelwright and Abe David, found in *The Third Wave*.[39] Wheelwright and David argued that Australia was on the verge of takeover by Asian investors who were replacing the British and the US as colonisers. A New Zealand follower of John Maynard Keynes, the unfortunate William Sutch (accused of treason), tirelessly tried to develop this left nationalism[40] by, among other things, arguing for economic protection to develop 'our' industry and reduce British control.[41] Kuhn argued that the bottom line with these populist perspectives is that they 'locate the main class division not between capital and labour, but in divisions within the capitalist class' leading them to be lulled into developing political strategies of class collaboration with competing ruling class fractions.[42]

Tom O'Lincoln suggests that 'power lies within an identifiable ruling class who individually and collectively control capital and the machinery of the state'.[43] And that this ruling class is a 'band of hostile siblings[44] located in class fractions denoted by industry, size, geography, etc.' such as pastoralists, financiers, mine owners, manufacturers, wholesalers, retailers and insurance brokers. Their interests often emerge as different political positions on issues like tariff protection or free trade. Members of these fractions of capital have also been called 'warring brothers' which is aptly attributed to Marx, but impossible to locate in his work.

This ruling class runs to no more than 2–3 per cent of the Australian population, yet it makes the major societal decisions.

The fractions dividing the capitalist class are clearly identified in the work of New Zealander, Bruce Cronin.[45] Cronin shows how the terms used to describe the fractions of capital (their forms of appearance) depend on the level of abstraction used in the particular analysis, as depicted in Table 1.1.

Table 1.1: A Conceptualisation of Capitalist Class Fractions

	Form of Appearance			
Differentiation in Distribution	1. Industrial Capital	2. Commercial Capital	Money dealing capital	
			3. Financial Capital	4. Land-owning Capital
Concrete Manifestations	Agriculture, Mining, Forestry, Fishing, Gas, Oil, Electricity, Manufacturing, Transport	Insurance Wholesale Trade, Retail Trade, Business Services, Hotels and Restaurants	Trading Banks Investment Banks	Real Estate

Source: Cronin (2001) p. 39

Cronin argues that in relation to the above schema, this type of 'conception of the capitalist class as a differentiated unity of distinct fractions helps move analysis away from structuralist forms of economic determinism, from individualist notions of class as a collective actor and from radical relativism'. Politics proceeds from 'the most abstract conception of capitalist accumulation'.[46] I have modified the four principal capitalist fractions as outlined in Cronin's diagram (above) to make use of the Australian and New Zealand data (using the data of William Rubinstein 2004 and Graeme Hunt 2003), based on the official statistical categorisation.[47] The divisions in the capitalist class then become 1. Industrial, 2. Commercial, 3. Financial, and 4. Land-owning. These become the basis of the empirical material used in chapters two and three.

These divisions within the capitalist class can be explained like this:

1. *Industrial capital* encompasses all of production and exchange and is therefore the dynamic force behind capitalism. This is the site where production takes place and surplus value is collected. Productive enterprises include

manufacturing, fishing, agriculture and transportation. In subsequent analysis, I have coded two areas of capital separately because of their unique character in the Australian data. They are agriculture (this includes the pastoralists) and the media (this includes printers, newspapers, advertising and publishers). Both of these categories are productive capital and therefore belong here but are of particular historic interest in Australian capitalist development.

2. *Commercial capital* exists as retailed commodity capital, different from industrial capital, where by 'commercial capital is, therefore, nothing but the producer's commodity capital which has to undergo the process of conversion into money to perform its function of commodity-capital on the market. Then it represents an incidental function of the producer, it is now the exclusive operation of a special kind of capitalist, the merchant, and is set apart as the business of a special investment of capital. This becomes evident, furthermore, in the specific form of circulation of commercial capital. The merchant buys a commodity and then sells it: M–C–M'.[48] This happens at the point of exchange (e.g. during the sale of an item by a retailer) or at other times during the circuit (e.g. during warehousing for a wholesaler or providing scientific information to the factory owner). I have included insurance here.

3. *Financial capital* is one of the two forms of money dealing with capital specialising in the circulation of money for the purpose of commodity purchase. Credit is used by money dealing capital to speed production (toward overproduction) to accelerate capital accumulation and expand the scale of production. Fictitious capital (as in 'futures') is a trade in ownership titles of future surplus value. The concrete form of financial capital is investment banks and trading banks.

4. *Landowning capital* is another form of fictitious capital because landownership provides the basis for a claim on surplus value (rent). The monopoly of land (a precondition of industrial production) is the basis of intense struggle between industrialists and landowners and forms one of the bases of their claims to surplus value. A concrete form of landowning capital is real estate ownership.[49]

These different forms of capital emerge at different times in history as a response to different needs that the capitalist system develops. Cronin using Marx explains how these capitalist class fractions emerge and dominate in six historical stages (see Table 1.2).[50] The implications of this become particularly clear in chapter two when we look at the historical evolution of these Australasian ruling classes.

Table 1.2: Recurring Emergence of Different Blocks of Capital

---

1. 1788–1849
Entry of merchant capital
- Foreign and domestic merchant capital critical
- Expansion and dominance of land capital, growth of non-pastoralism and then pastoralism
- Domestic industrial capital minor

---

2. 1850–1899
Entry of foreign finance capital
- Dominance of land capital — non-pastoral in gradual decline, pastoral capital peaks in 1880s
- Foreign and domestic finance capital stable
- Foreign and domestic industrial capital grow: manufacturing slowly grows, mining rushes in 1860s and 1890s
- Foreign and domestic commercial capital stable
- Comprador (national agents) capital emerges in the gold fields

---

3. 1900–1979
Industrialisation
- Growth to peak of foreign and domestic industrial capital, each split into domestic (dominant) and export orientation
- Decline of land capital
- Further emergence of comprador capital
- Foreign and domestic finance capital stable, large domestic finance capital protected from foreign competition
- Foreign and domestic commercial capital

---

4. 1980–2006
Major class fractions internationalising
- Further entry of foreign finance capital and internationalisation of domestic financial capital, remnant domestic-oriented finance capital
- Decline and internationalisation of industrial capital, remnant domestic industrial capital
- Growth of media capital
- Continuing decline of land capital
- Foreign and domestic commercial capital consolidates, growth of financial and business services
- Comprador capital consolidates

Chapter two refers to Table 1.2 as it develops the history of the ruling elites and uses a modified definition of these four epochs. In Australia, the first period (1788–1850) was when merchant capital dominated the convict colonies of New South Wales and Van Diemen's Land (now Tasmania). In the second period (1850–1899) the real dominance of land capital begins with the entry of foreign financial capital and the dominance of the pastoralists amongst the Australian ruling class. In the third period (1900–1979), there was a deepening industrialisation in which the competing politics of the ruling class came into play. It divided into fractions that either defended or fought against free trade and protectionism. This happened in both Australia and New Zealand. For example, car manufacturers wanted to be protected by tariffs so foreign manufacturers could be prevented from *dumping* cheap overseas cars onto the domestic market, whereas finance capitalists did not care about tariff control and actively wanted a freer, more speculative market open to them. This third period also saw the emergence of comprador capital — that is, native born agents acting for foreign businesses and serving as middle men or women, or collaborators, in business deals.

In the fourth or latest period (1980–2006) there has been an internationalisation of some forms of capital occurring in both Australia[51] and New Zealand.[52] In an updating of the ruling class literature since 1977, Connell suggests that Australian capitalism is still dependent capitalism, but in ways different from the old dependent industrialisation that ended in the 1970s.[53] The world economy has seen huge growth in capital mobility and the spread of transactions. There is a new mobility accelerated by, and in turn, motivating new interactive financial technologies. Financial capital has in particular, prospered through this new information and exchange mobility, enabling it to enhance its class hegemony. Hegemony refers to having authority, power and direction over people rather than just crude domination of them.[54]

Economic liberalism, the language of the market, underpins the politics of this period. The nature of this is explored in chapter six, but suffice it to say here that it been called 'hypertrophic'.[55] Hypertrophy as in an enlarged overgrowth of an organ usually a cancerous malignancy. This term was used due to the swarms 'of "consultants" around government including big [firms] such as Andersen, KPMG and their ilk, who have made colossal profits out of advising governments to undertake privatisations and then "managing" the privatisation process'.[56] New Zealand is a particularly good example of this (see chapter five).

Economic liberal market discourse is, according to Connell, a 'huge expansion of the logic of greed [that] has been sold as a moral triumph. The growth of the market is presented to us as a growth of individual freedom, an attack on rigid bureaucracy and stifling regulation, an expansion of choice, even in some of its more shameless propaganda for privatisation — as economic democracy, a return of property to the public'.[57] But, it is argued, this is an understanding that is carefully nurtured and funded by the ruling classes through their right-wing think tanks, state bureaucrats, politicians, and opinion leaders and then absorbed into a half hearted acquiescence by the general public.[58]

Connell makes three seminal points about economic liberalism.[59] The first is that it *dumbs down* class conflict. It occurs particularly in times when ruling classes are actively reducing wages and conditions in an attempt to retain the same level of profit in an unfavourable economic environment. The second point about its efficacy is that since the 1980s, when it came to dominate government policy, it has taken the market into new places, such as education, prisons, railways, health and telecommunications. Connell argues that the goods and services formerly 'provided by the public sector, voluntary agencies, and even families, have been turned into commodities sold for profit by entrepreneurs'.[60] The third, and perhaps the most important point for this book, is that economic liberalism has functioned to change the class structure in the following way: the number of managers has proliferated as a result of privatisations and de-mutualisations. These managers, whilst being classified as professionals by themselves, are in many senses part of the same social group as the owners of capital. Managers are that part of the ruling class who appropriate surplus profit principally or exclusively through the form of bountiful remuneration packages rather than simply in the traditional form of dividends (as discussed in chapter three). At the very top level of management, the balance shifts back to the traditional form 'as a large percentage of top executives' "compensation" now consists of shares and share options ... or outright gifts of part of the capital, called bonuses'.[61]

Chapters three, four and five develop these points by looking for evidence of political and economic power in the networks of the managers of the top companies in Australia and New Zealand. Broomhill suggests business has given widespread support to economic liberalism because it has reduced government regulation of business:

> by reducing government ownership of industry ... economic liberal policies seek to maximize the ability of (at least some sectors of) capital to restructure. In particular deregulation and privatization permit key sections of capital to shift investment out of areas of declining profitability while creating new areas for potentially profitable investment. At the same time labour market deregulation, the abandonment of corporatist compromise arrangements between capital, labour and the state and the reduction of state welfare expenditures all reinforce the disciplining of the workforce'.[62]

This disciplining of the workforce has taken the form of threats to downsize or to move interstate or offshore.

The Role of the State

Major questions exciting theorists are: in whose interests does the capitalist state exist and how does it organise to perpetuate the status quo? The state is the political apparatus of government, ruling over a given territory, through an organisation such as parliament or congress, and a bureaucratic civil service. The authority of the state is backed by a legal system and by the capacity to use military force to implement its policies.[63] The argument that the role of the state is to be a supporting structure for the ruling class is made by a number of Australian writers including Michael Pusey, Dick Bryan, Tom Bramble, Rick Kuhn, Michael

Rafferty, Frank Stillwell, Verity Bergman, Damien Grenfell and Damien Cahill.[64] This is another disputed theoretical area, however, with views ranging from economic liberals arguing that the state can be, and should be, socially minimalist,[65] to competing Marxist understandings of the capitalist state's role as either the ruling class's 'little helper'[66] or alternatively as being autonomous of the ruling class but structurally embedded within different fractions commonly divided, but at any one historical point guided by a dominant fraction.[67]

Liberal Perspectives on the State — Traditional Liberals

According to Max Weber, the historical uniqueness of the modern state lies in its freedom from feudal nepotism replaced by the potentially tyrannising rule from the desk by bureaucrats (bureau is the French word for desk) with rules of procedure enmeshed in a myriad of paperwork discernible only to those with the specialised expertise to read it. Specialist bureaucrats were full time, life long salaried professionals.[68]

The argument that the state has a life of its own was expanded upon by Weber in his theory of methodological individualism and is set out in the first chapter of *Economy and Society*. His central idea was that social action should be explained in relation to the results of individual human action and the intentional motives of actors.[69] Moving to the right of Weber's liberalism on the state is the dry liberalism of the present day economic liberals (as identified previously by Connell).[70]

Dry Liberalism versus the State

Milton and Rose Friedman wrote that they had 'spent much of our life trying to persuade our fellow men and women of the dangers of intrusive government and the key role that a free competitive economy plays in making a free society possible'.[71] This book will explore some aspects of how economic liberalism manifested in New Zealand and Australia as the result of the clever capture by economic liberals of the state's policy agenda.

This economic liberal attainment of the policy agenda has been irrespective of whether the government was either traditionally politically left or right. Bergman argues, when Labour parties were in power, they also became 'capital's little mate' on most issues.[72] She argues that the 1983 Hawke–Keating government was 'enthusiastically committed' to economic liberal ideology and 'policies that favored employer interests in direct opposition to working class interests'.[73] Overall, the ALP's 'infatuation with [the economic liberal] ideology and policies designed to increase profit levels and reduce the share of national wealth and income received by those who sell their labour to employers' was difficult to understand when the logic spelt out was 'to achieve increased profits for corporations and exorbitant packages for CEOs by means such as cutting real wages, privatising public assets, reducing progressive taxation and slashing social services'.[74]

Dry liberalism came into its own in both the Australian and New Zealand governments in. the 1980s, and it has remained there, to varying degrees, ever since. Whilst there, it is has been able to present itself as a stable form of government although never really enjoying popular support for its policy. Connell argues, however, that economic liberal leaders — Margaret Thatcher, John Howard, Ronald Reagan — did not get into power by saying that they wanted privatisation of public utilities, little welfare and indirect taxation favouring the rich — that is, economic liberal policy. Rather, they tapped into existing nationalist or racist issues.[75]

As we shall see throughout the following chapters, there was also some very strong economic liberal rhetorical support for the small state and denial of the role of the state's welfare role from top businessmen and women interviewed in this study of top businesses in Australia and New Zealand during 1984–2004. For example, when a New Zealand director was asked in the early 1990s about the new development of soup kitchens for the poor in Otara, he said:

> Cut out the drama! The state has paid us to be dependent ... Now it sees that the more money the state devotes to these problems, the more these problems are, and that's not surprising. It's because people change their behaviour ... the reality is that the state, in all its manifestations in the welfare industry, is a total failure worldwide.[76]

The Left on the State

Arguing against this economic liberal triumphalism, Damien Grenfell suggests that it is disingenuous for economic liberals to claim to have pursued policies that have made the small state happen in Australia; for what has actually happened is that the state is still very much there when it comes to regulation of ruling class interests: 'The state in Australia continues to contribute significantly to the regulatory, legal and ideological infrastructure, so as to secure the necessary preconditions for the advancement of the free market economics. The state remains intertwined in the processes that under-pin the reproduction of the market'.[77] As Connell also argues, in Australia since the 1970s, the upper levels of the state bureaucracy have been restructured to reflect the organisation of the top level of business:

> Senior public servants and executives of corporatised public agencies ... now work in conditions modeled on those of business executives. They are employed on contracts, at greatly increased salaries, with individually negotiated (and often secret) packages, and are subject to performance audits and restructures. They are more vulnerable to the displeasure of their political masters, while the rewards for compliance with the economic liberal agenda have rocketed.[78]

Pusey interviewed 200 senior bureaucrats and argued that policy-makers for the government favour ideas of small government, less powerful unions and generally exercise the voice of what he sees as a very narrow economic liberal training.[79] Pusey's work shows that the responsibility for the state using economically liberal ideas does not rest with its bureaucrats and it will not disappear with the restoration of non-economic liberal bureaucrats. Economic liberalism has been around since the beginning of capitalism and is cyclical in that it gets more demanding, and a wider state audience, in times of economic downturn.

This leaves the problem of where do state bureaucrats belong in the ruling class? Although they are not the focus of this work, they are clearly important in the dissemination of ruling class ideas. Marx argues that the 'ideas of the ruling class are in every epoch the ruling ideas, that is, the class that is the ruling material force of society is at the same time its ruling intellectual force'.[80] In this model, state bureaucrats and ideologues are the passive functionaries of the ruling class.

Marx locates ruling class membership as embedded primarily in the economy. It is here that capitalists, as the active exploiters of workers labour, are identifiable rather than being found at the level of distribution or exchange. His class model of social mobility is horizontal rather than vertical. Occupationally workers have the freedom to move sideways, for example, from carpenter to bricklayer, whereas capitalists largely inherit capital which is a 'live monster that is fruitful and multiplies' irrespective of the intelligence of its owner. Workers can only bring this imbalance of social forces to an end through their own struggle because nothing will be handed to them without their fight back.[81]

Elites

Others fatalistically believe that there will always be a divide between those who have and those who have not, or between those who are rulers and those who are ruled. These writers use the concept of elite rather than Marxian concepts of class. Indeed, elite has for some connotations of merit and achievement and, if not desirable, elites are at least unavoidable. These 'elite' writers include Vilfredo Pareto (1848–1923), who notes a circulation of elites based on their inherent weaknesses;[82] Gaetano Mosca (1858–1941), who maintains that ruling class membership is a violently contested political arena competed for by contending groups who manipulate ideologies or formula to stay there;[83] and Robert Michels (1876–1936), who argues that any organisation is inherently undemocratic because its leaders always gravitate towards oligarchy of which he later, as an active fascist, thoroughly approved.[84] Charles Wright Mills (1916–1962), using Weber more than Marx, argues that the capitalist elite share with the military and state elites a privileged status in society and they exist because of political decisions about the distribution of power and material resources.[85]

Pierre Bourdieu (1930–2002), also working primarily within a Weberian emphasis, considers Marxian definitions of who belongs to the ruling class as too narrow.[86] He sees economic capital as being reinforced by symbolic, social and cultural forms of capital — for example, a big business man or woman may donate a 'chair', a prize or a building to a university that will thereafter bear their name and enhance their individual cultural capital. The system of awarding knight or dame status to class members is seen as consolidating social capital and sponsorship of prestigious events (e.g. corporate sponsorship of tennis) gains companies symbolic capital.

Elite theory cannot, according to Boris Frankel, adequately explain the 'complex political and cultural forces Australians contend with'.[87] The 'paranoia and myths infusing the populist Right's version of "elites" and "ordinary" people are only an extension of the ideologically flawed theories of power' that dominate elite paradigm theorising. Instead, he argues that 'if alternative public policies are to emerge, they must be first grounded in concepts of culture and political economy that break free of discourse of "elites" and "masses"'.[88]

In the following chapters, we will examine these ideas of contested meanings of what is the Australian ruling class.

What is to Come?

To find out what it means to be in the ruling classes, chapter two begins by considering their history. This creates an evolving picture of Australia and New Zealand using historical references and raw data from books and primary sources. Drawing from this secondary source material a unique picture of Australian and New Zealand ruling class history from European settlement through to the twenty first century emerges. Amongst other wealthy colonies theirs remained a different brand of wealthy colonial power. Through secondary sources, this chapter describes these emerging business leaders, how many there were, what their backgrounds were and what we know about their social, business and political networks up until the present. The central class mobility question is; is their class evolution a vertical (from worker to wealthy) or horizontal (from wealthy to different type of wealthy) pattern?

Chapter three asks: if there are ruling classes what do they look like today? This empirically grounded chapter examines the modern ruling classes in Australia and New Zealand. It examines the *demography* of the ruling class. For example, what schools did they go to? What clubs do they join? What committees are they on? What do they do for leisure and how do they relate to the state through membership of government committees, government lobby groups and think tanks? This chapter considers the wealth of these richest Australasians and their social and cultural capital too. Subsidiary questions asked are: what type of capital (for example finance, industrial or commercial capital) is now dominant; what does that mean in terms of class power within the ruling classes; and how they organise?

The fourth and fifth chapters address how the Australian and New Zealand ruling classes are interconnected and networked and what the significance is of their interlocking company board networks. This traces directors of the top companies, their involvement on multiple boards and what this says about directions of their power. These chapters test, against the evidence, different theoretical perspectives to explore whether there are discernable forms of control, collusion, discretion and social embeddness amongst the networks of top 30 directors.

In chapter six, the ruling beliefs and their reproduction are examined as central to the perpetuation of the ruling class and the support that the class has. In modern Australia and New Zealand, these ideas are based around the economic liberal economic paradigm. Variants of this paradigm, from Dudley North and Adam Smith to the modern day, are examined to consider how the paradigm has been reproduced by, and for, specific class interests. This chapter looks at how liberal ideas are transmitted through lobby groups and think tanks that played a critical role in promoting the economic liberalism underpinning Australia and New Zealand government policy in the past two decades.

Chapter seven looks at who 'misses out'. The chapter points out that the ruling classes are not representative of the population at large — some groups are over-represented (for example, Caucasian males) and some miss out totally (that is, some ethnic minorities and indigenous people). But the chapter limits its focus to looking at a small group who have been sighted—female top directors. It ends by identifying alternative approaches that are taken to increase the numbers of women into top corporate roles.

The final chapter draws together the key points from the previous chapters and discusses their implications for Australasian patterns of power and policy. It relates this story to the wider global picture and the Australasian fit into this. Then it looks critically at the role of the corporation as a primary force in enabling the ruling class to organise our society.

Notes

[1] Abbott, T. (2003), *The Left the New Elites* according to David Flint, transcript from PM ABC, Friday 1, August, 6.39pm.

[2] Quoted in Probert, B. (2001), 'Class in the year 2001', *Australian Rationalist,* no. 56, pp. 1–14.

[3] Australian Election Survey [AES] (2004), Reference Computer File, Social Science Data Archive, Australian National University, Canberra.

[4] Australian Election Survey [AES] (2004).

[5] Pilger, J. (2002), 'Journalism in Australia has a courageous history, but Murdochism has turned it into a disgrace' 21 February, http://pilger.carlton.com/print/97358, p. 1.

[6] Hollier, N. (2004), *Ruling Australia: Power, Privilege and Politics of the New Ruling Class,* Melbourne, Victoria, Australian Scholarly publishing, p.xxxii.

[7] Communications Update (1999), 'Annual Media Ownership Update', *Communications Update,* issue 151, February, pp. 7–9.

8 Scott, J. (1991), *Who Rules Britain?* Oxford, Polity Press, p. 151.
9 Reich, R. (1991), *The Work of Nations, Preparing Ourselves for the 21st Century Capitalism,* New York, Alfred Knopf, Lind, M. (1996), *Up from Conservatism: why the Right is Wrong for America,* New York, Free Press.
10 Stilwell, F. & M. Ansari, (2003), 'Wealthy Australians, Economic Notes', *Journal of Australian Political Economy,* December, i.52. p. 143.
11 Marx, K. (1974), *Capital,* v. 1–3, London, Lawrence and Wishart. p. 1025.
12 Wheen, F. (2005), 'Why Marx is Man of the Moment: He had globalization sussed 150 years ago', *Observer,* London, Fourth Estate, Sunday, 17 July, p. 5.
13 Marx, K. (1974).
14 The director interviewed here is from Murray, G. (1993–1997), *Economic Power in Australia ARC Project* interview, Respondent 95. This is the first of the taped director interviews used illustratively throughout this book. Interviews of over 150 Australian and New Zealand directors of top 30 companies were done between 1984-1997.
15 Coser, L. A. (1977), *Masters of Sociological Thought: Ideas in Historical and Social Context,* second edition, New York, Harcourt Brace Jovanovich, p. 228.
16 'I continue to see exploitation as a central, analytically powerful concept', E. O. Wright (1997), p.11 http://www.theglobalsite.ac.uk/press/105wright.htm.
17 Butterworths Online http://www.butterworthsonline.com/lpBin20/lpext.dll/bw/L8/15/corps/1?f=templates&fn=bwaltmain-j.htm&contents=yes&szPath=/bw/L8/15/corps/1.
18 Root Quality Pty Ltd v Root Control Technologies Pty Ltd (2000) 177 ALR 231, 49 IPR 225, [2000], AIPC 37,826 (91-594), FCA 980.
19 Root Quality Pty Ltd v Root Control Technologies (2000).
20 Mourell, M. (2005), pers com, 10 May.
21 Bakan, J. (2004), *The Corporation: The Pathological Pursuit of Profit and Power,* New York, Free Press, p. 6.
22 Hadden, T. (1977), *Company Law and Capitalism,* London, Weidenfield and Nichollson, p. 16.
23 Mourell, M. (2005), p. 1.
24 Berle, A. & Means, G. (1932), *The Modern Corporation and Private Property,* New York, Macmillan, Burnham, J. (1943), *The Managerial Revolution,* Lexington, D.C. Heath.
25 Berle, A. & Means, G. (1932).
26 Connell, R.W. (2004), 'Moloch Mutates: Global Capitalism and the evolution of the Australian Ruling Class' in Hollier, N. (2004), Ruling Australia, Melbourne, Australian Scholarly publishing.
27 Connell, R.W. (2004).
28 Australian Stock Exchange (2000), 'ASX 2000 Survey', 8 February, http:www.asx.com.au p.
29 Dyer, A. (2003), 'The 'Haves' Have More', *Business Review Weekly,* 22 May – 18 June, pp. 30–31.
30 Dilnot, A. (1990), 'From Most to Least: New Figures on Wealth Distribution', *Australian Society,* July, p. 14.
31 Harding, A. (2002), 'Towards Opportunity and Prosperity, Trends in Income and Wealth Inequality in Australia', *NATSEM,* Canberra, University of Canberra, p. 11.
32 Dyer, A. (2003), p. 31.
33 Emmison, M. & Baxter, J, Western J. (1991), *Class Analysis and Contemporary Australia,* Melbourne, Macmillan.
34 Kuhn, R. (1996), 'Class Analysis and the Left in Australian History' in R. Kuhn & T. O'Lincoln *Class and Class Conflict in Australia,* Longman, Melbourne, pp. 145–162.
35 Campbell, E.W. (1963), *In Sixty Rich Families: Who Owns Australia,* Sydney, Current Book Distributors.

[36] Moran, A. (1990), 'Writing non-fiction: An Interview with E. L. Wheelwright', *The Australia Journal of Media and Culture*, v. 4, n.1.p.1. using Wheelwright, E. L. & Miskelly, J. (1967), *Anatomy of Australian Manufacturing Industry*, Sydney, Sydney Law Book Company.

[37] Moran, A. (1990), p. 1.

[38] Lavelle, A. (2001), 'Who Rules Australia?' *Socialist Workers Review*, n.4, May, p. 4.

[39] David, A. & Wheelwright, E. (1989), *The Third Wave: Australia and Asian Capitalism*, Sutherland, N.S.W, Left Book Club Co-operative.

[40] Easton, B. (2000), 'Sutch, William Ball 1907 – 1975' *Dictionary of New Zealand Biography*, v.5. (1941-1960), p.504.506.http://www.eastonbh.ac.nz/article 114.html.

[41] Sutch, W.B. (1966), *Poverty and Progress: A Re-assessment*, Wellington, A.H. & A.W. Reed. Sutch, W.B. (1973), *Takeover New Zealand*, Wellington, A. H. & A.W. Reed.

[42] Kuhn, R. (1996), p.145.

[43] O'Lincoln, T. (1996), 'Wealth, Ownership and Power, the Ruling Class', (ed.s), R. Kuhn & O'Lincoln, T. *Class and Class Conflict in Australia*, Melbourne, Longmans. p. 5.

[44] O'Lincoln, T. (1996), p. 15.

[45] Cronin, B. (2001), *The Politics of New Zealand Business Internationalisation 1972 – 1996*, v. 1 & v. 2. Auckland University, Unpublished PHD thesis, p. 37.

[46] Cronin (2001), p. 39.

[47] Australian Bureau of Statistics [ABS] (1993), Australian and New Zealand Standard Industrial Classification (ANZSIC), Government ABS Catalogue No 1292.0, ABS (1997), Australian Standard Classification of Occupations, (ASCO), ABS Catalogue No 1220.

[48] Marx, K. (1959), pp. 183–191.

[49] For further explanation of the categories read Bryan, D. (1995a), 'The Internationalization of Capital and Marxian Value Theory', *Cambridge Journal of Economics*, n.19, pp. 421– 440, Marx, K. (1974), Cronin, B. (2001), p. 37.

[50] Cronin, B. (2001).

[51] Bryan, D. (1996), *The Chase Across the Globe: International Accumulation and the Contradictions for Nation States*, Boulder, Westview Press.

[52] Cronin, B. (2001), Bedggood, D. (1980), *Rich and Poor in New Zealand*, Wellington, Allen and Unwin p. 17.

[53] Connell, R.W. (2002), 'Moloch Mutates: Global Capitalism and the Evolution of the Australian Ruling Class 1977–2002)', *Overland*, n.167, pp. 4–14.

[54] Using Gramsci, A. (1971), *Selections from the Prison Notebooks*; International Publishers, New York, 1971 http://www.marxists.org/archive/gramsci/editions/spn/state_civil/index.htm

[55] Connell, R.W. (2002), p. 6.

[56] Connell, R.W. (2002), p. 6.

[57] Connell, R.W. (2004), p. 8.

[58] Cahill, D. (2004), 'Contesting Hegemony: The Radical Neo Liberal Movement and the Ruling Class in Australia', in N. Hollier *Ruling Australia: The Power, Privilege and Politics of the New Ruling Class,* Melbourne, Australian Scholarly Publishers, p. 87.

[59] Connell, R.W. (2004), p. 6.

[60] Connell, R.W. (2004), p. 6.

[61] Connell, R.W. (2004), p. 6.

[62] Broomhill, R. (2001), 'Neoliberalism Globalism and the Local State: a Regulation Approach', *Journal of Political Economy*, n. 48, pp. 115–140, December, p. 124.

[63] Giddens, A. (2001), *Sociology*, Cambridge, Polity Press, p. 421.

[64] Pusey, M. (1991), *Economic Rationalism in Australia*, London, Cambridge University Press; Bryan, D. (1996); Bramble, T. & Kuhn, R. (1999), 'Social Democracy after the Long Boom: Economic Restructuring under Australian Labor 1983–1996', in M.

Upchurch (ed.) *The State and Globalisation: Comparative Studies of Labour and capital in National Economics,* London, Mansell, pp. 20–55; Bryan, D. & Rafferty, M. (1999), *The Global Economy in Australia: Global Integration and National Economic Policy,* St Leonards, Allen and Unwin; Stilwell, F. (2002), *Political Economy, the Contest of Economic Ideas,* Melbourne, Oxford Press; Bergmann, V. (2004), 'Active Citizenship against Marketisation: Community Resistance to Neo Liberalism' in G. Patmore (ed.) *The Vocal Citizen: Labor Essays 2004,* Victoria, Australian Scholarly Publishing, pp. 116–131, Grenfell, D. (2004), 'Getting the Government off our Backs? The Ruling Class and New Trends in the State's Management of Dissent', in N. Hollier (ed.) *Ruling Australia: the Power, Privilege and Politics of the New Ruling Class,* Melbourne Australian Scholarly Publishers, pp. 70–86; Cahill (2004).

[65] Friedman, R. & Friedman, M. (1980), *Free to Choose: A Personal Statement,* New York, Harcourt Brace Jovanovich.

[66] Marx, K. & Engels, F. (1977), *The Communist Manifesto,* in the Collected Works of Karl Marx and Fredrich Engels, Moscow, Progress Publishers: and neo Marxists — Miliband, R. (1969), *The State in Capitalist Society,* London, Weidenfield & Nicholson; Connell, R.W. (2004), Bergman, V. (2004), or Grenfell (2004).

[67] Marx, K. (1974); Poulantzas, N. (1972), 'The Miliband and Polantzas Debate' (ed.) R. Blackburn *Ideology in the Social Sciences,* London, Fontana; Bedggood, D. (1980); Cronin, B. (2001); Stillwell, F. (2002), p. 351.

[68] Weber, M. (1968), *Economy and Society,* G. Roth & C. Wittich (ed.s) 1922 New York, Free Press.

[69] Weber, M. (1968).

[70] Connell, R.W. (2004), p. 6.

[71] Friedman, M. (2005), p. 1.

[72] Bergmann, V. (2004), pp. 48–69.

[73] Bergmann, V. (2004), p. 50.

[74] Bergmann, V. (2004), p. 51.

[75] Connell, R.W. (2002), 'Moloch Mutates, Global Capitalism and the Evolution of the Australian Ruling Class, 1977–2002' *Overland,* n.167, Winter, p. 10.

[76] Murray, G. (1993-1997), Respondent 91.

[77] Grenfell, D. (2004), p. 70.

[78] Connell, R. W. (2004), p. 7.

[79] Pusey, M. (1991).

[80] Marx, K. (1977), *The German Ideology,* [first published 1932] Marx-Engels, *Collected Works,* v.5, London, Lawrence and Wishart, p. 47.

[81] Marx, K. (1976), *Capital,* v.1, London, Penguin/New Left Review p.189.

[82] Pareto, V. (1973), *Mind and Society,* London, Dover.

[83] Mosca, G. (1896), *The Ruling Class,* New York, McGraw Hill.

[84] Michels, R. (1911), *Political Parties: A Sociological Study of the Oligarchical Tendencies of Modern Democracy,* New York, Free Press.

[85] Wright Mills. C. (1956), *The PowerElite,* New York, Oxford University Press.

[86] Bourdieu, P. (1973), 'Cultural Reproduction and Social Reproduction' in R. Brown (ed.) *Knowledge, Education and Social Change,* London, Tavistock, pp. 71–112.

[87] Frankel, B. (1998), 'Elites', *Arena Magazine,* October, pp. 29–42 (1) p. 32.

[88] Frankel, B. (1998), p. 40.

Chapter 2

The History of the Australian and New Zealand Ruling Classes

New Zealand and Australia have quite distinct colonial origins and class structures that are to be explored in this historical chapter. The empirical data used comes primarily from a number of mixed Australian and New Zealand secondary sources:

- the *All-time Australian 200 Rich list from Samuel Terry 'the Convict Rothschild' to Kerry Packer* written by William Rubinstein in 2004 in conjunction with *Business Review Weekly (BRW)*;
- the *Business Review Weekly (BRW)* Rich 200 lists published annually;
- the *Australian Dictionary of Biography* which uses material from the Research School of the Social Sciences at the Australian National University, Canberra;
- its trans-Tasman counterpart *The New Zealand Dictionary of Biography* and the *Te Ara Encyclopaedia of New Zealand*;
- *The Rich List, Wealth and Enterprise in New Zealand 1820–2003* by Graeme Hunt, written in 2003; and
- the National Accounts from the *Australian Bureau of Statistics* (ABS).

All except the latter deal with the histories of the richest men and women.

Rubinstein's Australian sample covers 183 men and women who were included only if they possessed, on death, a probate worth over a billion dollars in 2003 values. Rubinstein's *BRW* data has to be treated with some caution.[1] For example, he uses National Accounts from Australian Historical Statistics to convert past wealth holdings into modern values by expressing wealth as a proportion of GDP. Thus, his concept of wealth is relative to the size of the economy rather than an absolute concept that simply takes account of price inflation.[2] And the main data sources are from public records and business intelligence drawing upon 'public company records and property listings, obtaining value estimates on known assets, and questioning reliable and key industry contacts'.[3] This data capture method can neglect wealth held by old families in hidden accounts, foreign bank accounts or family trusts. This qualification also relates to the work of Graeme Hunt.[4] Both authors were uncritical, sharing the dominant liberal belief in the potential upward mobility of the individual with entrepreneurial savvy.

The New Zealand wealth data comes from the work of Hunt and originated in his work on the *National Business Review*'s (NBR) rich lists. These form the basis of his book.[5] In his sample there are 85 men and women listed from 1840 to 2003.

Unlike Rubinstein, Hunt's sample is 'highly selective', drawn as an 'inspiration to those who place individual endeavour before that of the state'. He admits a 'number of assumptions have had to be made' and here the author credits as exemplary, *Forbes Journal*'s rich list, excluding those it considers 'too boring'.[6] He cites his unnamed sources for the top ten wealth lists as 'based on available information, some of it limited'.[7]

Using these secondary sources the material is then divided into the four key periods:

- *Period 1, 1788–1849*, when the Australian and New Zealand colonies were an export enclave sending primarily agricultural and marine products back to Britain;
- *Period 2, 1850–1899*, when the pastoral industry continued to dominate the economy witnessing the rise of manufacturing and industrialisation;
- *Period 3, 1900–1979*, which saw deepening industrialisation. The manufacturing contribution to GDP in Australia doubled between 1901 and 1951;
- *Period 4, 1980–2005*, the period in which there has been a major change in the importance of distribution and services (mainly financial services) and a decline in manufacturing.

This chapter looks at how the ruling class developed through these four periods.

Background to the History of Ruling Class Crooks

In 1786 the British government decided to make Botany Bay a penal colony. When the First Fleet arrived in Port Jackson on 26 January 1788, they had already visited and rejected Botany Bay, a few kilometers south, as being unsuitable for settlement. At the time of this landing there were an estimated 250,000 Aboriginal people already living in this ancient 45 million-year-old continent. Theirs was one of the world's oldest surviving cultures, dating back 60,000 years[8] with over 500 different tribal groups and dialects. In New Zealand, Maori settlement was relatively new, that is, 'less than 1,000 years'.[9]

The first European settlers were 788 convicts (only one in six of whom was a woman) and the military to guard them.[10] Organised under the authority of Governor Arthur Phillip, the First Fleet arrived in eleven ships with 1,350 people on board. The European settlers behaved as if the land was 'empty' in a legal sense and hence able to be appropriated and improved.[11] As early as 1791, sealers from New South Wales (NSW) had established bases in New Zealand but European

(*Pakeha*) settlement generally had slower beginnings there. In both countries by the early 1800s, Europeans were predominantly whalers and sealers. There were also some small traders, included amongst them the NSW Military Corps, who were 'prepared to go to almost any length, geographical or otherwise, to enrich them-selves'.[12]

The British government national archives suggest that in the 80 years in which transportation took place, 158,702 convicts arrived in Australia from England and Ireland and 1,321 from elsewhere, making a total of 160,023 men and women starting a new life in the colonies.[13] At the start the convicts, settlers and military found themselves in a colony (in NSW but also similarly in New Zealand) where nothing of great significance was known about the climate, the animals, the plants or the indigenous people. Their relationships with the latter became hostile, with harmful consequences for the Aborigines, who lost their land and were exposed to new deadly diseases such as smallpox and measles. None of the earliest settlers had experienced land of this type and few had previous farm experience. They often made poor locational choices. They tried, for example, to farm the poor soil around Parramatta and were subsequently subject to widespread starvation.

The second fleet, or Death Fleet, as it subsequently became known, landed 692 people at Sydney Cove in June 1790. Two hundred and sixty seven people, 27 per cent of the 1017 that left Portsmouth, died on the voyage. The convicts had travelled shackled and lying in their own body wastes throughout the voyage. They arrived emaciated, covered in their own dirt and lice, with many unable to walk. A total of 488 were too sick to work when they landed. Instead of able-bodied workers being delivered to employers, the sick and dying arrived and a tent hospital had to be quickly constructed to accommodate them.[14] Only 67 of the survivors were women. 1791 saw the arrival of the third fleet and the first Irish convicts.[15]

From these sad beginnings, a vibrant economy and a dynamic society grew. Sydney, Parramatta and, later, Hobart, grew into prosperous towns. The new arrivals, while experiencing the undeniable extreme pain of exile, were able to enjoy some leverage on power because of the shortage of labour. They worked fewer hours (pre 1819 convicts worked for 48 hours a week, post-1819 convicts worked for 56 hours a week) than children working 72–84 hours in factories at that time in Britain.[16] They enjoyed a good climate, a better diet (convicts had 4,903 calories daily in 1819, compared with 3,178 calories daily for the soldiers in the British army from 1813–57) and they were able to experience limited social mobility. This was because, until the mid-1830s, only 6 per cent of the convicts were in prisons like Moreton Bay and Port Arthur and the rest lived and laboured with masters throughout the colonies.[17] As Raymond Evans and Bill Thorpe argue, there is danger in overstating how good things were, because there is horrific evidence from the Moreton Bay Penal colony, such as this convict's words: 'my back had been cut and chopped, until it was scarcely ever well ... as if being scorched by a red hot iron ... we felt we were slaves'.[18] Convictism was 'a system of coercion centred primarily upon processes of exile and labour. It was reinforced by means of re-transportation, or renewed exile, and the intensification of work. Public executions, treadmills, solitary cells, branding, iron collars, heavy leg irons, withdrawal of privileges, floggings, in effect fell like scarlet filigree across the garment of penal coercion'.[19] Evans suggests this was all done in the name of 'penal discipline ... needed to incarcerate a minority, in order to subjugate the mass'.[20] O'Lincoln points out that colonial convicts were unwilling pioneers and their forced labour was used not just in Australia but by expanding capitalism throughout the Pacific, Africa and Latin America; anywhere the British rulers wanted to add to their empire.[21]

Period 1 (1788–1849): The Export Enclave

The real dynamic of European settlement in Australasia from 1788 through to the 1850s (and on to the 1870s) came from the high profits earned from non-pastoral (agriculture) and the pastoral industry (see Figure 2.1). Colonial agriculture fed into the industrial revolution taking place in England and Scotland. Sheep were at the base of this growth. In 1797 the first Merino sheep were sent to Australia from the Cape of Good Hope and from these a fine wool industry rapidly grew. In 1813 William Charles Wentworth, Gregory Blaxland and William Lawson went over the Blue Mountains looking for more 'empty land' for this farming. Others followed them. By 1849 white settlers held 73 million acres deep inside both NSW and (what later became) Queensland.[22] The colony's export commodities included wool, coal, woods, barks, gums, salts, salt fish, seals and the products of whale fishery.

The non-pastoral and pastoral industries, plus the revenue from land sales to pastoralists, attracted and provided the profit basis for growth in manufacture, commerce, public services and house building. An unusual feature of the patterns of production shown in Figure 2.1 was the demand for public services from the military and the convict guards and for the infrastructure for business including railways, roads, houses, shops and offices. At this time there was huge amounts of British investment securing capital developments by local compradors (agents for the British capitalists) and allowing them to secure and consolidate their economic power and giving rise to an emerging ruling class. The billionaires identified in this time are not the entire ruling class but they represent its most significant part.[23]

The Australian Billionaires 1788–1848

Rich men and women in this earliest period are those with wealth at modern values of more than '0.170 per cent of Australian GDP — about $1.22 billion'.[24] Some of them lived in Van Diemen's land (21 per cent), others lived in New South Wales (76 per cent) and three lived overseas.

Figure 2.1: GDP by Industry in Australia 1800–1850

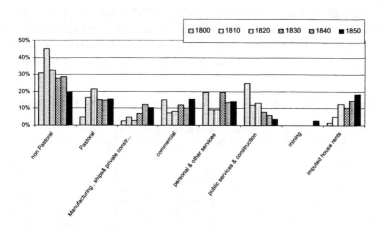

Source: Collated from Butlin, 1987.

Their number included 109 men and one woman, Mary Cooper. Mary Cooper began her Australian life as a convict but on her death, her wealth by modern values would make her Australia's richest woman ever, with a probated wealth equivalent to $2.30 billion.

Mary Cooper (1788–1842)
Source of wealth: marriage and manufacture
Wealth: equal to 0.32 per cent of GDP, 2003 value: $2.30 billion
Mary Cooper is in relative terms the richest woman in Australian history. She arrived in Australia as an 18-year-old convict in 1806. She married a fellow convict, Thomas Cooper, who was 21 years her senior. Thomas was a farrier and a blacksmith with premises at George Street, Sydney. There is no information on how she made her money. She died in 1828 aged 61.
Source: Rubinstein (2004), p. 42.

Merely being a woman makes Mary Cooper significant as part of a minority in the colony where men outnumbered women in a ratio variously described as 6:1[25] or 3:1[26] in 1830 and shifting to 7:3 in 1851.[27] But as a married convict, Mary Cooper was also unusual in that 62 per cent of all convict women were unmarried.[28] Anne Summers wrote that when these women arrived in the colonies most faced enforced whoredom.[29] This was because of the lack of paid female work and the 'lusts of men were so urgent as to require the prostitution of the most abandon women to contain them,' according to Governor Arthur Phillip.[30]

What Wealth?

In 1815, Australia's Gross Domestic Product (GDP) was small, worth only £500,000 pounds but compared to the wealth in England at the time, and in relation to wealth today, the colonial rich who shared this small amount appear to be seriously rich.[31] Analysis of their wealth in Table 2.1 shows the predominance of pastoralism.

Table 2.1: Type of Wealth of the Richest Australians 1788–1849

Wealth also held in these sectors	Number of richest Australians who hold wealth in these sectors						
	Industrial	Financial	Commercial	Agriculture	Real Estate	Media	All
Industrial	--	5	15	19	8	0	37
Financial	5	--	8	15	7	0	19
Commercial	15	8	--	37	9	2	53
Agriculture	19	15	37	--	14	3	76
Real estate	8	7	9	14	--	2	19
Media	0	0	2	3	2	--	5
No other wealth source	9	1	11	23	0	2	46
Total	37	19	53	76	19	5	109
	34%	17%	49%	70%	17%	5%	

Source: Collated from W. Rubinstein, data (2004).
Multiple response: totals are multiple choices, numbers in the columns will not sum to the totals.
Categories for coding the source of wealth were from the ANZSIC classification
Number of cases: 110 valid cases; 1 missing case.

How to read Table 2.1. The numbers in each cell indicate the number of people with wealth in the column category that also have wealth in the row category. So the top cell in the second data column indicates that 5 (out of 19) people with financial wealth also had industrial wealth, while the cell two rows below that indicates that 8 (out of 19) people with financial wealth also had commercial wealth. As wealth holders can hold wealth in several sectors, the numbers in the columns do not add to the total in the bottom row. The percentages in the bottom row indicate the proportions of all wealth holders with the wealth category in that column. Again, multiple holdings mean the percentages add to more than one hundred per cent.

Table 2.1 shows the sectors most commonly acquiring wealth, and also how sectors associate with each other. For instance, those who were involved in agriculture were also most likely to be in commerce, then in industry, then finance, then real estate and least likely to be in media. By the 1820s and 1830s, convict labour was the mainstay of the colony's agriculture. Pastoralists and squatters were loud in their demand to hasten more transportation and increase the number of convict workers for their farms. But slowly the politically stronger urban classes who did not want competition for jobs defeated them. When the pastoralists realized that this was a battle they were not going to win, they tried (with limited success) to indenture labour from the Pacific Islands (e.g. Vanuatu), China and India.[32]

A good example of a man who was wealthiest through commerce but had multiple sources of revenue was Samuel Terry (see below), the richest man of this period (and any Australian period).[33] Samuel Terry, worth 24 billion dollars in modern value, would be four times richer in modern terms than the late Kerry Packer, Australia's richest man in 2005 ($6.9 billion).[34]

Samuel Terry (c 1776–1838)
Sydney merchant and landowner
Wealth: £200,000, equal to 3.395 per cent of GDP, 2003, modern value $24.37 billion
Terry was known as the 'Botany Bay Rothschild'. An ex-convict who, in 1800, as a 24 year old labourer was transported from Manchester to Australia for seven years for stealing 400 pairs of stockings. He arrived in Sydney in June 1801 on board the ship, *Earl Cornwallis*. As a convict, he worked in a stonemason's gang and was flogged. Before being freed he set up a stonemason business and by 1809, he also owned a farm at Parramatta. In 1810 as an innkeeper, he married a higher status woman, Rosetta Madden. By 1817, he was a contract trader to the government, dealing in meat and flour provisions. His expertise was real estate and by 1820 he owned one-fifth of all mortgages in NSW. He owned 1,450 cattle, 3,800 sheep and 1,900 acres including what is now the central Sydney CBD, Martin Place. His business methods were ruthless and extortionate but Governor Macquarie regarded him highly. He was a spokesman for the 'emancipists' (the ex convicts) and a prominent freemason. He is still relatively speaking Australia's richest man.
Source: Rubinstein (2004), p. 11.

In 1821, giving land grants to emancipists like Samuel Terry was stopped because Governor Brisbane (1773–1860) was warned by Commissioner Bigge acting on strong popular prejudice[35] that if he did not 'distinguish between emancipist and immigrant in society he might disgust the free section of the population'.[36] The warning came from Brisbane's system of land grants was that for every hundred acres granted, 'the grantee would maintain free of expense to the crown one convict labourer'.[37]

Class Backgrounds

Approximately two-thirds of the earliest wealthy (1790–1849) were free settlers and approximately one third were convicts. Although at first glance this looks like proof of great social mobility it must be seen in the 1820 context that the convicts were two thirds of the total white population and even to 1837 in NSW, convicts numbered 42,000 of a total population of 75,000. Nonetheless, the social mobility of these convicts is unique to their ruling class. Interestingly, however, and consistent with later data,[38] is that their fathers were still predominantly from managerial and administrative backgrounds.[39]

Table 2.2: Father's Occupation 1788–1849

Occupation	Frequency	Per cent	Percent known
Free settlers			
Managers & Administrators	16	14.5	44.4
Professionals	5	4.5	13.9
Associated Professionals	1	.9	2.8
Tradespeople	8	7.3	22.2
Advanced Clerks	1	.9	2.8
Intermediate Clerks	1	.9	2.8
Convicts	4	3.6	11.1
Total	36	32.7	100.0
Not stated	74	67.3	
Total	110	100.0	

Source: Murray collating Rubinstein's original data (2004), classifications ABS ASCO codes.[40]

Table 2.3: First Occupation 1788–1849

Occupation	Frequency	Per cent	Per cent known
Free settlers			
Managers & Administrators	10	9.9	10.6
Professionals	23	22.3	24.4
Associated Professionals	3	2.9	3.1
Tradespeople	18	17.8	19.1
Advanced clerks	6	5.9	6.3
Intermediate clerks	2	1.9	2.1
Production workers	3	2.9	3.1
Convicts	29	28.7	30.8
Total	94	93.0	100.0
Not stated	7	6.9	
Total	101	100.0	

Source: Murray collating Rubinstein, original data (2004).

The second most common 'paternal occupation' amongst the early wealth was 'convict' (see Table 2.2). The first jobs of these first billionaires were most likely to be prison work with 28 per cent arriving in the colony as convicts (see Table 2.3). The earliest Australian free settler billionaires were most often professionals doing work that included being clergy, captains of ships and holding public office.

By the 1870s, the British had stopped sending convicts to the colonies (New South Wales in 1851, Tasmania in 1853 and Western Australia in 1868).

Religion

On 3 February 1788, the Reverend Johnson held the first Christian service in Botany Bay. The early wealthy were mostly Anglicans (80 per cent). There were few Roman Catholic ruling class members and they (along with all other Catholics in the colonies) were denied a cleric until 1803. O'Lincoln suggests that the state relented because of their fear of Irish rebellion. The authorities knew the priests would counsel submission to authority. This was important after the 300 convicts had unsuccessfully rebelled at Castle Hill in 1804. Six convict leaders were hung.[41]

Table 2.4: What Religion were they in 1788–1849?

Denomination	Frequency	Per cent	Known Per cent
Anglicans	21	19.1	80.8
Methodists	2	1.8	7.7
Roman Catholics	2	1.8	7.7
Jewish	1	.9	3.8
Total known	26	23.6	100.0
Unknown	84	76.4	
Total	110	100.0	

Source: Murray collating Rubinstein's original data (2004).

One of the richest, and least popular, of evangelical ministers operating in both Australia and New Zealand at this time was Reverend Samuel Marsden (1764–1838). He arrived in Australia in 1793 and later in New Zealand in 1814. He was renowned for his immense personal wealth and his extreme cruelty as an anti-Catholic 'flogging judge.' He harboured a lifelong hatred of Irish Catholics but paradoxically a fondness for the Maoris whom he thought a 'very superior people … in point of mental capacity'.[42]

Missionaries like Marsden were crucial for capitalist expansion; they taught indigenous populations literacy, they put the fear of God and obedience into an often less than cooperative convict-dominated workforce and they articulated support for the status quo among their parishioners.[43]

Samuel Marsden (1764–1838)
Anglican missionary and landowner
Wealth: £30,000, equal to 0.509 per cent of GDP, 2003, modern value $3.65 billion.
The son of a British blacksmith, he became a Methodist lay preacher in the Church of England. In 1793 he went to NSW where he became the only Anglican minister. By 1827 he was a very large landowner (owning 5000 acres); a sheep breeder and woolgrower. He was also a magistrate renowned for his harsh sentencing. Governor Macquarie disliked him and had him removed. Socially he would not mix with ex-convicts or Catholics. He was keen to convert Maoris and Pacific islanders but despaired of Aborigines.
Source: Rubinstein (2004), pp. 30–31.

The State

From the outset, the organisation of the state was split along class lines. The pastoralist squatters and the British government were happy to have a plantation state and economy, whereas the urban capitalists, labourers and emancipists wanted a modern, capitalist society of free men working cooperatively as free labour in a business market.[44] Republicanism was treated harshly. In 1806, a convict received 100 lashes because he expressed a liking for the revolutionary views of Thomas Paine.[45] There were other politically savvy convicts who had arrived including the Scottish 'martyrs' sent as convicts for committing sedition in 1794[46] and there were 1,200 Chartists transported to Australia for social or political protest in the wake of the 1839, 1842 and 1848 protests.[47] And there were the English Tolpuddle Martyrs, the six men transported to NSW in 1834 for trying to form a union. They received 'especially harsh treatment from their masters'.[48]

Dissidents were not what the British state wanted (though they did not want them at home either). They wanted colonies full of loyal British subjects who would support their imperialist ambitions while simultaneously providing a South Pacific military bulwark against the French and any other imperialist interests. Meanwhile the governors also needed a bulwark against their own military — who were a constant thorn in their side. The military developed ambitions for personal excess based on their control of trade monopolies.

Governor Arthur Phillip

In the first days of the colony an embryonic ruling class emerged from the mentoring mantle of early governors. The first such mentoring governor was Governor Arthur Phillip (1738–1814), a British naval officer and a farmer who was largely credited with founding Sydney and Parramatta. He started a system whereby emancipists helped to control and organise convict workers. Phillip did not want slavery although his forms of punishment were not unlike that meted out to slaves; he frequently disciplined by flogging.

The military considered it beneath them to work and cultivate food but they were hungry for land that Governor Phillip was reluctant to give them. Soldiers became increasingly antagonistic toward Phillip until his 1792 return to England. Then their belligerence transferred to subsequent governors up until the 1820s.

John Macarthur (1767–1834)
Military Officer, pastoralist and merchant
Wealth: £40,000, equal to 1.047per cent of GDP, 2003, modern value $7.54 billion.
Born in England, he joined the Second Fleet as an army lieutenant. He arrived at Sydney Cove in 1790 and was given a 100-acre grant of land from Governor Hunter in return for his services as inspector of Public Works. This land grant became Elizabeth Farm. In 1797, he purchased two merino sheep that started his famous flock largely cared for by his wife. After igniting and leading a

tense period of military friction, he returned to England from 1801 to 1805. He wounded his commanding officer in a duel (one of a number) because he would not join him in acting against Governor King. He was instrumental in deposing Governor William Bligh in the Rum Rebellion of 1808. He returned permanently to NSW in 1817 becoming the colony's most successful sheep breeder. By 1830 he owned 60,000 acres around Parramatta. He established the Australian Agricultural Company to promote the pastoral development of NSW. In 1832, Governor Bourke removed him from the NSW Legislative Assembly on the basis that he was a lunatic. His descendants became pillars of the Australian upper class.
Source: Rubinstein, W. (2004), pp. 16–18.

Governor William Bligh[49]

William Bligh (1754–1817), after experiencing one mutiny on the *Bounty* in 1787, was unenthusiastic about his appointment to become Governor of NSW. He arrived in Sydney in 1806 and one of his first orders was that no alcoholic spirits should land in the colony without his consent. This order became a huge challenge to the military that had excluded the settlers from the alcohol trade. Not only was there a military monopoly over sales but there was also persecution of non-military spirit traders such as Isaac Nicholls (1770–1819) who was sent to Norfolk Island for fourteen years for reasons that thinly veiled his rival alcohol trading interests.[50]

Governor Bligh's order to allow himself (as the state) to control the rum trade fired the already existing military antagonisms, flaring into open rebellion against him in 1808. Behind these machinations was the infamous John Macarthur who was gaoled for igniting a military rebellion against Governor Bligh. This led to a mutiny of officers begun by Lieutenant-Colonel George Johnston, arresting Bligh. Macarthur, Johnston's superior, was freed. Johnston made Macarthur Colonial Secretary. He immediately restored the military's rum trade monopoly and the officers or supporters of the rebel administration were given government cattle handouts. In the period of Bligh's arrest there was in place a military junta, nominally and formally headed by Johnston but controlled by Macarthur. Bligh was recalled to London in 1810.

By 1820, taking a form of public office, held at the behest of the Governor, was clearly the way to amass a fortune or being in control of the government stores (see Table 2.5).

Table 2.5: Public Office 1788–1849

Public Office	Frequency	Per cent	Known per cent
Free settlers and convicts			
Government store keeper	3	2.7	18.8
Superintendent of Public Work	2	1.8	12.5
Law Enforcers	6	5.5	37.5
Inspector of Agriculture	1	.9	6.3
Surveyor	1	.9	6.3
Governor or Lieutenant Gov.	1	.9	6.3
Member of Parliament	2	1.8	12.5
Total	16	14.5	100.0
Missing number	94	85.5	
Total	110	100.0	

Source: Murray collating Rubinstein's original data (2004).

William Field was one of the 20 per cent of the wealthy who were government suppliers or storekeepers.

William Field (1774–1837)
Pastoralist and Meat Contractor
Wealth: £69,400, equal to 1.238 per cent of GDP, 2003, modern value $8.86 billion
Field was the son of an auctioneer, becoming a farmer and a butcher while still in England. In 1780 he was accused of illegally receiving nine sheep. He was convicted and sentenced to 14 years' transportation to NSW. By 1814 he was a merchant, farmer and grazier and in 1820 he became the principal meat supplier and trader in Van Diemen's Land. His wife, Elizabeth, was a former convict. By 1828, he owned nearly one third of the buildings and land in Launceston. At his death he was a publican and racehorse owner with 16,000 acres of Van Diemen's Land.
Source: Rubinstein (2004), p. 14.

Starting as a law enforcer in the colony was another way to achieving social mobility. Among the most interesting examples of this was an ex convict, Thomas Howard (1819), who left probated wealth with modern value of $2.06 billion. He had been a chief constable at Port Dalrymple in Van Diemen's Land. Others were a superintendent of convicts or public works and extraordinarily an ex-convict William Hutchinson (1772–1846) became the director of the Bank of NSW (the forerunner of Westpac). The numbers of members of parliament, amongst the wealthy, was low.

Edward Wollstonecraft (1783–1832)
Pastoralist
Wealth: £6000, or 0.250% of GDP, at current 2003 value $1.79 billion
Wollstonecraft's main claim to fame was that he was the brother of Mary
Wollstonecraft. In 1792, Mary had written a central liberal feminist text on
female rights called *The Vindication of the Rights of Women* and her equally
famous daughter, Mary Wollstonecraft Shelley, at 18 wrote *Frankenstein* in
1818. Edward Wollstonecraft was believed to be on the run from these female
relatives; as women writers at the time were referred to by their contemporaries
as 'Our unsex'd female writers' [51]
Source: Rubenstein (2004), p. 53.

Governor Lachlan Macquarie[52]

All governors gave land to 'the deserving' but the most enthusiastic land giver was
Governor Lachlan Macquarie (1761–1824). Governor Macquarie was a key person
at this time because it was he who helped build and consolidate this new ruling
class. He arrived in Sydney on 31 December 1809 after Governor Bligh's
ignominious recall to England. Wisely his first vice regal act was to send back to
England the New South Wales Corps and replace them with his own 73rd
regiment.[53] He then started parceling out land to those he favoured. One to whom
he gave land was a sardonic, bitter man with an irascible temper, Edward
Wollstonecraft.

Macquarie had a vigorous building policy that was to become a feature of his
administration. He straightened streets, commissioned buildings and improved new
barracks to be built for his regiment. Professionally and socially, Macquarie sought
to bring prominent emancipists into the organisational life of the colony. He
appointed four to the magistracy. But his thoughtfulness on this issue gave rise to a
schism between the free settlers and the military on one side and the emancipists
on the other. However, these emancipists were not to be easily ostracized by free
settler snobbery for they were brutalised ex-convicts used to risk-taking; they were
ex-thieves, insubordinate and mutinous. In short, they had learned skills suited to
their upwardly mobility in a capitalist colony. Wealthy emancipists numbers
amongst the billionaires, however, continued to decline to little more than a third
of what they had been in 1788–1849.

Period 2 (1850–1899): Free Trade and Limited Land Reform

Pastoralism was embedded in the new Australian colonies by 1850 with the
economy becoming increasingly dependent on the sale of merino sheep bred on the
vast new estates (see Figure 2.2). From this nineteenth century peak right up until
its twenty-first century decline, the contribution of has fluctuated, but in June 2001

still represented 3 per cent of the total Australian merchandise exports.[54] Non-pastoral agricultural areas 'under cultivation almost doubled from four and a half million acres to eight and three quarter million acres'.[55] Australian colonies were now answering a world (not just British) demand for their agricultural products. This was a period of immense growth particularly from the 1860s when these loosely joined Australian colonies developed sustained primary production with substantial (in some cases domestically invented) capital equipment and achieved a great deal of wealth. Wool production, gold mining and manufacturing provided the basis for economic growth for a 'powerful ruling class, a stable working class and predictable political institutions'.[56] These were only temporarily set back by the depression lasting from the mid-1880s to mid-1905.

Away from the farms, an urban infrastructure was building to service the industrial needs of agriculture. Manufacturing earnings increased quite sharply over this period as earnings from mining and distribution (retail and wholesale industries) and 'other' services grew after 1890. Government services were not as substantial a proportion of GDP in 1850–1899 as they had been in 1788–1849 when the state had been maintaining a prison colony. Mining became increasingly important after discoveries of gold first found by J. McBrien in 1823 in the Fish River, then again in Hartley in 1839 by Sir Paul de Strezlecki. In Otago, New Zealand, Gabriel Reed discovered gold in 1861. During this gold-rush period, a comprador merchant class associated with wholesaling and retailing emerged. These were colonial conduits or agents for larger overseas interests; they acted on peripheral colonialies for global capital.

Billionaire wealth was made in agriculture often combined with commercial, then industrial, then financial capital (see Table 2.6). Table 2.6 shows that numbers of the wealthy were down from the more populous billionaire 1788–1849 period, but particularly down in agriculture and commerce. This pattern of decreased participating wealthy principally represents what is happening in the population at large — each rich person is a smaller slice of a larger pie. William Clarke was Australia's richest man in this second 1850–1899 period.

Figure 2.2: GDP by Industry in Australia 1861–1900

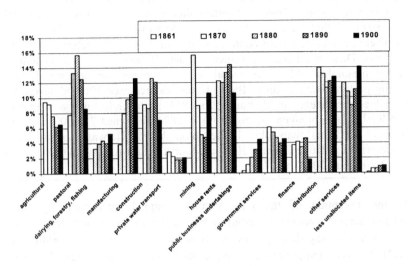

Source: Collated from Butlin (1987).

Table 2.6: The Type of Wealth of the Richest Australians 1850–1899

Sector	Number of richest Australians who held wealth in these sectors						
	Industrial	Financial	Commercial	Agriculture	Real Estate	Media	All
Industrial	--	9	13	15	5	0	22
Financial	9	--	9	11	6	0	18
Commercial	13	9	--	16	9	1	29
Agriculture	15	11	16	--	6	1	62
Real estate	5	6	9	6	--	1	17
Media	0	0	1	1	1	--	2
No other wealth source	2	0	3	30	3	0	38
Total	22 28%	18 22%	29 36%	62 78%	17 21%	2 3%	80

Source: Murray collating Rubinstein's original data (2004).

Percentages and totals based on respondents' multiple choices i.e. the % will not add up to 100%.

Note: Categories for coding the source of wealth were from the ANZSIC classification.

How to read this table: see Table 2.1.

William John Turner Clarke (1805–1875)
Pastoralist, Banker and Insurance Broker
Wealth: £1640, equal to 1.49 per cent of GDP, 2003 value $10.74 billion
Clarke was a free settler, born in London though his father was a Somerset farmer. After his father's death, he became a cattle drover and in 1829 he went to Hobart where he became a meat contractor. Within 24 years he acquired 80,000 acres in Van Diemen's Land and rented another 50,000 acres, making him a substantial pastoralist. When provincial Victoria opened up he moved into purchasing pastoral licences there. By 1842, he had acquired 100,000 sheep. In 1850, he lived permanently in Melbourne. In 1851, as the Gold Rush grew so did demand for his farm produce. At his death in 1874 he owned 215,000 acres in and he was a substantial shareholder in the Colonial Bank. He was also a member of the Victoria Legislative Council. He is the fourth richest Australian ever.
Source: Rubinstein (2004), p. 77.

With the exception of the UK, financial capital investment by core industrialised European countries started slowly in the 1850s. It increased slowly until 1890 then fell away sharply in the cyclical financial crisis of the 1890s (see Figure 2.2). The core and peripheral ruling classes were able to counter the crisis and raised profits by lifting the level of colonial labour exploitation. The popular clamour for land rose with increasing numbers of migrants. This meant that the squatters (the big landowners or pastoralists) were increasingly exposed to political pressure to either pay for their land or relinquish some of it.

European economic depression meant that European money needed new outlets to be realised. Colonial capital investment was their solution and the scale in which their capital was introduced was enormous. Late in the 1880s over 20 million pounds a year was invested (seen as pastoral investment in Figure 2.2). Overseas capital developed a colonial economy that was largely, though not exclusively, based on the wool industry and its productive infrastructure. Industries and infra-structural developments such as manufacture distribution, wholesale and retail trade, export, and transportation by rail, road and sea all flourished with the large injection of British investment.[57]

Phil Griffith argues that the cyclical crisis and subsequent crash of the 1890s was because British investment dried up; new marginal lands needed more, not less, investment, and over production resulted in a massive wool glut in 1892. In addition, the colonial governments had acquired massive debt.[58] For example, by 1890, 160 million pounds was borrowed to build 12,800 miles of railway.

Class

The background status of the Australian billionaires rose in this second period, with their fathers likely to have come from higher status jobs, and less likely to be convicts.

Table 2.7: Father's Occupation 1850–1899

Occupation	Frequency	Per cent	Known per cent
Free settlers			
Managers & Administrators	36	44.4	50.0
Professionals	4	4.9	5.6
Associated Professionals	15	18.5	21.1
Tradespeople	4	4.9	5.6
Advanced clerks	5	6.1	7.0
Convicts	7	8.6	9.8
Total known	71	87.6	100.0
Missing Unknown	10	12.3	
Total	81	100.0	

Source: Murray. collating Rubinstein's original data (2004).

In this period, 1850 — 1899, the ruling class became uniquely visible as state actors with many entering parliamentary politics. The first jobs of the ruling class had dramatically improved with only 9 per cent of Australian billionaires having begun their working lives in prisons (see Table 2.8).

Table 2.8: First Occupation 1850–1899

Occupation	Frequency	Per cent	Known per cent
Free settlers			
Managers & Administrators	35	43.8	43.8
Professionals	6	7.5	7.5
Associated Professionals	12	15.0	15.0
Tradespeople	12	15.0	15.0
Advanced Clerks	5	6.3	6.3
Intermediate Clerks	1	1.3	1.3
Other	2	2.5	2.5
Convicts	7	8.8	8.8
Total	80	100.0	100.0

Source: Murray collating Rubinstein's original data (2004). No missing data.

Managerial and/or administrative jobs were common. There were much smaller numbers associated with professions or trades than in the first half of the century. Changes were happening in the distribution of religions, too. Presbyterians entered their numbers at this time in both Australia and New Zealand. Presbyterians become 32 per cent of the total sample (after not registering at all through 1788–1849).

The State

One of the most outstanding features of this period is the number of ruling class members who became visible as active politicians. Some 28 per cent of the very wealthy were members of parliament and this occupation covered 79 per cent of all office holding amongst these very wealthy people (see Table 2.9). This enabled them to create legislation that gave them further access to migrant workers who were necessary for their factories and it enabled them to use the state to provide the public sector infrastructure necessary for business expansion.

Table 2.9: Public Office 1850–1899

Public Role	Frequency	Per cent	Known per cent
Industry related role	1	1.3	3.6
Councillor/Alderman/Mayor	3	3.8	10.7
Law Enforcer	1	1.3	3.6
Surveyor	1	1.3	3.6
Member of Parliament	22	28.0	78.6
Total	28	35.0	100.0
Missing	53	66.2	
Total	80	100.0	

Source: Murray collating Rubinstein's original data (2004).

An example of a billionaire whose earlier public office was as a government surveyor was Henry Dangar (1796–1861). Dangar was infamous as the owner of Myall Creek station, where an Aboriginal massacre took place in 1838. A group of 40 Aborigines had set up camp on his land, when a posse of stockmen and squatters took the opportunity to avenge cattle losses. The men knew that these Aborigines had no involvement in attacks on their stock but they decided to kill the 28 old men, women and children anyway. Children were decapitated, people hacked to death and a young woman was forced to watch the deaths and was then repeatedly raped.[59]

The two big issues of the political parties, and hence the dividing issues of the ruling class before 1890, were immigration and free trade or protection. Protection was an economic measure to raise domestic revenue and to protect local producers from overseas competition through the erection of sizable tariff barriers or through restrictive quotas.[60] This policy was strongly advocated by key political leaders, Edmund Barton (1849–1920) and Alfred Deakin (1856–1919). Later, both became prime ministers. Australian citizens, they argued, should be protected through state legislation against overseas corporate monopolies and wage guarantees should be provided.[61]

The background to the Free Trade Movement was the economic liberalism of the Manchester School, particularly the politics of two of its UK parliamentarians, Richard Cobden (1804–1865) and John Bright (1811–1889). Both Cobden and Bright promoted free trade and opposed protectionism. They wanted an end to aristocratic privilege in commerce (specifically by repealing the *Corn Laws* in 1846) and to allow free trade without state or union interference. NSW Premier George Reid was a strong advocate of free trade.

Henry Dangar (1796–1861)
A pastoralist, surveyor and Member of Parliament
Wealth: £280,000, equal to .434 per cent of GDP, 2003 value $3.11 billion
Dangar was a free settler from Cornwall. His father was a farmer. His first job was as a public surveyor surveying the Hunter River area where he built up a pastoral estate. He was dismissed for using his office for personal gain. He published a surveyed guide to the Hunter Valley region and was reinstated. A further 300,000 acres on the Liverpool Plains where acquired by 1850. He entered the NSW parliament in 1845–51 and ended his life in a Potts Point mansion.
Source: Rubinstein (2004), pp. 89–90.

With a rising economic crisis in the 1890s, class struggle increased and the divided ruling class regrouped to oppose labour.[62] The Australian Labor Party (ALP) grew out of working class distress. Support was given by the whole labour movement to events such as the 1890 Maritime Strike and the 1891 and 1894 Shearers Strikes. On each occasion the workers suffered badly; the strikers were beaten and starved into capitulation but after 1891 they hit back through the use of their new ALP voice.

Another dynamic was that the Australian economy was moving away from its agricultural base to explore other industries such as manufacturing and distribution. This changing economic dynamic was paralleled by an emerging rural-to-urban drift and brewing political fights for female suffrage.

Period 3 (1900–1979): Protectionism Dominates

In 1910, pastoralism was still dominant but it was soon replaced in significance by manufacturing, distribution and services, as shown in Figure 2.3.

The wealth of the billionaires in the sample (see Table 2.10) reflects the distribution of the economy of the colony. Big changes came to differentiate this period from the 1788–1900 wealth distribution patterns. The billionaires no longer depended primarily on agriculture, but rather industry and commerce, and there were wealthy financiers, real estate and media men. Again, there are common combinations of wealth, centring on industry and commerce. Individuals' wealth was not only in one fraction of capital.

Table 2.10 shows a declining number of relative billionaires based on percentage of GDP as their numbers drop to 42 per cent less than in 1850–1900 and 86 per cent less than in 1788–1949. The growing population meant each individual's share of wealth would be smaller, coupled with a growing disincentive to declare wealth because of tax avoidance and the use of trusts.

Figure 2.3: GDP by Industry in Australia 1910–1939

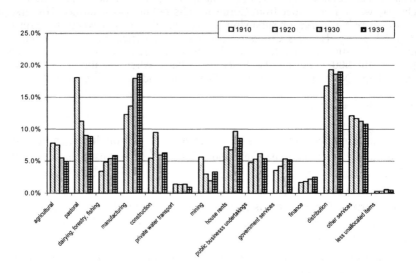

Source: Collated from Butlin (1987).

Table 2.10: The Type of Wealth of the Richest Australians 1900–1979

Sector	Number of richest Australians in these sectors						
	Industrial	Financial	Commercial	Agriculture	Real Estate	Media	All
Industrial	--	4	4	2	0	0	15
Financial	4	--	4	1	2	0	8
Commercial	4	4	--	0	3	0	14
Agriculture	2	1	0	--	0	0	9
Real estate	0	2	3	0	--	0	3
Media	0	0	0	0	0	--	2
No other wealth	6	0	6	7	0	2	21
Total	15 44%	8 29%	14 41%	9 27%	3 9%	2 6%	34

Source: Murray collating Rubinstein's original data (2004).

Multiple responses: Percentages and totals based on respondents' multiple choices i.e. the % will not add to 100%. Categories for coding the source of wealth were from the ANZSIC classification.

Number of cases: 34 valid cases; 0 missing cases.

How to read this table: see Table 2.1.

Class Background

By the 1900s, the newly federated state was now enjoying the benefits of its past. Manning Clark wrote of the role of 'semi slave labour in transporting a civilisation without handing on to posterity either the social problems, or the sense of guilt, that the use of slave ... labour often engenders'.[63] There was only one wealthy man left with a convict father amongst this 1900–1979 sample.

Table 2.11: Father's Occupation 1900–1979

Occupation	Frequency	Per cent	Known per cent
Free settlers			
Managers & Administrators	16	47.1	53.3
Professionals	2	5.9	6.7
Associated Professionals	3	8.8	10.0
Tradespeople	8	23.5	26.7
Convicts	1	2.9	3.3
Total	30	88.2	100.0
Unknown	4	11.8	
Total	34	100.0	

Source: Murray collating Rubinstein's original data (2004).

Total number of cases: 34 cases, missing cases 4.

Both the class of origin (Table 2.11) and the first occupation of the ruling class had improved dramatically for these rich men and women in this period from 1900–1979. The percentage of those starting in this period first as convicts was now very low (only 3 per cent of the sample).

The ruling class had well established class confidence as they held state power. Prior to federation in 1901, they were unchallenged in the colonial parliaments until the rise of the new Labor Party in 1890. This party became a very real and visible threat to their interests in Queensland when, in 1892, there were four Labor members elected into the state parliament. The situation became even worse for the ruling classes in 1899 when, from the first to the seventh of December, Andrew Dawson led the world's first Labor government in Queensland. Although something of 'a temporary aberration in the Continuous Ministry', it was a breakthrough for Labor, and it set the stage for a federal labor victory in 1904, two years after federation in 1901.[64]

The Australian State

ALP leader Chris Watson led his party to federal parliamentary success in 1904. Watson seriously took up the gauntlet and class struggle took on a new form by working through the parliamentary process. This was the time when the arbitration court system was introduced after the successful passage of the *Conciliation and Arbitration Act* in 1904. This meant that the working class now obtained the benefits of, and operated through, legal structures.

The next fourteen years of federal politics from 1901 to 1915 illustrated the volatility of the state, control of which fluctuated between parties supporting protection, free trade and labour. From 1915 onwards, things settled down to at least three-year periods of government for political parties; however, the demise of free trade — the victory of Alfred Deakin over Reid — signalled Reid's inability to get an Australia-wide mandate.

Griffith suggests that the ruling class at this time systematically used the state to contain class struggle. The ruling class fought from disparate class fractional bases built up by charismatic leaders like Sir Henry Parkes and their defining issues were free trade or protectionism.[65] Conflicts were to be resolved by the political parties, represented by labour and capital, acting within state organisations. Potentially, revolutionary movements were avoided. However, this development of the 'neutral' state using legal forms of coercion and persuasion through a 'layer of professional mediators' gave indirect power to the ruling class, enabling them to operate from a small and relatively weak social base.[66]

A test case for the protectionists involved manufacturer and inventor Hugh McKay. He was also an astute political operator who was virulently anti-union. He developed the Sunshine Stripper Harvester business through the 1890s employing up to 3,000 workers in Ballarat and Melbourne.

Hugh Victor McKay (1865–1926)
Agricultural and Machinery manufacturer at Sunshine and Ballarat in Victoria
Wealth: £2123945 equal to .272 per cent of GDP, 2003, value $1.95 billion
McKay's father was a farmer and staunch Irish Presbyterian. He arrived in Australia in 1852 becoming a manufacturer by 1883. His break was the multi functional harvester invented as the result of a government incentive scheme. In 1911 he developed the Sunshine Harvester plant into a model anti union based village called Sunshine.
Source: Rubinstein (2004), pp. 158–59.

Sunshine Harvester's rapid expansion threatened rival North American companies and in 1905 rumours circulated that these rival companies were preparing to dump their excess machinery on to the Australian market. McKay stimulated nationalistic sentiments that he used to pressure Prime Minister Deakin to protect Australian industry by increasing tariff protection through the *Excise Tariff (Agricultural Machinery) Act* 1906. Deakin agreed to the protection of domestic industry but, sensitive to the increased voting capacity of the newly enfranchised working class voters, he tied the excise exemption to the manufacturer's willingness to pay a fair and reasonable wage. This fair and reasonable basic wage was subsequently determined by the newly established Conciliation and Arbitaration Court in what was known as the *Harvester Judgment*. The *Excise Tariff (Agricultural Machinery) Act* 1906 was subsequently overturned by the High Court, but the basic wage concept remained in place as a centrepiece of wage fixing for six decades.[67]

Period 4 (1980–2005): Deepening Industrialisation and Economic Liberalism

By the 1980s, the high growth industries of the nineteenth and early twentieth centuries were registering sharp decline. Agriculture, the largest individual industry in 1900–1901 accounted for only 3.8 per cent of GDP by 2005. Manufacturing fell dramatically from 20 per cent of GDP in 1975 to 12.3 percent in 2005, the same as in 1900–1901. Mining and construction began at a starting point of 3.8 per cent in 1980 going to a slightly higher 4.6 per cent of GDP in 2005, having been as high as 10 percent of GDP in 1900.

Figure 2.4: Australian Industry by GDP 1976–2005

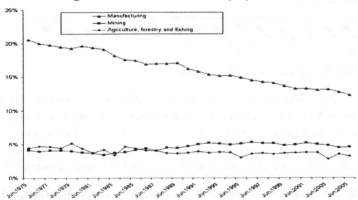

Source: ABS (2005) Industry gross value added, chain volume measures ($m) 5204.0 Australian System of National Accounts, Table 9. 07/11/2005.

The biggest growth was in property and business services; these contributed 12.7 per cent of GDP in 2005 (see Figure 2.5), growing from just over 8.3 per cent since the 1980s. The industry group includes a wide variety of services: wholesale trade and retail trade, accommodation, cafes and restaurants, property and business services and community services. Finance and insurance grew from 6 per cent of GDP in 1980 to 7.5 per cent in 2005. Communication services, including the big telecommunications firms such as Telstra and Optus, went from 1.1 per cent of the GDP in 1980 to 3 per cent in 2005.

Figure 2.5: Australian Industry by GDP 1976–2005

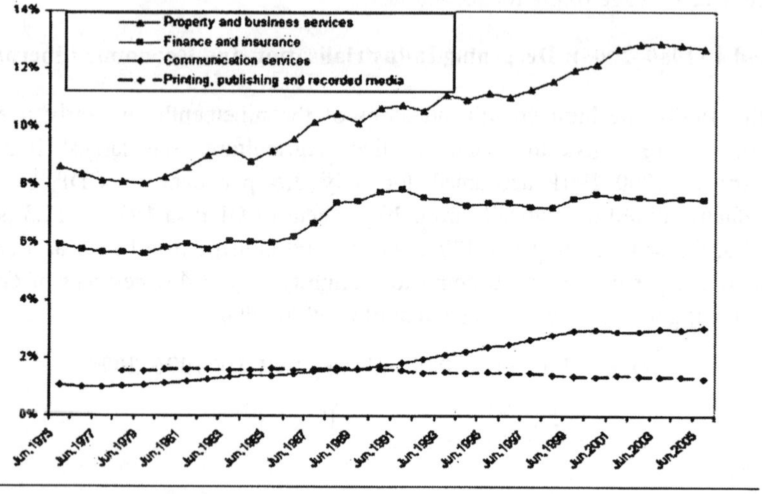

Legend:
- Property and business services
- Finance and insurance
- Communication services
- Printing, publishing and recorded media

Source: ABS (2005), Industry Gross Value added, 5204.0.

The major new development in terms of wealth in this period was the spectacular rise of those who control the media. Kerry Packer, who was Australia's wealthiest man, was a good example. Packer was described in an obituary as 'the most powerful man in Australia' and 'his decisions and leanings would decide elections that he could make kings and destroy those he disliked in an instant'.[68]

Table 2.12: Types of Wealth Owned by Wealthiest Australians 1980–2001

Sector	Number of richest Australians who held wealth in these sectors					
	Industrial	*Financial*	*Commercial*	*Real Estate*	*Media*	*All*
Industrial	--	3	4	2	0	5
Financial	3	--	4	3	1	4
Commercial	4	4	--	5	1	7
Real estate	2	3	5	--	1	5
Media	0	1	1	1	--	3
No other source of wealth	1	0	0	0	2	3
Total	5 50%	4 40%	7 70%	5 50%	3 30%	10

Source: Murray collating Rubinstein's original data (2004).
Categories for coding the source of wealth were from the ANZSIC classification.
Percentages and totals based on multiple choices i.e. % will not add up to 100%
Total cases: 10 valid cases; 0 missing case.
How to read this table: see Table 2.1.

With the number of relative billionaires (based on a percentage of GDP) just 10 in 1980–2005, they accounted for only 4 per cent of the total original 1788–1849 sample of billionaires.

Kerry Packer (1937–2006)
Media magnate and investor
Estimated personal wealth: $7 billion or $1 million a day (2005).
Biographical details: The Packer family dynasty began with Robert Packer (1869–1934). Robert was a Tasmanian customs official who left Hobart in 1879 moving to Sydney at age 21 and worked his way up from reporter to editor. During the 1920s, Robert joined forces with the newspaper owner, Sir Joynton Smith. His son, Frank, 'an honest man but a thug',[69] extended his father's newspaper interests and continued to make a fortune from the Australian Woman's Weekly. In 1959 Frank's close association with the Liberal Party and his relationship with the Prime Minister, Sir Robert Menzies meant a knighthood. Kerry Packer went to Geelong Grammar. 'He did not suffer the disadvantage of a good education. He was purely intuitive.'[70] At school, Packer was 'unpopular; taunted because of his huge size and by the vulgar way his family made their money'.[71]
Career: His success was attributed to his micro management of his empire.
Private Interests: Consolidated Press Holdings, a wide diversity of investments including media, gaming, property, chemicals, gems and fashion, Consolidated Pastoral Company, one of Australia's largest privately owned cattle companies, a 25 per cent stake in Challenger Financial group, a 50 per cent stake in Australia's biggest ski resort, Perisher Blue in Victoria.
Public Interests: Publishing and Broadcasting (36 per cent), Nine Network, Australian Consolidated Press (publishing *Women's Weekly*, *The Bulletin*, *Cosmopolitan* and other magazines), Crown and Burswood Casinos, Foxtel (25 per cent), Seek (25 per cent), Betfair, Ticketek, Ninesmsn, Hoyts Cinema groups (50 per cent), New Regency movie and television production (25 per cent).
Recreation: Polo, golf, tennis, cricket.
Clubs/societies: Royal Sydney Golf, Elanora Country, Tattersalls, and Athenaeum.
Sources: Rubinstein (2004), p.188, *BRW Rich list* (1996, 1997, 1998 1999, 2000, 2001, 2002, 2003, 2004, 2005). *Who's Who in Business in Australia* (2006), online, *Who's Who in Business in Australia* (1998), p. 796, Barry (1993), pp. 1–18, Jones (2005), p. 1, *Courier-Mail* 28 December 2005, p. 1.

In this period a unique pattern of wealth indicates the economic power of the media and the development of their subsequent close relations with the state and politicians.

Media and the State

Australia was arguably the first country in which the press was 'authentically popular' in that it was integrated into people's everyday lives.[72] In 1883 there was a peak of 600 newspapers in the six colonies.[73] But by 1980 the major newspapers and their major shareholders were reduced in number to a few key players, two of whom are the billionaires, Packer and the Australian expatriate, Rupert Murdoch.[74] The power of the media is great. One-writer notes the way that the Murdoch media are 'feared by politicians above all others'.[75] An example of a political relationship that went sour for the politician was Murdoch's relationship with Gough Whitlam after 1972.[76] Before the 1972 election 'only some key people in the Labor party put more energy into the campaign than Murdoch'.[77] In return, Murdoch revealed diplomatic ambitions 'to be Australian High Commissioner in London'.[78] This would have given Murdoch 'enormous business value at that time'.[79] Gough Whitlam, when made aware of Murdoch's ambitions, said, 'No way'.[80] Two years later, Murdoch in his own words, 'tore down' the Whitlam government.[81] Governments allocate and control the use of licenses; 'this function is why Newscorp is interested in governments'.[82]

After Packer's death, it was said 'Kerry used politics as an arm of business'.[83] Prime Minister John Howard highlighted this shatterproof link at Packer's death by giving him a state memorial service and saying Mr Packer was 'a friend...[and] of all the impressions he left me with none was greater or more indelible than his passionate commitment to the interests of Australia and the Australian people'.[84] At this time it was also said his 'feudal type company' or 'core businesses' rely heavily on government decisions, which restrict the entry of competitors.[85] Nine network television and Packer's share of Foxtel pay TV are protected from more vigorous competition by government policies. Even more restrictive entry conditions apply to his ownership of casinos in Melbourne and Perth.'[86] He was known to express his displeasure with on air programmes by saying 'Get this s--- off air!'[87] This interventionism in the media was something of a family trait. Kerry's father, Frank Packer, 'was certainly not averse to using his media outlets to express his displeasure when governments threatened to stand on his toes'. As owner of the Sydney *Telegraph* in the 1950s, Packer used his paper to unleash a series of virulent attacks upon politicians, including then coalition treasurer, Sir Arthur Fadden. Fadden's mistake had been 'to crack down on a particular tax avoidance scheme admired by Packer'.[88]

1980–2004 Billionaire Demographics

Class in 1980–2004 holds no surprises: there are no convict fathers nor had any billionaires started their first jobs in prison work. Nine billionaires (one has untraceable data) have fathers who are either managers or administrators (67 per cent of the sample) or are trades people (33 per cent of the sample). The billionaires' first jobs are similar to those of their fathers. Out of the nine valid cases they were managers and administrators (78 per cent of the sample) and trades people (22 per cent of the sample).

Their religion is interesting in that there is a notable 'over representation' of Jewish Australians who are nearly all 'Eastern European refugees or holocaust survivors and their families'.[89] As Michael Gilding points out, this may mean that wealth accumulation is a learned cultural skill with values instilled in a child's socialisation.[90] This is what a Jewish director said:

> Frequently, too, in the 50s and 60s, the migrants that came to Australia came from societies that were very affluent, and therefore they knew what being wealthy was. They knew what living by high standards was. And even though some of them may not have been rich in their own country of origin, they knew what being rich was about. Whereas here in Australia in those decades, there was no concept of wealth at that extreme. So the migrants knew what they were aiming for whereas the average Australian achieved a certain level of success and compared to his or her peer group felt comfortable. On the other hand, the migrant reached that level of success and said this is nothing compared to my European counterpart. [91]

Australia and New Zealand share this religious similarity and other parallels among the wealthy. There was much economic symbiosis occurring between the two countries. Until 1901, there was a real possibility that New Zealand would be included in Australia's federation. This was resisted by New Zealand whilst maintaining close cultural and trade links with Australia.

New Zealand's Wealthy

Graeme Hunt's sample included 85 men and two women. Note that this sample starts approximately 52 years later than the Australian sample.[92] Table 2.13 shows where different fractions of capital lie and embed with each other. New Zealand's early wealth, like Australia's, is shown to be primarily rural and these wealthy pastoralists were also likely to own real estate, be involved with commerce but be less likely to be involved with finance. Wealthy New Zealand farmers were unlikely to be involved with industry.

To make the New Zealand data comparable with the Australian data, I have recoded the wealthy as individuals and put them into the same time periods as the Australian sample by coding them by their death (as Rubinstein did using probate data).[93] Unlike the Australian data, Hunt's lists of top ten wealthy are occasionally listed as family wealth but from this individuals have then been identified and used. The individuals are noted as being amongst the top ten wealthy but the amount of their wealth is not recorded.

Table 2.13: Multiple Holdings by New Zealand's Wealthy 1840–2003

Sectors	Number of richest New Zealanders who held wealth in these sectors					
	Industrial	Financial	Comm-ercial	Agricu-ltural	Real Estate	All
Industrial	-	0	5	0	0	10
Financial	0	-	4	4	6	9
Commercial	5	4	-	5	9	23
Agricultural	0	4	5	-	7	30
Real estate	0	6	9	7	-	16
No other source of wealth	0	0	0	0	0	0
	10 18%	9 16%	23 40%	30 53%	16 28%	57

Source: Murray using Hunt data (2003).
Percentages and totals based on multiple responses.
Number of cases: 58 valid cases; 28 missing cases.
How to read this table: see Table 2.1.

The Weller Brothers:
Edward Weller (1814–1893), George Weller (1805–1875)
Whaling, Farming, Timber, Land Speculation
The Weller brothers came in 1831 from NSW and did not stay long in New Zealand. They developed an Otago whaling station with 80 cottages, slipways and sheds. Edward was kidnapped by Maoris in 1833 and held to ransom. They made their money selling timber, flax, fish, Maori artefacts, and preserved Maori heads. They moved into land speculation and by 1840, the brothers had three million acres. Edward drowned in NSW in 1893.
Source: Hunt, G. (2003), pp. 6–7.

Table 2.14 shows how New Zealand wealth creation continued to be dominated by agriculture from the 1900s to the 1980s. Agricultural wealth grew greatly in the 1890s when farmers with refrigerated shipping to sell their products to markets outside the colony. As in Australia, wool was the staple early source of wealth creation and agricultural declines after 1979.

Table 2.14: Sectoral Wealth Holdings 1840–2003

Decades	Industrial	Financial	Commer-cial	Agricultural	Real Estate
1850–1899	5	4	14	12	7
1900–1979	4	2	6	18	8
1980–2003	1	3	3	0	1
Total	10 17%	9 15%	23 40%	30 53%	16 28%

Source: Murray using Hunt data (2003).
Percentages and totals based on multiple responses.
57 valid cases; 29 missing cases.

Commerce, which is interlocked with farming, was the early starter with the sale of timber, fish, whale oil and seal skin products and flax. In the earliest period, these things had to be negotiated with the Tangata Whenua (people of the land) also known as Maori (ordinary people) with whom they traded artefacts and preserved Maori heads. Industrial wealth was more popular in earlier periods than in the later period (1980–2003) when the trend was for it to go offshore. As manufacturing too went offshore, financiers took control.

Period 1 (1790–1849): Pre-Treaty Wealth

Prior to European settlement, the Maori people had incalculable wealth in land, waka (canoe), pounamu (green jade) and goods that were collectively owned by the tribe.[94] Western wealth creation began with white settlers who brought from Europe a primitive form of capitalism revolving around commodity trade; first as traders in seal and whale and then flax fibre. There was no parallel first fleet landing in New Zealand in the eighteenth century and no convicts directly settled in New Zealand as it was not a penal colony.

> **Reverend Henry Williams (1792–1867)**
> Land, Farming
> Williams was a leading Anglican missionary from genteel Welsh stock who began his career as a navy midshipman fighting against the Danish. He left England on January 1822 on the *Lord Sidmouth*, a female-carrying convict ship on which he succeeded in banning the lewd songs of women convicts. In 1823 he met Samuel Marsden who was then working in New Zealand. He sailed for New Zealand where he acquired large land holdings in the 1830s. Governor Grey called him *land grabbing*. This reference got Williams sacked by the London Home Office. He assisted in the creation of the Treaty of Waitangi (1840). He was a fluent speaker of Maori and had an extensive knowledge of their culture He was reinstated to the Church Missionary Society (CMS) in 1852. His 800 descendents today own land worth at least $30,000,000.
> *Source:* Hunt (2003), pp. 22–23, *New Zealand Encyclopaedia*.

Although the Maori have never been among the top wealthy, they were always entrepreneurial, technologically adept and vocal in their dealings with white settlers. Relations between the ethnic groups ranged from tense to violent, culminating in the land wars of the 1860s. Both the Maori and the Pakeha had a similar low life expectancy (30 years) at the earliest period of white settlement.[95] The richest early settler was a NSW man called Johnny Jones who was known to be a man of irascible temper.[96] Jones was instrumental in prolonging the signing of the Treaty of Waitangi by persuading Maori not to sign it because he rightly believed that British Home Office rule would mean he would have to return extremely large amounts of land he had acquired from South Island Maoris.

> **Johnny Jones (1808/9?–1869)**
> Whaling, shipping, land speculation
> Jones was once described as one of Sydney's 40 thieves; he migrated to New Zealand before 1835 to become a whaler and sealer. Thomas Jones was his father and his unknown mother was rumoured to be a convict. He married Sarah Sizemore and they had 11 children. In 1838–1839, he purchased approximately 40,500 acres from Maori elders and he joined with William Wentworth (1790–1872) in an almost successful attempt to buy all unsold Maori land. They were stopped by NSW Governor George Gipps and allowed only a maximum of 2,560 acres, but later Jones acquired an additional 8,650 acres. He printed his own bank notes and founded the forerunner of the Union Steam Ship Co called the Harbour Steam Navigation Co. He died in a stately home in Dunedin.
> *Sources:* Hunt (2003), pp. 3–7 and Tapp (2005).[97]

Period 2 (1850–1899): Merchant Wealth[98]

Settlers were able to fully realise the value of New Zealand's fertile soils, its temperate climate and its high rainfall. Peasant-like arable farming soon gave way to pastoralism, particularly among those wealthy enough to buy and ship stock. Corriedale sheep with their long fleece continued to be New Zealand's economic mainstay until 1882. Exports were enhanced by canned meat exports from 1869 and further by refrigeration invented in 1882. These technologies helped give New Zealand its disproportionately significant role, for its size, in food production for the UK. It maintained this role until the 1970s when Britain entered what later became the European Union.

Wealth to be found in farming led to aggressive competition for land, usually Maori land. The *Native Land Acts* of 1865 and 1873 opened up Maori landholdings by breaking down communal land ownership. The first ten tribe members were able to list as owners making individual ownership possible. Hunt suggests 'virtually every nineteenth century settler who could be described as rich and a number of public servants to boot' entered into land speculation.[99] 'Scabby Moore' is an example of one of these pastoralists of this period (see below).

From 1879 to 1896, New Zealand went into a 'long depression', a period characterised by heavy borrowing by the colonial treasurer (later premier), Julius Vogel. Vogel's conservative government went through 1869 to 1875 and later from 1884 to 1888 when Vogel was the colonial treasurer in the government of Robert Stout. Rural colonial gentry and their cronyism dominated the National government.[100]

George Henry 'Scabby' Moore (1812–1905)
Pastoralist
Moore in 1854 with his friends William Kermode, Dr John Lillie and his son, William, Moore purchased the Glenmark leases in Canterbury. Although very wealthy he became renowned for his mean and suspicious personality. In his large mansion, on his 150,000 hectares farm, there was strangely no back door. Moore was widely seen as a hard employer and a bad neighbour with scab-ridden sheep. Thus he was known as 'Scabby Moore.' In 1864 he was fined 2,400 pounds for owning distressed sheep.
Source: Hunt (2003), New Zealand Dictionary of Biography.

Class Background

Crony capitalism characterised this period with riches and resources being given to buddies within the same class and passed on to their sons. The very wealthy in the sample came primarily from high-class origins with many of their fathers being administrators or managers (this includes those who owned and managed farms). The rest had fathers who were professionals or associate professionals.

Table 2.15: Class Origin, Father's Occupation 1850–1899

Occupation	Frequency	Per cent	Known per cent
Managers & Administrators	7	8.1	77.9
Professionals	1	1.2	11.1
Associated Professionals	1	1,2	11.1
Total	9	10.5	100.0
Unknown	77	89.5	
Total	86	100.0	

Source: Murray using Hunt data (2003).

Crony capitalism permeated late nineteenth century business. Central figures at this time were Sir Frederick Whitaker, John Grigg and Thomas Russell who were all land speculators (in confiscated Maori land) and members of parliament. They were the core of Auckland's business and social network core. Russell had begun this network from his Wesleyan church contacts enlarging it to become what became known as the 'Limited Circle'. Grigg was his brother-in-law. The seven original trustees of the Bank of New Zealand were Russell's cronies from the Limited Circle. Russell is an excellent example of very wealthy leadership in this period (see below).

Thomas Russell (1830–1904)
Estimated wealth: 160,778 pounds
Law and land speculation
Russell was arguably New Zealand's most 'outstanding commercial figure in the nineteenth century, he was born in Ireland. His father became a farmer in Maitland, NSW. The family settled in New Zealand in 1840 and his mother later ran a drapery in Auckland but she died in 1847 aged 36. His father left New Zealand for the Californian gold fields, leaving the family with the young Russell. In 1851 Thomas was licensed to practice as a lawyer. He was an active supporter of the Progress Party that in 1850s represented Auckland business interests. He took Sir Frederick Whitaker (later the Premier) as his legal partner. He founded the Bank of New Zealand the year he became an MP in Premier Alfred Domett's government (1862–1863). In 1863 he was Minister for Defence and pursued a policy of no compromise with 'rebel' Maoris. He then profited from the sale of confiscated Maori land. His business deals were corrupt and in 1872 Cyrus Haley attempted to shoot him. In 1878, Russell was only able to avoid bankruptcy through his 'Limited Circle' friends but by 1886, he financially recovered due to the success of the Waihi Gold Mine.
Source: Hunt, G. (2003), *New Zealand Dictionary of Biography.*

Religion

From 1850 through to 1899 there were only eight New Zealanders with noted religions among the wealthy. These were three Anglicans, one Presbyterian, one Catholic and three Jews. Again, the last is disproportionate to the number in the general population recorded in 1886. Congregations, that year, were 40 per cent Anglicans, 14 per cent Catholics, 23 per cent Presbyterians and .27 per cent Jews.[101] Caughey writes that the Jewish Nathans sought 'to marry into other Jewish families and are therefore not likely to be a part of this network'.[102] Jews were not a part of Russell's Limited Circle.[103]

Period 3 (1900–1979): Protectionist Wealth

From 1900, the now defunct 'Limited Circle' took on a new life as an Auckland group known as the 'Kelly Gang'. They were financiers and lawyers associated with the Auckland Northern Club and linked in politics to the Reform Party.[104] They were businessmen (unnamed by Hunt) who were said to control 180 million pounds of the country's funds and assets and had a 'hand in every nefarious business deal going'.[105]

The political voice of business was the conservative New Zealand Political Reform Party. Discontentment with Richard Seddon (1845–1906) and the Liberals came from both the small farmers and some workers who drifted toward the Reform Party too. The new Reform Party was led to victory by Prime Minister

William Massey who, in 1915, showed his tough anti socialist line as a militant response to striking Waihi miners and dockers.

At this time a most noteworthy development began—cooperative farming. This was a small farmer defensive response to growing multi-national (MNC) agribusiness. A leading individual in the movement was Sir William Goodfellow who set up the Waikato Dairy Company in 1908. With future amalgamations, but still cooperatively owned by the farmers, this grew into the successful MNC Fonterra (formerly New Zealand Dairy Company).

Sir William Goodfellow (1880–1974)
Pastoralist Cooperative farmer.
Goodfellow's father Thomas was a farmer. He was born in Pirongia in the Waikato in 1880 and educated at Auckland Boys Grammar School. In 1908, he set up the Waikato Dairy Company in 1918 it became the New Zealand Dairy Company. He was its first managing director. In 1925–1926, he formed the Amalgamated Dairy and Phosphate Company. 1923 was knighted in 1923.
Sources: Te Ara Encyclopaedia (1966), [Accessed online June, 2005], *Dictionary of New Zealand Biography* [Accessed online July, 2005].

Only two extremely wealthy women were noted in the New Zealand rich lists. The first was Anne Quayle Townend (1844–1914), the daughter of 'Scabby' Moore. She was completely dominated by her cantankerous father. The other wealthy woman was Lady Agnes Wigram (1862–1957) who similarly inherited her wealth.

Class Background

Class backgrounds in 1900–1979 appear to be similarly concentrated in high-status occupations. A clear majority of fathers were managers and administrators.

Table 2.16: Father's Occupation 1900–1979

Occupation	Frequency	Per cent	Known per cent
Managers & Administrators	19	46.3	73.1
Professionals	3	7.3	11.5
Associated Professionals	2	4.9	7.7
Intermediate clerical	1	2.4	3.8
Intermediate production	1	2.4	3.8
Total	26	63.4	100
Missing	15	36.6	
Total	41	100.0	

Source: Murray using Hunt. data (2003).

Period 4 (1980–2005): Economic Liberalism

This latest period up until the present witnessed a change in the business community from a productive to a finance orientation then back to land capital. Hunt denies the existence of any 1920s Kelly-type gang of the powerful in this later period but he contradicts this when he refers to the New Zealand Business Roundtable in the 1990–2000s as the 'big boys' club'.[106] The idea of these men as a cabal can also be found in the work of Jesson: 'Speculative finance has gutted New Zealand ... it is no exaggeration to say that while the means of the financial dealers may be sane — and in fact highly rational — their purpose is mad'.[107] And 'a generation ago the economy was controlled by producers; these days the economy is run by financiers'.[108] Finance had consistently been a source of wealth but suddenly in the 1980s it also became a source of policy direction.

One of the strongest members of this 'small but strategically influential team' was Allan Gibbs.[109]

Allan Gibbs (1939–)
Investment, Land, Inheritance
Estimated wealth: $300million (2003)
Allan Gibbs is a strong advocate of 'new right' economic liberalism. Early in 1979 he partnered Trevor Farmer in the acquisition of Tappenden Motors. He has a reputation as an astute businessman 'if not always ... affable'. He was a diplomat. Gibbs and Charles Bidwell became very successful in Ceramco.
Source: Hunt (2003), pp. 225–56.

Allan Gibbs, a New Zealand Business Roundtable (NZBR) member, personally profited from the privatisation of state assets particularly, in his case, the sale of Telecom. Jane Kelsey and Bill Rosenberg wrote of this time of privatisation:

> The key players in this process were a select group of merchant bankers and consultants for whom privatisation was especially lucrative. They collected a transaction fee for advising on potential privatisations; there were brokerage and underwriting fees if the sale proceeded (which they invariably recommended); afterwards, the buyer would need financial and other investment services, which the broker would often provide. Sometimes they blurred the boundaries by advising the government and also acting as buyers.[110]

NZBR members did well out of privatisation[111] in a period described by Easton as a 'Wild West show of corporate greed and dishonesty'.[112] Many overseas corporations also benefited from the privatisation sales — 'State railways went to Wisconsin; telecommunications to US companies Bell Atlantic and Ameritech; the major banks passed into Australian and British hands; steel ended up with Australian mining giant BHP; state forests were shared among the US, China,

Japan and Malaysia, as well as New Zealand-based but foreign-owned transnationals'.[113] There was a great deal less privatisation occurring at the same time in Australia, largely because of the political complexion of the government and because, after the Liberals took office in 1996, the Senate blocked the passage of some privatisation Bills such as the sale of Telstra.

According to Easton the evidence as to the extent of the greed of 1980s and 1990s emerged 'among other places, in some of the evidence to the *Wine Box Enquir'y.*[114] This alleged affair of theft, corruption and murder committed by big business is outlined in Wishart's book, *The Paradise Conspiracy.*[115]

Conclusion

We have found two ruling classes in Australia and New Zealand; they are not the same as each other or internally cohesive but two discernable ruling classes with some similarities. Nowhere else in the world is there a beginning for the wealthy like that found in the Australian penal colony where 28 per cent of the earliest known wealthy were ex-convicts. But still, New Zealand and Australia's ruling classes both have generally high social origins and are largely horizontal rather than vertical in their movements. There is some evidence here to show that the ruling classes have moved away from directly involving themselves in the running of the state (as they clearly did in the period 1850–1900). Most recently the ruling classes may have withdrawn from this direct method of state control because they have indirect control through their monopoly over the media and the power of finance. The ruling classes have emerged as predominantly Protestant though Judaism is outstanding amongst the ruling class because, although Jews are only 0.4 per cent of the total religious population in Australia and 0.16 per cent in New Zealand, they achieve so highly.[116]

The Australasian indigenous peoples fared very badly in this history of rapacious land grabbing and are notable by their absence from the elite on both sides of the Tasman Ocean. Amongst the wealthy who won? The overall winners were white, Protestant, middle class and male. Fractional ruling class dominance passed from pastoralists, to miners, to both media and finance magnates. Class mobility is shown here to be primarily horizontal as in Marx's model. But whether the state's relationship to the ruling class, whether instrumental or autonomous, still remains to be seen in chapters three and beyond.

Notes

[1]   Rubinstein, W. (2004), *The All-time Australian 200 Rich list from Samuel Terry 'The Convict Rothchild' to Kerry Packer*, Crows Nest, Allen and Unwin.

2   Australian Historical Statistics (1987), http://www.library.usyd.edu.au/subjects/govern
     ment/austhist .html#WPTOHTML11.
3   Gilding, M. (1999), p. 171.
4   Hunt, G. (2003), *The Rich List, Wealth and Enterprise in New Zealand 1820–2003*,
     Birkenhead Auckland, Reed Publishers.
5   Hunt, G. (2003).
6   Hunt, G. (2003), pp. xii–xiv.
7   Hunt, G. (2003), p. *xiv.*
8   Adcock, G. & Dennis, E., Eastal, S., Huttley, G., Jermiin, L., Peacock, J. Thorne, A.
     (2001), 'Mitochondiral DNA sequence in Ancient Australians: Implications for Modern
     Human Origins', *Proceeding of the National Academy of Sciences of the United States,*
     1998, 16 January, p. 537 and the *SBS Australian Almanac,* (2000), South Yarra, Hardie
     Grant Books, p. 252.
9   Kirch, P. V. (2000), *On the Road of the Winds: An Archaeological History of the Pacific
     Islands before European Contact,* Los Angeles University of California Press, Berkeley.
     quoted in Adele L.H. Whyte; S. J. Marshall; G. K. Chambers, (2005), 'Human evolution
     in Polynesia' *Human Biology,* April, v.77, i.2, p. 157(21).
10   Carmichael, G. (1992), 'So Many Children: Colonial and Post Colonial Demographic
     Patterns', in K. Saunders & R. Evans, (1992), *Gender Relations in Australia:
     Domination and Negotiation,* (ed.s) Harcourt, Brace & Jovanovich, Sydney, p. 103
11   Borch, M. (2001), 'Rethinking the Origins of Terra Nullius', *Australian Historical
     Studies,* v. 32, no.117, pp. 222–39.
12   Tapp, R. quoted in O'Lincoln, T. (2005), p. 3.
13   British National Archives
     www.catalogue.nationalarchives.gov.uk/RdLeaflet.asp?sLeaflet ID=347&j=1.
14   French, J. (2005), 'The Convict Death Fleet, Australia's Second fleet' — 1790, *IFHAA
     Shipping Pages,* IFHAA, [Accessed 6 August, 2005].
     http://freepages.genealogy.rootsweb.co/ ~ifhaa/ifhaa/ships/2ndfleet.htm).
15   *SBS Australian Almanac 2000*, South Yarra, Hardie Grant Books, p. 253.
16   Paul, A. & Southgate, D., McCrane, D, Widdowssons, S. (1987), 'The Compensation of
     Food', 4th edition, *MRC Special Report,* no. 297.
17   Australian Government (2005), *Culture and Recreation Portal website* [Accessed 21
     July, 2005]. http:/www.cultureandrecreation.gov.au/articles/australianhistory/
18   Evans, R. & Thorpe, W. (1998), 'Commanding Men: Masculinities and the Convict
     System', *Journal of Australian Studies,* n.56, p. 17.
19   Evans, Professor R. & Thorpe, W. (1998), p. 17.
20   Evans, R. (2006), pers com, 20 January.
21   O'Lincoln, T. (2005), 'The Most Outrageous Conduct, Convict Rebellions', *Marxist
     Interventions,* http://www.anu.edu.au/polsci/marx/interventions/convicts.htm, p. 1.
22   Griffiths, P. (2005), *Understanding Australian History,* Unpublished PhD, ANU,
     [Accessed 25 July, 2005] line http:/members.optsnet.com.au/~griff52/crisis-ah.html.
23   Rubinstein, W. (2004).
24   Rubinstein, W. (2004), p. v.
25   Frances, R. (1994), 'The History of Female Prostitution in Australia', in Perkins, R. &
     Prestage G. Sharp, R. Lovejoy, F. (ed.s) *Sex workers and Sex work in Australia,*
     University of New South Wales Press, Sydney, pp. 27–52.
26   Carmichael, G. (1992), p. 10.
27   O'Lincoln, T. (2005).
28   Oxley, D. 'Data from Convict Maids', *International Centre for Convict Studies,*
     [Accessed 1 July, 2005] http://iccs.arts.utas.edu.au/data/convictmaids.html#9.
29   Summers, A. (1975), 267–85.
30   Rutter, O. (1937), *The First Fleet,* London, Cockerel Press.
31   Rubinstein, W. (2004), p. 1.

32 Griffith, P. (2005), p. 4.
33 Source of original data Rubinstein,W. (2004). See how to read the table description under Table 2.1.
34 *Business Review Weekly*, 11 March, 2005.
35 *Australian Dictionary of Biography*, John Thomas Bigge [Accessed 1 January, 2006] http:/Gutenberg.net.au/.
36 Clark, M. (1961), p. 53.
37 Clark, M. (1961), p. 53.
38 Murray, G. (1990), *New Zealand Corporate Capitalism*, PhD Thesis, University of Auckland, Auckland, p.216.
39 McGregor, C. (1997), *Classes in Australia*, Ringwood, Victoria, Penguin, pp. 1–19,
40 From classifications found in the ABS ASCO catalogue 1220.
41 *SBS Australian Almanac 2000*, (2000), p. 252
42 Marsden, S. (1932), *The Letters and Journals of Samuel Marsden 1766–1838*, (ed.) John Rawson Elder, Dunedin, Coulls Sommerville Wilkie, A.H. Reed. pp. 325–6.
43 O'Lincoln, T. (2005), p. 3.
44 Griffith, P. (2005), p. 4.
45 O'Lincoln, T. (2005), p. 2.
46 Clune, F. (1969), 'The Scottish Martyrs', *HRNSW* v2 p. 826. p. 7.
47 Chartist Ancestors [Accessed 21 January 2006] http://chartists.net/Transported-to-Australia
48 Hughes, R. (1987), *The Fatal Shore: the History of the Transportation of Convicts to Australia, 1787–1868*, London, Vintage, p. 320.
49 This material is from Langmore, D. et al [Accessed 5 June, 2005] the *Dictionary of Australian Biography*
50 Rubinstein, W. (2004), p. 23.
51 Polwhele, R. (1798), *The Unsexed Females*, London, Cadwell and Davis, p.238.
52 Dictionary of Australian Biography, Lachlin Macquarie, [Accessed 5 June, 2005].
53 Dictionary of Australian Biography, John MacArthur, [Accessed 18 June, 2005].
54 Australian Bureau of Statistics (2003), *1301.0 — Year Book Australia*, p. 5.
55 Clark, M. (1961), p. 147.
56 Clark, M. (1961), p. 147.
57 Griffith, P. (2005), p. 3.
58 Griffith, P. (2005), p. 6.
59 Elder, B. (1988), *Blood On the Wattle — Massacres and Maltreatment of Australian Aborigines since 1788,* Sydney, National Book Distributors.
60 Clark, M. (1961), p. 177.
61 Probert, B. (2001), 'Class in the Year 2001', *Australian Rationalist,* n. 56, p. 4.
62 Griffith, P. (2005), p. 7.
63 Clark, M. (1961), p. 109.
64 Evans, R. [Accessed 20 January, 2006] Pers com.
65 Griffith, P. (2005), p. 9.
66 Griffith, P. (2005), p. 9.
67 Plowman, D. (2005), 'Protection and Labour Regulation' [Accessed 28 December 2005] http://www.hrnicholls.com.au/nicholls/nichvo13/vol134pr.htm.
68 Courier Mail (2005), 'Powerful Man Packs a Political Punch', 28 December, p. 4.
69 Barry, P. (1993), *The Rise and Rise of Kerry Packer*, Sydney, Vantage Books.
70 Walsh, R. (2006), 'The Bully and the Charmer', *The Weekend Australian Financial Review,* 2 January, p. 18.
71 Walsh, R. (2006), p. 18.
72 Page, B. (2003), *The Murdoch Archipeligo*, London, Smart & Schuster, p. 15.
73 Page, B. (2003), p. 16.
74 The other major player is the Fairfax Press.

[75]   Page, B. (2003), p. 16.
[76]   Page, B. (2003), p. 6.
[77]   Page, B. (2003), p. 159.
[78]   Page, B. (2003), p. 161.
[79]   Page, B. (2003), p. 161.
[80]   Page, B. (2003), p. 161.
[81]   Page, B. (2003), p. 163.
[82]   Page, B. (2003), p. 486.
[83]   Clark, A. (2006), 'Media Giant who used Politics as an Arm of Business', *The Weekend Australian Financial Review,* 2 January, p. 3.
[84]   Allen, L. (2006), 'Hats off to a Master Tactician', *The Weekend Australian Financial Review,* 2 January, p. 4.
[85]   Chanticleer (2006), 'Demerger Issue Looms large', *The Australian Financial Review,* 3 January, p. 48.
[86]   Toohey, B. (2006), 'Licences to Print Money', *The Weekend Australian Financial Review,* 2 January, p. 16.
[87]   Courier Mail (2005), 'The Many Faces of an Empire Builder', 28 December, p. 4.
[88]   Toohey, B. (2006), 2 January, p. 16
[89]   Rubinstein, W. (2004) p. 184.
[90]   Gilding, M. (2002), *Secrets of the Super Rich,* Pymble, NSW, Harper Collins, p.55.
[91]   Murray, G. (1994), *Economic Power in Australia ARC Project* interview, Respondent 2.
[92]   Hunt, G. (2003).
[93]   Rubinstein, W. (2004).
[94]   Hunt, G. (2003), p. 1.
[95]   *New Zealand Official Yearbook* (2002), Auckland, Statistics New Zealand, p. 16.
[96]   Tapp, E. 'John Jones' *Dictionary of New Zealand Biography,* [up dated 7 July 2005] URL http/www.dnzb.govt.nz/.
[97]   Tapp, E. [up dated 7 July 2005].
[98]   This material is primarily from *Encyclopedia of New Zealand* [Accessed 28-29 July, 2005] *Te Ara Encyclopaedia of New Zealand* 1966 [online] and the *New Zealand Official Yearbook* (2004).
[99]   Hunt, G. (2003), p. 35.
[100]   *New Zealand Official Yearbook* (2004), p. 16.
[101]   Line ham, P. (2005), 'Using Department of Statistics Census of Population and Dwelling 1186', in *The Religious History of New Zealand,* [Accessed 7 July, 2005] http://www.massey.ac.nz/ Dept. of Statistics Census 1886.
[102]   Cagey, A. M. (1988), *An Auckland Network,* Auckland, Shoal Bay Press.
[103]   Hunt, G. (2003), p. 144.
[104]   Hunt, G. (2003), p. 254.
[105]   Hunt, G. (2003), p. 254.
[106]   Hunt, G. (2003), p. 176.
[107]   Jesson, B. (1999), *Only their Purpose is Mad, Money Men take over New Zealand* Palmerston North, Dunmore Press. p. 12.
[108]   Jesson, B. (1999), p. 39.
[109]   Brash, D. (1996), quoted in Jesson, B. (1999), p. 13.
[110]   Rosenberg, B. & Kelsey, J. (1999), 'The Privatisation of New Zealand's Electricity Services', *International Seminar on Impact of privatization of the electricity sector at the global level,* 20 September, Mexico City.
[111]   *The New Citizen,* January/February/March (1997), p. 9.
[112]   Easton, B. (1996), 'Philosophers, Kings and Public Intellectuals', *Auckland University Winter Lectures,* Auckland University, Auckland, Tuesday, 20 August, p. 2.
[113]   Rosenberg, B. & Kelsey, J. (1999), p. 3.
[114]   Easton, B. (1996).

[115] Wishart, I. (1995), *The Paradise Conspiracy*, Wellington, Kowhai Gold Books.

[116] ABS (1994), 'Australian Social Trends, 4102.0, the New Zealand data is 6,636 Jews in New Zealand in 2001, Te Ara Encyclopædia of New Zealand [Accessed 23 January, 2006] [http://www.teara.govt.nz/] or 0.16 of the total population 4,125,485 on 15 February 2006.

Chapter 3

What do the Australian and New Zealand Ruling Classes Look Like Today?

In 1972, Nicos Poulantzas wrote about the false problem of managerialism whereby managers are considered as merely one group within an elite.[1] He argued that managers are the ruling class because of their objective position within the production process. This empirically grounded chapter examines the part managers play in Australia. Are they just the de facto controllers and organisers of top business with no deeper commitment to a structural ruling class role? We will look at top directors of the top companies through primary and secondary source data and exmine the demography of the ruling class. We will look at their world of work, their salaries, the sector they come from and their location. We will find out how they acquire social capital, what schools they went to, what clubs they join, what committees they are on and even what they do for recreation.

The theoretical base for this chapter comes from an *embeddedness perspective,* focusing on the meanings of the director and their social location. Mark Granovetter identifies four core principles around which these complex socially embedded interactive meanings revolve. Embeddedness occurs where there are meetings between people:

1   with shared norms including ideas about the proper way to behave, and where enforcement depends largely on the closeness of contact and the size of the network;[2]
2   where strong and weak ties will determine the extent and the diffusion of information in and between social structures;[3]
3   where there are bridging ties, significant between those who hold (or withhold) multiple networks, which will affect structural holes in organisations;[4] and
4   with social life orbits around non-economic axes, having multiple functions, that operate strongly within economic considerations — for instance, job recruitment at the golf club.[5]

Apparently, for these top players in business, 'work often resembles leisure, and leisure pursuits resemble work ... At play as at work the competitiveness, the manipulation, and the excitement of apparent risk is what obsesses ruling class men'.[6] The following material will test this take on the ruling class as competitive, manipulative and obsessive risk-takers.

Who are the Top Directors?

The demographic sources for the data in this chapter are:

1. an Australian report called *The Buck Stops Here: Private sector Executive Remuneration in Australia* by Shields, O'Donnell and O'Brien;[7]
2. their self-description written by the directors in *Who's Who in Business in Australia* and *Who's Who in New Zealand*. These have been collated and put into table form but come from these original sources;[8]
3. the *Business Review Weekly* (*BRW*), and the book written in conjunction with the *BRW* by William Rubinstein (2004); and
4. taped anonymous interviews done by the author since 1984 with the top Australian and New Zealand directors. These are used to illustrate different points of view.

The sample, used to explore the social capital of the ruling class consists of 248 men and women who were directors of the 2004 top 30 Australian-listed companies as scored by the *Business Review Weekly*.[9] The sample includes a number of New Zealanders who are in top 30 companies in both countries. Of those in the sample, 141 had entries in the Almanac, *Who's Who in Australia*. All the material in this chapter is publicly available. The names of the directors are those on the top 30 listed Australian companies in 2004 and, where identified, they have either voluntarily given all the information to publicly available secondary sources or, when not on the public record, their words are anonymous.

Work — What Directors Earn

Nationally and internationally, corporate executive remuneration is large. Henwood suggests that in the US 'the richest 10 per cent account for over three-quarters of the total wealth'. And with that wealth comes power — the 'power to buy politicians, pundits, and professors, and to dictate both public and corporate policy'.[10] Are there parallels in Australia? When asked how his income was calculated, one executive director said:

> Income that executives get is normally part of the costs of production derived from the income that the company earns. It is a charge against the income derived by the company before profit is struck. Sometimes executive remuneration can have two components; one a basic salary and secondly it's related to the profit on the basis that a percentage of the profits are shared. For example, an executive is employed at $600,000 a year but if the profit is above a certain level he (the employer) shares the profit as a bonus. That becomes part of the expenses of running the business. If income is tied to bonuses then it comes directly from company profit. It can vary widely.[11]

The work of John Shields, Michael O'Donnell and John O'Brien,[12] shown in Table 3.1, alerts us to the very large salaries earned by executives in Australia.[13]

They are able to give a comprehensive overview of remuneration patterns for the top twenty highest paid executives in Australia in 2001–2002. (Those directors in the sample are noted with an asterisk).

Table 3.1: Australian Directors' Earnings

CEO	Company	Year	Base Salary A$m	Bonuses A$m	Total An Cash A$m
1. R. Murdoch (& chair)*	News Corp.Ltd	2003	10.98	5.31	16.29
2. P. Anderson	BHP Billiton	2003	10.53	3.51	14.04
3. F. Lowy (& chair)	Westfield Holdings	2003	.98	10.94	11.92
4. W. King	Leighton	2003	2.19	6.85~	9.04
5. M. Chaney*	Wesfarmers	2003	1.22	6.71	7.94
6. D. Murray*	CBA Bank	2003	1.68	5.32~	7.00
7. D. Eck	Coles Myer	2003	5.46	0	5.46
8. A. Moss	Macquarie Bank	2003	0.65	4.19	4.83
9. T. Degnan	Burn Philip	2003	3.17	0.72	3.89
10. P. Smedley	Mayne	2003	2.10	1.75	3.85

Sources: Shields, J. O'Donnell, M. & O'Brien, J. (2003), p.6 using *AFR* 6 November (2002) and (2004/5) figures from Lee, T. (2005) 'In the Money: the long distance boss', *Financial Review*, November, pp. 58–6. and *The Age*, (2004) 'Murdoch tops CEO Pay Packets' http://www.theage.com.au/articles/2004/11/09/1099781351705.html?from=storylhs&oneclick=true
! Remaining executives in Murray, G. sample of top 30 companies 2004 (revenue based), *BRW*, 14 Nov–15 Dec. 2004.

In February 1999, Statistics New Zealand released a report tracing changes in the distribution of New Zealanders' incomes from 1982 to 1996. This report found that 'the gap between high and low income households had grown significantly and that this increase in income inequality occurred at both personal and household levels'.[14] As shown in Table 3.2, pay for New Zealand CEOs and Chairpersons was high, relative to the average male wage in New Zealand, which was approximately $36,000 per annum before tax in 2005. The *New Zealand Herald*, running the same story, used a headline proclaiming 'Executives raking in the cash'.[15]

Table 3.2: New Zealand Executives' Earnings

Company	Names	Role	Pay 2003	Pay 2004	change
Telecom Corp. of NZ	Roderick Deane	chair	$384,031	$402,090	5
	Theresa Gattung	CEO	$1,771,577	$2,829,130	60
Contact Energy Ltd	Phil Pryke	chair	$80,000	$390,742	388
	Stephen Barrett	CEO	$1,226,228	$1,092,553	-11
Carter Holt Harvey	John Masland	chair	$90,000	-	-
	Peter Springfield	CEO	$919,800	-	
Fletcher Building	Roderick Deane	chair	$180, 000	$191,250	6
	Ralph Waters	CEO	$800,000	$1,640,000	105
Fisher & Paykell	Gary Paykel	chair	$80,000	$88,00	10
	Michael Daniel	CEO	$512,257	$690,641	35
The Warehouse	Steven Tindall	MD	$200,000	$594,000	197
	G. Inger	CEO	$547,000	$534,000	-2
Fonterra	A. Ferrier /H.	CEO		$2,000,000	
	Van Der Heyden	chair	$161,667	$194,107	20
ANZ	Sir John Anderson	CEO	-	$1,443,323	-
NZ Post	Jim Bolger	chair	$64,976	$63,345	-3
	John Allen	CEO	$905,000	$795,000	-12

Sources: Shields, J. O'Donnell, M. & O'Brien, J. (2003) p.6 using *AFR* 6 November 2002 and 2004/05 figures from Lee, T. (2005) 'In the Money: the long distance Boss', *Financial Review*, November, pp. 58–6 and *The Age*, 2004 'Murdoch tops CEO Pay Packets.'

These tables suggest that the incomes of the Australians (Murdoch's top remuneration of $23 million plus) far outstrips the incomes of the New Zealanders. Executives' earnings in Australia went from 22 times to 74 times the average Australian's wage in this period from 1992 to 2002 (see Figure 3.1).[16]

Figure 3.1 Growth Indicies for CEO Remuneration 1992-2002

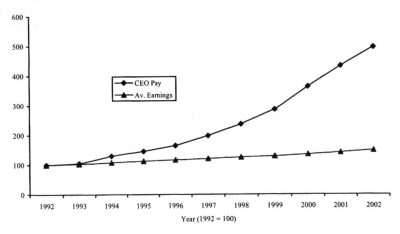

Source: Shields et al, p. 6

Shields and colleagues further showed that, throughout the same period (1987–1998), executive option packages (share bonuses, share purchase plans and share option entitlements) increased from 6.3 per cent of their total payment to 35.2 per cent of their total remuneration[17] (see Table 3.3).

Table 3.3: Average Top Twenty CEO Packages 1988–1998

	Base Salary	Allowances & Benefits	Total Fixed Pay	Incentive Bonuses	Total Cash Remuneration *
			$AU		
1988	112,104	59,912	170,016	12,207	184,263
1993	160,932	72,307	233,239	22,914	256,153
1998	237,476	91,046	328,522	59,533	388,055
change 1988–98	(+112%)	(+52%)	(+125%)	(+386%)	(+111%)

* Excludes income from share options.

Sources: Vaughan, G (2005) New Zealand Herald, C1.

There was no apparent link between high pay and high performance.[18] Rather, Shields et al. found the opposite correlation existed. When executive pay increased, the profit made by the company decreased. A performance optimising remuneration level was suggested to be between 17–24 times the average wages; above this the average company profits fell. Average CEO pay was three times the performance optimising level, that is, average corporate performance could have been improved if CEO pay had been cut by two-thirds. The clear winners were CEOs in the finance sector, with the four major (national) banks (ANZ, Westpac, CBA and National) having their executives earning 188 times more than their customer service staff, with no commensurate part of the considerable bank profit growth going as returns to shareholders.[19]

Work — The Number of Directorships Directors Held

When Ronald Burt writes of the centrality of those who can bridge structural holes in the social network, he refers to multiple directors who are on at least two company boards.[20] Table 3.4 shows that 68 per cent of those on top Australian boards fall into this category, for only 32 per cent of these Australian directors held only one directorship.

Table 3.4: Number of Directorships

Numbers of Boards Directors are on	Frequency	Known per cent
1	45	31.9
2	19	13.5
3	35	24.8
4	19	13.5
5	9	6.4
6	8	5.7
7	2	1.4
8	1	.7
9	2	1.4
19	1	.7
Total	141	100.0

Source: *Who's Who in Business in Australia*, (2005) Information Australia, Melbourne, www.cserver.com.au/wholive/
Valid cases 141 missing cases 0.

Interestingly, one director, a former Premier of NSW, Nick Greiner, held eleven board chairperson positions, three deputy chairs, five directorships and six consultancies.[21] But the pinnacle of career directorships has to go a New Zealander, Keith Smith, who was reported to be on 97 boards, one of which is a top 30 company — The Warehouse — which leads him to be included in our sample.[22] Twenty of Smith's 97 companies are associated with The Warehouse. He said, 'I am busy, but really no busier than some of the managing directors that work for me'.[23]

Work — Where Directors Locate their Offices

Where directors locate their offices is important in regard to their access to their formal economic and informal non-economic networks. This is where social embeddedness occurs.[24] Location in a central capital state location suitable to the economic location of the company and socially within easy reach of professional, sporting or leisure clubs opens easy networking for directors. Directors will often be operating from a number of different companies and even in different countries but where they locate their 'workplace' in the *Who's Who in Business in Australia* is with one institution or company:

Table 3.5: Where Australian Directors' Workplaces are Located

Geographic location of workplace	Frequency	Per cent	Known per cent
Sydney/NSW	36	25.5	35.0
Melbourne/Victoria	23	16.3	22.3
Brisbane/Queensland	12	8.5	11.7
Perth/Western Australia	3	2.1	2.9
Adelaide/South Australia	9	6.4	8.7
United States	15	10.6	14.6
Wellington/New Zealand	1	0.7	1.0
China	2	1.4	1.9
Singapore	2	1.4	1.9
Total number	103	73.0	100.0
Missing	38	27.0	
Total	141	100.0	

Source: Who's Who in Business in Australia, (2005)
Valid cases 103, missing: 38 cases.

Table 3.5 suggests that little has changed since the 1800s in regard to where Australian business is primarily located — that is, principally in Sydney and Melbourne. The other state capitals are less likely to be the principal location for Australian executives than the US.

Work — The Sectors to which Directors Belong

Poulantzas and other structuralists argue that what matters are that we recognise amongst the ruling class their differences; where they come from, what different sector and different capital interests they represent and which sector dominates at any one time.[25] These are the basic building blocks for understanding capital as disparate — whether it is comprador monopoly capital, national monopoly capital,[26] non-monopoly capital,[27] industrial capital or financial capital. In Australia in 2004, the directors defined their sector by nominating the type of major company on which they were a director or major shareholder (or both).

Table 3.6 shows that, in 2004, the biggest proportion of Australian directors name the finance and/or insurance industries and related services as their corporate work base.

Table 3.6: Sector Location of Company that Directors Direct

Sectors where directors say they work from	Frequency	Known per cent
Finance/Insurance and services to both	15	26
Farming	10	17
Oil and Gas Extraction	7	12
Consulting	5	9
Publishing	5	9
Mining	2	3
Manufacturing	2	3
Energy	2	3
Construction	1	2
Food Retailing	1	2
Personal & Household Retail	2	3
Air Transport	1	2
Communications	1	2
Defence	1	2
Education	1	2
Commercial Fishing	1	2
Total	57	100

Source: *Who's Who in Business in Australia* (2005)
Valid cases 57 missing cases 84.

The next section looks at the public face of directors and their relations with the state in their formal ties to it on committees, through lobby groups or the public offices they held. Here we look at the truth of Poulantzas's surmise that the state is not a mere tool, toy or instrument of the ruling class because they share ideas in a common social, political and cultural environment.[28]

Work — The Professional Groups Directors Join

Festinger et al identify the power of rewards and sanctions where there is a dense network with clear-shared norms about goals.[29] The lobby group is a clearly defined professional interest group. When organised on a national basis, cutting across sectoral lines, interests are pooled for the ruling class's interests as a whole ('let's join together to fight the industrial relations battle against labour'). Anyone in the lobby group who deviates from this stated interest can easily be identified and ostracised. Lobby groups function to create these strategic alliances between group members, and between group members and the state.

Table 3.7: Directors' Professional Groups

Professional Group	Frequency	Known per cent
BCA	18	47
Australian Institute of Company Directors	9	24
Grains Council of Australia	4	10
International Business Leaders	3	8
Australian Bankers Association	3	8
Institute of Management	2	5
Financial Sector Advisory Council Australian	2	5
Accounting Standards Association	1	3
The Copper Association	1	3
Australian Business Foundation	1	3
NZBR	1	3
World Economic Forum	1	3
International Global Corporate Governance	1	3
Other	4	10
Total Multiple Responses	51	134.2

Source *Who's Who in Business in Australia* (2005).
Valid Cases: 38, missing cases 103.

Using their own words to describe the function of the professional group, I will first describe the most frequented business lobby group of the directors in 2004. This is the BCA's description:

1. The Business Council of Australia (BCA) is 'an association of Chief Executives from leading Australian corporations with a combined national workforce of almost one million people ... established in 1983 to provide a forum for Australian business leadership to contribute directly to public policy debates ... the BCA Board [includes] Mr Michael Chaney AO, President, Business Council of Australia; Mr Philip Bullock, CEO and Managing Director, IBM Australia/New Zealand; Mr Tony D'Aloisio, Chief Executive Officer, Australian Stock Exchange; Mr Geoff Dixon, Chief Executive Officer, Qantas Airways Limited; Mr Greg Gailey, Chief Executive Officer, Zinifex Limited; Mr Angus James, Chief Executive Officer, ABN AMRO; Ms Katie Lahey, Chief Executive, Business Council of Australia; Mr Charlie Lenegan, Managing Director, Rio Tinto — Australia; and Mr Rod Pearse, CEO & Managing Director, Boral Limited'.[30] The Board was elected on 28 October 2005. Main criterion for membership to BCA is to be a CEO of a sufficiently large size company.

2. The New Zealand Business Roundtable (NZBR) is 'an organisation comprising primarily chief executives of major business firms committed to contributing to the development of sound policies that reflect overall national interests. It is founded on the belief that a healthy, dynamic business sector and open and competitive markets are fundamental to the achievement of a prosperous

economy and fair society ... [members] are drawn from all parts of the business sector. Their organisations comprise listed and private companies and other types of business enterprise, both domestically and overseas owned, primarily in the private sector ... The NZBR believes ... the New Zealand community is best served by a free enterprise system and market-oriented economy. It supports the concepts of competition, entrepreneurship and risk-taking as vital to achieving economic and social progress'.[31]

Of less impact nationally and more industry specific related, are the following industry or professional organisations to which some of the directors belong:

3. The Australian Bankers' Association (ABA) 'works with its members to provide analysis, advice and advocacy and contribute ... to the development of public policy on banking and other financial services ... The ABA works to ensure that the banking industry's views are put forward when governments determine policy or legislation'.[32]

4. The Australian Institute of Company Directors (AICD) is a 'peak body for directors, offering board level professional development, director specific information services, and representation of directors' interest to government and the regulators ... [began] in 1906. With more than 19,500 members, AICD has a strong presence in the business and government communities.[33]

The most popular Australian membership, among the top directors, is in the BCA. This lobby group is becoming increasingly visible to the public partly because of their interventionist strategies to support the Howard government. In 2005, they undertook a member-paid expensive advertising campaign in support of the Howard government's proposed Industrial Relations legislation. The BCA takes seriously its role to disseminate information that legitimates itself and the role of liberal government (this is developed in chapter 6.

Work —Trusts of which Directors are Trustees

Legally, a trust is a device to help set aside money or property that belongs to one person for the benefit of an organisation or a group of individuals 'The key element of a trust is that once transfer of ownership to the trust is complete, the trustees, rather than the settler, own and control the assets'.[34] Directors on trusts become the trustees and shareholders are unit-holders.[35]

There is a mixture of economic and non-economic trusts, again conforming to ideas of social embeddedness; using a mixture of activities to widen and consolidate your position within a community of interest. The directors record themselves to be trustees of overseas financial institutions' trusts, such as Deutsche Bank Trust Company Americas, Rothschild Investment Trust or major Australian companies such as Westpac Trust and BHP Trust. Non-profit trusts include the Mary McKillop Trust, the National History Museum Trust, the Carnegie

Endowment for International Peace, the Opera House Trust, Medical Research and Compensation Foundation, the Walter and Eliza Hall Trust, the Australian Charities Foundation and the Property Industry Foundation. Two University trusts belong to Monash University. These are the Monash University Foundation and the Monash Superannuation Foundation.

The most popular form of trust, although predictably absent here, is the very under-researched family trust. Family trusts have been used to take money out of individual accountability. This lack of wealth accountability is the source of the unstated difference between the earliest parts of Australian wealth history from 1788–1850 relative to the later period 1980–2004.[36] The family trust is a way for those with wealth to put money into overseas, nationally unaccountable accounts, for taxation purposes.

In the next section, social capital is shown to be very significant for directors at the public interface.[37]

Public Face — Through the Public Office(s) Directors Hold

Granovetter's theory about the strength of weak ties is that, when a person moves outside his/her usual circles into unknown networks, then his/her interconnections with these new people are weak, but the plus is that these new weak relationships are diverse with people who are dissimilar therefore offering new ideas and solutions.[38] A businessperson schooled in commerce and given a public office is then open to operate in an entirely new field of weak ties.[39] This top business director can now move in and out of new circles which he/she has gained access to or, in most cases, previously accessed, such as the government bureaucracy, university, local government, the defence force, the state or federal parliament. These links between disparate worlds makes the multiple linked directors uniquely useful as the holder of select information and knowledge valued by the mixed worlds within which they now operate.

In this context too, public office is a reward for services done. This is public recognition that social capital has been acquired. During its period of political leadership, a government will characteristically reward directors of its own ilk in the form of membership of public offices, membership of government committees and ordinary committees as a part of a symbolic and symbiotic ongoing relationship. A conservative government, such as the Australian Liberal–National coalition in 2004, which is wedded to the pro-business, neo-liberal policies that a working population sees as having no inherent advantages to them, needs strong allies in the business community. There is only a small portion (9 per cent) of the sample saying that they either held, or had held, public roles (see Table 3.8).

Table 3.8: Number of Public Offices Held

Public Office	Frequency	Known per cent
Member of Parliament	4	30.7
Treasury	2	15.3
Commissioner	2	15.3
Chairperson of major committee	1	7.6
Chancellor of a University	1	7.6
Mayor	1	7.6
Army posting	1	7.6
Trade Negotiator	1	7.6
Total	13	9.00
Missing	128	90.00
Total	141	100.0

Source: *Who's Who in Business in Australia* 2005.
Valid cases 13, missing cases 128.

The roles taken by those who hold, or held, public office are significant because of the established networks that they have been privy too. Examples of highly networked ex-politicians are; the Liberal member for Ku-ring-gai 1981–1992, Nick Greiner; ex liberal deputy Queensland Premier 1978–1983, Sir Llewellyn Edwards; and ex Labor member for Lowe 1997–2001, Mary Easson. Those directors who held public office also have a great deal of knowledge that they bring to the network. For example, Ted Evans was the head of treasury; while Heng Keat in Singapore is still a permanent secretary. Some also hold, or held, roles in the universities as Chancellors (Jeremy Ellis has been Chancellor at Monash University since 1999), mayors (Maree Callaghan) or commissioners (Elizabeth Alexander was a member of the federal government Commission of Audit 1996). In sum, it can be seen that direct relations between top business and the state do happen. These emerging patterns are different to those observed earlier where key roles in formal ruling-class networks began whilst occupants held public office.

Public Face — The Government Committees on which Directors Sit

Closely related to holding public office is the honour involved with being put onto important government committees. There were 24 committee memberships held. These ranged from belonging to a Prime Ministerial Committee; to being included as a trade envoy; to being on the Prime Minister's Supermarket to Asia Council scheme; or on an advisory committee to the PM. Also notable were Foreign Affairs committees and state and federal talk fest panels and Austrade.

An example of close committee membership ties between a private company, AWB (the former Australian Wheat Board, in the top 30 companies) and the Coalition government came to light with the exposure of what was said to be a

$300 million kickback by AWB, and given to Sadam Hussein as his regime's 'largest source of funding'. Several of the key players were on the public payroll.[40]

Murray Rogers
Qualifications: AM 1998, FAIM, FAICD
Occupation: Chairperson McLaughlin Consolidated Fishermen Ltd since 2003; Chairperson AAB Holdings Pty Ltd since 2002; Chairperson, Quarantine and Exports Advisory Council since 2002; Chairperson National Management Group 2001; a member of the Food Processing Sector Advisory Committee.
Career: Suspected as being involved in Iraqi corruption or 'derelict in his duties' when Managing Director of AWB (formerly The Australian Wheat Board) 1997-2000, and President of the Surf Life Saving Association.
Sources: Who's Who in Australia (2005), Milne, G. (2006) p.15.

The Keating–Hawke ALP government appointed various union officials to government committees; the Howard government has subsequently removed them.[41]

Public Face — The Non-Parliamentary Committees

Cultural capital is the acquisition of merit for services to the arts and cultural pursuits. This can be gained from belonging to theatre committees, museum committees, art gallery committees, Aboriginal-related committees or charities.[42] Of the 104 non-government committees the sample acknowledges in the *Who's Who in Business in Australia 2004,* two types of non-government committees were most popular. These were university committees and think tanks.

Table 3.9: Number of Directors on Non-government Committees

Non-parliamentary committee	Frequency	per cent of directors
Think Tanks	16	11
University Committees	15	10
Company Committees	13	9
Theatre Committees	12	8
Medical Committees	9	6
Art Gallery Committees	8	5
Museum Committees	5	3
School Committees	5	3
Charity	3	2
International Marketing Groups	3	2
Sports Committees	3	2
Aboriginal Related Committees	2	1
Superannuation	1	.7
Religious Committees	1	.7
ASX Supervisory Committee	1	.7
Technological Reference Group (NZ)	1	.7
Other	7	4
Total Responses	105	

Source: *Who's Who in Business in Australia* (2005
Valid cases: 141 total with 44 directors noting a committee.

The highest commitment of top business directors to non-parliamentary committees was shared between their commitment to the committees of Universities and to right-wing think tanks (of which there are a far greater number than left wing think tanks).[43] This high commitment and involvement with these ideology-generating institutions is further explored in chapter 6.

Here are the think tanks committees that are used by the top directors with (shortened) self-descriptions giving their central points of interest.

1. The *Centre for Independent Studies* (CIS) is an economic liberal think tank which describes itself as 'Australia's leading economic and social research institute. Founded by Greg Lindsay in 1976, the Centre's main concern is with the principles and institutions underlying a free and open society'.[44]

2. The *Institute for Public Affairs* (IPA) is an older establishment conservative-liberal institute 'dedicated to preserving and strengthening the foundations of economic and political freedom. We believe in the free market of ideas, the free flow of capital, a limited and efficient government, the rule of law, and representative democracy ... By the close study of Australian policy, we can recommend the best path for our politicians, policy-makers and businesses to take'.[45]

3. The *Tasman Institute* (TI) is an economic liberal think tank with a 'research institute associated with Tasman Asia Pacific (TAP) with the objectives to provide research, advice and strategies on a broad range of issues, including economic restructuring and reform in Australia, New Zealand and the region.' Dr Michael Porter chairs TAP and TI. 'The 1990 founding Chairmen of Tasman Institute were S. Baillieu Myer AC and Sir Roger Douglas, former Finance Minister of New Zealand. Tasman Institute ... is an affiliated institution of the University of Melbourne and was formed from the key leadership of the Centre of Policy Studies ... [it specialises] in areas such as economic policy and reform, efficient forms of government regulation and governance issues, economically efficient solutions to environmental challenges, infrastructure and taxation policy issues'.[46]

4. The *Committee for Economic Development of Australia* (CEDA) is a centre-right think tank that Prime Minister John Howard describes as 'mak[ing] an important contribution in Australia to emerging public policy debates. It is independent and bipartisan, and continues to engage leaders not only from business but also from government, academia and community organisations. The essence of good public policy-making is a thoughtful and intelligent dialogue between the government and the business community, and others who are interested in the development of policy. Of the many organisations that might claim ownership of that description, CEDA ... has been in the forefront'.[47]

5. The *Institute of Policy Studies* (IPS) is a New Zealand economic liberal institute located at Victoria University where 'The Institute of Policy Studies

exists to promote study, research and discussion of modern issues of public policy, both foreign and domestic. As a link between academic research and public policy, it provides opportunities for independent, detached study and for neutral and informed discussion of issues that are important to New Zealand.[48]

The next section looks at the persona of the directors — where they were born, their ages, their schools and university and the type of education and the qualifications that they received.

Personal Information on the Directors' Backgrounds

The directors' entries from the *Who's Who in Business in Australia* show that the highest proportion of this mainly-male top director sample (there are only ten women directors in the total sample of 141) were born in NSW and Victoria, with the UK being their next most probable birthplace.

The Directors' Ages

Amongst the sample, 94 directors gave birth dates ranging from between 1931 to 1981. The major birth grouping was from 1941 to 1950 (that is, they were aged in their 50s and early 60s). The youngest director was Lachlan Murdoch, born on 8 September 1971.

Table 3.10: Directors' Birth Decade

Decade of birth	Frequency		Known per cent
	Females	*Males*	
1931–1940	0	22	23.4
1941–1950	4	35	41.5
1951–1960	7	21	29.8
1961–1970	1	3	4.3
1971–1990	0	1	1.1
Total	12	82	100.0
Missing	2	45	
Total	14	141	

Source: *Who's Who in Business in Australia* (2005).
Valid cases: 94 Missing cases: 47.

The fourteen women, comprising 10 per cent of the sample, are younger. (Two female birth dates are missing.) Many women (seven out of a sample of fourteen) were found in the 1951 to 1960 period, whereas more men (37 per cent of the total number) were born in the earlier decade 1941 to 1950.

Directors' Education

While some scorn elite education as 'where the boys of insecure parents are sent to fulfill the distorted ambitions of their father',[49] it is generally recognised as enhancing, by association and expectations, chances of class mobility. As Herscher, a woman chief executive officer at Simplex Solutions Inc., said of her school, 'I went to an all-girl boarding school in England and I was good at maths and physics. I was generally told that what I could do with that was to teach or maybe go to London town in banking'.[50] Forty-two per cent of these directors who responded to the question 'What was your school?' went to high-fee-paying schools, which represent just 3 per cent of the total Australian schools.[51]

Table 3.11: Status of Directors' Schools

Schooling	Frequency	Known per cent
Elite private high-fee-paying	17	41.5
Second-tier elite	6	14.6
Elite Public	6	14.6
Non elite Private	8	19.5
Non elite Public	4	9.8
Total	41	100.0
Missing	100	
Total	141	100

Source: Who's Who in Business in Australia (2005)

The names of their private high-fee-paying secondary schools are Sydney Church of England Grammar School (9 per cent of the sample at annual fees of $14,349 per year), Scots College (9 per cent at $13,772 per year), Geelong Grammar (5 per cent at $16,760 per year), Wesley College (2 per cent at $14,706 per year), Melbourne Church of England Girls School (2 per cent at $14,508 per year), Cranbrook (2 per cent at $13,195 per year), Ascham (2 per cent at $17,142 per year), Kings College (2 per cent at unknown fees, New Zealand) and St Ignatius (2 per cent at $13,140 per year).

Other schools attended by directors in the sample were second-tier elite schools such as Knox College, St Aloysius, Malvern Grammar, Ipswich Grammar, Hale and Silver-Stream (New Zealand).[52] Similarly numbers went to elite public schools: Fort Street High School, Sydney High School, Melbourne High School, Brighton High School, and Warragul High School. Non-elite private schools included poorer Catholic schools such as Waverley College, Star of the Sea College, St Bernard's College, St Saviour's College, Monte Olivetto Convent and Trinity School. A small number of directors came from non-elite public schools such as Bankstown High School and Lismore High School.

Interestingly, when the status of the school is cross-tabulated with the ages of the directors, it shows that the numbers of elite private high fee paying enrolments are higher in the younger generation (73 per cent) than in the older generation (31 per cent). This contrasted with analysis of a New Zealand sample of top directors' interviews by the author in the 1980s. That sample showed the youngest New Zealand top directors came primarily from public schools (70 per cent) whereas the oldest New Zealand directors came primarily from private schools (47 per cent).[53] Therefore, in the 2000s, 'young' Australian entrepreneurs rising from public education systems are fewer, with most coming from ruling class educational institutions, reflecting a changing cycle of capitalism.[54] Surprisingly, more women went to non-elite schools than elite schools.

Table 3.12: Status of Directors' Schools

School	Year of Birth		Total
	1931–1950	*1951–1981*	
Elite private high-fee-paying	9	8	17
% within year of birth	31%	73%	42%
Other	20	3	23
% within year of birth	69%	27%	58%
Total	29	11	40
	100%	100.0	100%

Source: *Who's Who in Business in Australia* (2005).
Valid cases: 40, missing cases 101.

Seventy-six per cent of the top directors went to elite universities, either in Australia (the group of eight was the benchmark) or overseas.

Table 3.13: Status of Directors' Universities

Status of the University		Frequency	Valid per cent
Elite Australian University		26	44.1
Elite Overseas University		19	32.2
Non-Elite Australian University		3	5.1
Non-Elite Overseas University		11	18.6
	Total	59	100.0
	Missing	82	
	Total	141	

Source: *Who's Who in Business in Australia* (2005).
Valid cases 59, missing cases 82.

In Australia, 44 per cent of the sample went to elite Australian universities; these were the University of Melbourne, the University of Sydney, the University of Western Australia, the University of NSW and the University of Queensland. The overseas elite universities favoured were Harvard, Cambridge, Oxford, the University of Edinburgh, London School of Economics, Stanford University, MIT or Princeton.

Fonterra, the New Zealand dairy cooperative, inflated the numbers of directors going to non-elite overseas universities as its directors largely went to New Zealand agricultural universities at Massey or Lincoln; as far culturally from Oxbridge as the miles between them.

Social embeddedness as a causal explanation really comes into its own in relation to the education system. 'Recruiting from within homogeneous social categories can be an employer strategy to derive benefit from the loyalty and social control that already exists in such categories and networks.'[55] Bosses know they will share cultural and social norms and trust people who share their elite education.

Table 3.14: Directors' Qualifications

Qualifications	Frequency	Valid per cent
Master of Business Administration (MBA)	24	27.3
Bachelor of Commerce/Master Commerce	20	22.7
Bachelor of Laws/D Hons	16	18.2
Bachelor of Economics/Master Economics	14	15.9
Bachelor of Engineering/ME/D. Engineering	10	11.4
Bachelor of Science/MSC	12	13.6
Bachelor of Arts/MA	11	12.5
Doctorate (PhD)	8	9.1
Bachelor of Agriculture	8	9.1
Other	14	15.9
Total Responses	137	155.7

Source: Who's Who in Business in Australia (2005).

Valid cases: 88, missing cases 53.

Gilding quotes a director as saying:

However good an education you get, the best it's going to do for you in terms of economic advantage is to get you into a high-paid profession. But even doctors and lawyers are only going to get paid while they are themselves working. But to make any real money, any serious money, and this is what the capitalists themselves are telling us, you have to get other people to work for you.[56]

It appears that some others shared this view, with relatively few top directors obtaining higher qualifications. There were 123 university qualifications (given that some directors have more than one degree) shared between 141 directors (Table 3.14).

Here are generations of ruling class members being socialised into elite schools and universities and forming networks that recruit them through both formal and informal ties into careers of privilege. This relates straight back to the assumptions challenged at the beginning of this book that Australasia is a classless society. It shows that it is not, because our education system creates and reinforces tiers of those who learn to labour and those who learn to make labourers labour. The tiers are based on a person's (or their parents') ability to pay the high fees.

The last part of this chapter looks at directors' recreation. That is, what types of recreation they do, the number of clubs they join, the type of clubs they join and contrasts between the traditional and newer recreational golf and surf clubs.

Recreation

Recreation, occurring in networks that are not overtly economic (sport-based, arts-based, family-based, etc.) is often a venue for many economic deals to be settled and social embeddness to occur.[57] Donaldson and Poytning use a methodology called *found life history,* whereby life-history methods are linked with information systematically gathered from 'autobiographies and biographies' to gain insights into these 'distant and unavailable men'.[58] Using this secondary evidence, they argue that for big business people 'at dinner parties or in the boardroom, relations with their peers are instrumental. Close friendships are rare ... spurred by a keen sense of their superiority and ceaseless acquisitiveness reinforced by their feelings of deservedness ... it involves the habitual exercise of power expressed in hierarchy, bullying, manipulation and determination to win. They are detached from, and ruthless towards, almost everyone'.[59]

Table 3.15: Types of Recreation used by Directors

Recreation	Frequency	Known per cent
Sports	63	140.4
The Arts	13	29.0
Reading	9	20.0
Gardening	4	9.0
Farming	3	7.0
Fishing	3	7.0
Photography	3	7.0
Travel	3	7.0
History Society	3	7.0
Wine	2	4.4
Political Association	2	4.4
Woodwork	2	4.4
Cooking	2	4.4
Languages	2	4.4
Bridge	1	2.2
Dinner with Friends	1	2.2
Quilting	1	2.2
Cars	1	2.2
Family	1	2.2
Total Multiple Responses	120	266.7

Source: Who's Who in Business in Australia (2005).
Valid cases: 45, missing cases 96.

It is true the directors' recreational choices are predominantly sports (Table 3.15). But the sports category divides into competitive sports that include golf, tennis, squash, horse riding, cycling, yachting, boating, sailing, motor bike riding, rugby, running, swimming, skiing and surfing and the lesser number of non-competitive sports that include walking, hiking and diving. Directors were also interested in the arts, in political associations and historical societies. But individualist pursuits like farming, reading, gardening, photography, fishing, woodwork and cars predominate, rather than social activities like bridge, dinner with friends, family or just cooking for pleasure. Quilting, which is often done in groups, was a surprise.

Recreation — What are Directors' Social Clubs

Donaldson and Poynting suggest that the boundaries between the working day and leisure of the rich are blurred as the 'leisure activities of ruling class men tend to be those cultural processes which resemble their life work'.[60] Club membership is the means to business mobility in Australia as a newly arrived mining American director described:

> My experience is that, as the CEO of a significant Australian company, this is a very clubby small community. I run into the same people all the time. We all get invited to the same things. There is a great deal of socializing; much more than in the US. I could be out every night of the week at cocktail parties, launches — we are always launching things. This is a great mystery to me … What gets attention here is what your title is. If you're the managing director of Alpacca then you are included in everything. If you get your head chopped off like Gil Hoskings did at National Mutual then you are never seen again. Here today and gone tomorrow in all of these things that go on around this town.[61]

Table 3.16: Number of Clubs to which Directors Belong

Number of Clubs	Frequency	Known per cent
1	10	25.6
2	6	15.4
3	10	25.6
4	4	10.3
5	3	7.7
6	2	5.1
7	2	5.1
8	1	2.6
11	1	2.6
Total	39	100.0
Missing or zero	102	
Total	141	

Source: Who's Who in Business in Australia (2005).
Valid cases 39, Missing cases 102.

The numbers and types of clubs, that directors belong too, were significant enough for a third of those in the sample to mention them.

Most of the directors were involved in one to three clubs but some had more, including Norman Adler, a non-executive director who belonged to eleven. Chenoweth and Maley suggest that there has been a sea change toward less stuffy establishment clubs among a new generation of businessmen and business women who no longer patronize the traditional Sydney or Melbourne Clubs and are instead venturing into new places for camaraderie such as at the Savage Club.[62] Table 3.17 shows this to be an incorrect assumption.

Table 3.17: Types of Directors' Clubs

Clubs	Frequency	Valid per cent
Golf Clubs	31	79.5
Australian Club	14	35.9
Cricket Clubs	12	30.8
Melbourne Club	9	23.1
Yacht Clubs	9	23.1
Horse Riding Clubs	9	23.1
Rugby Clubs	7	17.9
Union Club	4	10.3
Weld	3	7.7
Athenaeum	3	7.7
Car Clubs	3	7.7
Surf Clubs	2	5.1
Skiing Clubs	2	5.1
Chief Executive Women	2	5.1
Tattersalls	2	5.1
Wellington Club	2	5.1
Lyceum	2	5.1
Savage Club	1	2.6
West Australian	1	2.6
Brisbane Club	1	2.6
Adelaide Club	1	2.6
Harvard Club	1	2.6
Sandhurst	1	2.6
Selangor (Malaysia)	1	2.6
The Queens (UK)	1	2.6
Rotary	1	2.6
Total Multiple Responses	127	325.6

Source: *Who's Who in Business in Australia* 2005.
Valid cases 39, missing cases 102.

The data shows that Chenoweth and Maley are wrong because successful directors still stick loyally to their traditional clubs (that is, the Melbourne, Athenaem and Australian type-club). Cornell writes of the great import of 'membership of the Australian Club and — most significantly — a position on the committee of the Melbourne Cricket Club, a club where to gain membership, children are put on a waiting list before birth'.[63]

Recreation — Do Directors go to Traditional Clubs?

Exclusive clubs used by the Australian directors are The Australian Club, The Melbourne Club, Weld, Union, the Athenaeum, Tattersalls, the Wellington Club, Lyceum, the Savage Club, the West Australian, The Brisbane Club, The Adelaide Club, Harvard Club, Selangor (Malaysia) and Queens (UK). They are all based on an exclusiveness that is guaranteed by their structured membership protocols, their high fees and nominations for membership. Clubs choose their members with care:

> Wealth alone does not guarantee admittance, but without it one cannot get a hearing. Once in, one shares all the privileges and obligations associated with institutions but there is usually a strict social order. A new member is expected to take a back seat even if he has more millions than any of the others ... it is taken for granted that everyone is rich: the actual amounts do not matter.[64]

John Pilger describes his introduction to the Melbourne Club as the following:

> Entering the Melbourne Club, we were greeted by a huge moose head and a tiger skin...The assistant secretary, a colonel from out of pre-war Punch, shook my father-in-law's hand and led us through the Doric columns to the Lawn Room where members were drinking gin and brandy ... The grandfather clock had just struck noon and those in the leather chairs rose and funeral marched to the dining room where, beneath chandeliers, the members eat off monogrammed plates in an atmosphere of a minor English public school common room ... Etiquette dictates that you join a table and your 'leader' who sits at the head, takes your order and gives it to the waitress. But first our leader calls us to order. 'Gentlemen, the Queen!' he said, and those who were able stood.[65]

Traditional clubs such as the Melbourne Club have reputations that 'savor ... the ancient art of blackballing'.[66] (Blackballing refers to the classical Greek and Jewish method of using white (yes) and black (no) balls placed in an urn to signal a decision. But it takes a threateningly negative meaning when addressing a practice of exclusion based on race, religion, gender or skin colour.) Established in 1838, the Melbourne Club's anti-Semitic reputation followed the blackballing of Kenneth Myer in the 1950s and Baillieu Myer in the 1970s.[67] Exclusion practices in clubs also relate to the barring of women. These are 'men's spaces and as exclusive of women as in the boardroom'.[68] Women have often only had access through their husbands or fathers. As this New Zealand female director said:

> We [her female friend and fellow director also being interviewed] have been unusual because our husbands belong to the Northern Club ... so we know most of those people

socially and personally... and it has been a huge strength to [the company] that we have had these contacts... the old boys network is hard to overcome.[69]

Exclusionary practices against women extended to leisure clubs such as golf clubs. There is no evidence that Aboriginals are absent. Whether they ever tried to enter is another question.[70]

Recreation — Directors and Golf Clubs

The highest proportion of the directors said they belonged to a golf club. Why is golf so important to the wealthy? Donaldson and Poynting suggest that it is because golf embodies the individualism that they enjoy at work. Expensive membership ($40,000 upwards for private clubs) excludes the poor.[71] Membership can be obtained by either owning your own private golf club (e.g. as Kerry Packer did — the Greg Norman-designed Ellerston in the Hunter Valley) or obtain a nomination for entry into a public or private club.[72] Private golf clubs are those most frequently used by the sample ensuring their more exclusive networks.

At the Manly Golf Course a morning's game of golf and a two course lunch will cost you (if you are a member or a member's guest) between $105–$150 per person and you will need a 'minimum deposit [of] ... $1,000 and confirmation in writing' for a round of golf. There are also dress codes applied. At Australia's oldest golf course, the Royal Melbourne Club, women must wear — 'Neat slacks, tailored golf shorts, culottes and skirts. Shirts should be collared and of neat appearance'. Unacceptable female dress includes:

[d]enim, jean-cut or tight legged pants and shorts, track suits, cargo pants and cargo shorts, draw string pants and shorts, rugby jumpers, shirts and jumpers bearing writing or advertising material other than small badges or logos. Shoes not designed as golf shoes. Smart casual dress is acceptable in all areas of the Clubhouse. Golf Attire is acceptable; however, in extreme weather conditions, it is expected that members change wet clothes. Golf shoes may be worn providing that shoes have non-metal spikes and are clean. Some Special Events require more formal attire, such as jacket and tie for men and this will be notified at the time of promoting the event ... Caps, hats and visors are not permitted in the Clubhouse.[73]

Recreation — Directors and Surf Clubs

Surf clubs are an Australian institution. The surf clubs of top directors are exclusive, such as Cabbage Tree Club and Palm Beach Club. Sean Brawley wrote a book called *Beach Beyond: A History of the Palm Beach Surf Club 1921–1996,* describing how the clubs work. Brawley suggests 'few, if any' people join Palm Beach club because they wish 'to protect the surf bathing public' but rather to take advantage of the social activities.[74] Booth adds that the club members are from exclusive Anglo-Saxon and Celtic Protestant North Shore and Eastern suburbs, private schools and Sydney University.[75] Palm Beach developed a reputation as a 'finishing school for Sydney Grammar students on their way to becoming barristers and judges with members referred to as "Gin Boys' or 'poofters', or 'gentlemen lifesavers whose competitive strengths lay in polo and clay pigeon shooting'.[76] Palm Beach club stopped women entering competitions or performing rescues 'except by invitation of the Committee'.[77] In 1980, many members believed that women threatened the club's 'greatest asset': 'mateship'.[78] Female acceptance came in 1985. Comments noted in the Patrol register were that members would 'make life hell for any female who dared to try and join'.[79] And that 'the good and somewhat refreshing character of this patrol I believe is attributed to the fact there are no pogs, or "Clayton's Lifesavers". Oops, sorry, they are useful at parties???'[80] A pog is a mixture of pig and dog or a synonym for a female lifesaver at Palm Beach.

Conclusion

Granovetter's social embeddedness explanation is a useful explanation as to what is happening to Australian top directors.[81] There is evidence here of the importance of both strong (family and educational networks) and weak (committee networks) cohering the power of these men and the few women. There is also room for Marx's argument that 'the mode of production of material life conditions the general process of social, political and intellectual life'.[82] Ruling-class clubs and professional groups exist to create spaces for the interaction and dissemination of multiple interests such as providing the social bases for forming partnerships, friendships, mate ship and spouse-ship, (where women are allowed and if the player is heterosexual). Their social life in turn helps to determine their consciousnesses.[83]

Bernard Mandeville's (1670–1733) metaphor of bees and business, with the directors as the drones of the beehive living the good life, unless they disastrously wear cargo pants into the Royal Melbourne Club, works here too.[84] Here is the evidence of the integrating social networks between the ruling business class and members of the state that sustains a structuralist argument. These men (sic) have a totality of interests that coincides with those of the capitalist state. The key results show that executives of the top companies earn more than 74 times the average Australian worker's pay and this is enlarged by large bonus packages. They identify with wealth because they have a small part of it and it works for them. They can hold anything up to 19 noted directorships (or 97 in the exceptional case of Keith Smith). They are largely located in New South Wales and Victoria, and come primarily from the finance sector. They have a strong beehive that keeps them apart from work and the vicissitudes found in the world of workers, the workers make them large amounts of honey (money) and they sleep with the queen (the state) in a warm world of financial plenty. Theoretically, Milliband was right to argue that managers share 'personal ties ... [with] state members thus enabling them to expand their ruling class networks and power base into the state.[85] But Poulantzas was right too to insist that managers are the ruling class because of their location in production and that their power is embedded in shared networks from top institutions whereby the 'very process of institutionalisation' is an integrating glue of capitalism.[86]

Notes

[1] Poulantzas, N. (1972), 'The Problems of the Capitalist State' (in) *Ideology and Social Science*, (ed) R. Blackburn, New York, Random Press.

[2] Associated most clearly with the work of Festinger, L. & S. Schachter, K. Back (1948), *Social Pressures in informal Groups*, Cambridge, Mass. MIT Press.

[3] This idea is original to Granovetter, M. (1973), 'The Strength of Weak Ties: a network theory revisited', *Sociological Theory*, 1. pp. 201–33.

[4] The original theorists here is Burt, R. (1992), *Structural Holes: the Social Structure of Competition,* Cambridge, Mass. MIT Press.

[5] Granovetter, M. (1985), 'Economic Action and Social Structure: the Problem of Social Embeddedness' *American Journal of Sociology*, 01:3, pp. 481–510.

[6] Donaldson, M. & Poynting, S. (2004), 'The Time of Their Lives: Time, Work and Leisure in the Daily Lives of Ruling Class Men', in Hollier, N. (ed.) *Ruling Australia: Power, Privilege and Politics of the New Ruling Class*, Melbourne, Victoria, Australian Scholarly Publishing, p. 148.

[7] Shields, J. & O'Donnell, M., O'Brien, J. (2003), *The Buck stops here: Private sector Executive Remuneration in Australia*, A Report prepared for the Labor Council of New South Wales, pp. 1–57.

[8] *Who's Who in Business in Australia*, (2006), Information Australia, Melbourne.

[9] The sample is taken from the top 30 companies listed in the *Business Review Weekly* [*BRW*] (2004), 'Top 1000 Companies', *Business Review Weekly*, November 11-17th, p.88. Then the individuals are found in the individual company reports and their details are then found in the (2005), Accessed on line *Who's Who in Australia*.

[10] Henwood, D. (2005), *Wall Street*, http://www.leftbusinessobserver.com/WSDownload. html, p. 14.

[11] Murray, G. (1990), *New Zealand Corporate Capitalism*, Auckland, University of Auckland PHD, Respondent 7, p. 167.

[12] Shields, J. et al (2003), pp. 1–57.

[13] Shields, J. et al (2003), pp. 1–57.

[14] Statistics New Zealand, (1999), *Income* accessed November 25th, 2005. http://www.stats.govt.nz/products-and-services/Articles/income-distrib-May99.htm?print=Y.

[15] New Zealand Herald (2005), 'Executives Raking in the Cash: What Executives earn' p.9, C1.

[16] Shields, J. et al (2003), pp. 1–57.

[17] Shields, J. et al (2003), pp. 1–57.

[18] Shields, J. et al (2003), pp. 1–57.

[19] Shields, J. et al (2003), pp. 1–57.

[20] Burt, R. (1992).

[21] Mayne, S. 'Nick Greiner's Record number of Board Seats' *Crikey dot com,* 28 April 2004 [Accessed 1 January, 2006] http://www.crikey.com.au/articles/2004/04/28-0003.html.

22   Vaughan, G. (2004), 'One man 97 jobs no Problem: Governance the Busiest Directors oppose any limits', *New Zealand Herald,* Monday, 27 December, C1.
23   Vaughan, G. (2004), C1.
24   Granovetter, M. (1985), pp. 481–510.
25   Poulantzas, N. (1972), p. 244.
26   National monopoly capital refers to home owned businesses joining together in a cartel.
27   Non national monopoly capital refers to overseas corporate cartels.
28   Poulantzas, N. (1972), p. 247.
29   Festinger, L. et al (1948), pp. 481–510.
30   BCA website: http://www.bca.com.au/.
31   NZBR website: http://www.nzbr.org.nz/statement_of_purpose.asp.
32   Bankers Association website: http://www.bankers.asn.au/default.aspx?FolderID=2.
33   AICD website: http://www.companydirectors.com.au/0fra/a/fa0.html.
34   Shirley Trust Company Limited, (2005).
35   Westfield Trust Reports 10.4% increase in full-year distribution to $525.5 million', [Accessed online 5 February 2004] http://www.westfield.com/corporate//newsroom/announcements/ trust_archive/2004/20040205.html.
36   Rubenstein, W. (2004).
37   Bourdieu, P. & Wacquant, L. (1992), *An Invitation to Reflexive Sociology,* Cambridge, Polity Press, p. 119.
38   Granovetter, M. (1973).
39   Granovetter, M. (1973).
40   Milne, G. (2006), 'Key Staff at AWB on Public Payroll', *Sunday Telegraph,* 5 February, p.15.
41   Peetz, D. (2005), pers com 28 November.
42   Bourdieu, P. (1979), *Distinction: A Social Critique of the Judgment of Taste,* Harvard, Harvard University Press.
43   Herd, B. (1999), *The Left's Failure to Counter Economic Rationalism in Australia: Classical Economists Legacy to Government, Bureaucracy, Think Tank and the Union Movement,* to be submitted Doctorate of Philosophy, Griffith University.
44   Centre for Independent Studies [CIS] http://vs19901.server-store.com/store/about.inetstore.
45   Institute for Political Affairs [IPA] http://www.ipa.org.au/about.asp.
46   Tasman Institute http://www.tasman.com.au/institute.htm.
47   Hon. John Howard, MP, Prime Minister of Australia, November 2002 http://www.ceda.com.au/New/Flash/html/about_ceda.htm.
48   Source: http://www.vuw.ac.nz/ips/about/overview.aspx.
49   Maloney, S. Address to Scotch College, [online] http://archives.econ.utah.edu/archives/ marxism/2004w35/msg00251.htm [Accessed 26 July, 2004], p. 3.
50   Reported by Costlow, T. (2000), 'Design automation suffers a gender gap', *Electronic Engineering Times,* 19 June, p. 183.
51   Latham, M. (2004), *Great Australian Schools,* Campaign 2004, ALP policy paper. pp. 1–20.
52   See Latham, M. (2004), pp. 19–20.
53   Murray, G. (1990), p. 219.
54   Mandel, E. (1972), *Late Capitalism,* London, New Left Books.
55   Granovetter, M. (2005), p. 42.
56   Gilding, M. quoted by Connell, R. in Cathcart, M. & Burgmann, V. Connell, R., Mayne, S., McGregor, C. (2004), 'Class in Contemporary Australia', pp. 154-181 reprinted in Hollier, N. (2004), *Ruling Australia,* Melbourne, Victoria, Australian Scholarly Publishing.
57   Granovetter, M. (1985), pp. 481–510.

58 Donaldson, M. & Poynting, S. (2004), pp. 127–28.

59 Donaldson, M. & Poynting, S. (2004), p. 148.

60 Donaldson, M. & Poynting, S. (2004), p. 128.

61 Murray, G. (1993–1996), *Economic Power in Australia ARC Project,* Respondent 75.

62 Chenoweth, N. & Maley, K. (1997), pp. 1–10.

63 Cornell, A. (2005), 'In the Belly of the Beast,' *The Australian Financial Review Magazine*, p. 59.

64 Davis, W. (1982), '*The Rich a Study of the Species*, London, Sedgwick & Jackson, p.140 quoted in Donaldson, M. & Poynting, S. (2004), p.133.

65 Pilger, J. (2004), *Tell me no Lies Investigative Journalism and its triumphs*, Jonathan Cape, London.

66 Chenonweth, N. & Maley, K. (1997), 'Australia's New Establishment' *AFR Net Services*, Saturday, 13 September, pp. 1–10.

67 Chenonweth, N. & Maley, K, (1997).

68 Donaldson, M. & Poynting, S. (2004), p. 133.

69 Murray, G. (1990), Respondent 43, p. 215.

70 The evidence for their non indigenousness is that no directors in this sample have other than European or Asian names and they look either European or Asian in their photos in company reports or elsewhere on the web. This is, of course, not conclusive evidence.

71 Donaldson, M. & Poynting, S. (2004), p. 130.

72 Oliver, D. (2005), *Australia's Finest Golf Courses*, http://www.ausgolf.com.au/ellerston.htm p.1.

73 Royal Melbourne Golf Club, (2005), http://www.royalmelbourne.com.au/

74 Brawley, S. (1996), *Beach Beyond: A History of the Psalm Beach Surf Club 1921–1996*, Sydney, University Press, p. 103.

75 Booth, D. (2001), *Australian Beach Cultures: The History of Sun, Sand, and Surf,* London: Frank Cass, quoting Brawley (1996), p. 151.

76 Booth, D. quoting Brawley, S. (1996), p. 151.

77 Booth, D. quoting Brawley, S. (1996), p. 151.

78 Booth, D quoting Brawley, S. (1996), p. 202.

79 Brawley, S. (1996), p. 208.

80 Brawley, S. (1996), p. 212

81 Granovetter, M. (2005), p. 44.

82 Marx, K. (1971), *Contributions to the Critique of Political Economy*, London, Lawrence Wishart, pp. 20–21.

83 Marx, K. (1971), *Contributions to the Critique of Political Economy*, London, Lawrence Wishart, pp. 20–21.

84 Mandeville, B. (1711), *The Fable of the Bees; or, Private Vices, Publick Benefits*, 1714 reprinted Indianapolis, Liberty Fund, pp. 493–502.

85 Miliband, R. (1969), pp. 48–68.

86 Poulantzas, N. (1972), p. 251.

Chapter 4

Australian Networks of Power

This chapter looks at the Australian ruling class's web of interconnecting threads maintained by their membership on one or more company's board of directors. If they are on more than one board then they are defined as multiple directors on interlocking directorates. The big question is: what does access to the network created by these interlocks mean in relation to their personal power and the power of their class? The hypothesis is that *interlocking company board networks* link class members and help them to discover shared political interests, to hone common strategies and to listen and tell others about perceived class wisdoms. We trace the interlocking webs made by directors over a period of time to look at the centrality of key individuals and key companies and try to understand what these changes mean and why the network patterns occur. Why this focus? Because, although chapter three establishes that managers are a key part of the ruling class because of their objective role in production, giving them financial rewards and privileges of power that most of us can only dream of, we do not really know how they obtain or sustain this access to power and material reward. These people are able to enjoy this wealth and privilege largely in anonymity. 'We really only see networks after the fact in the traces they leave ... you know they are powerful, you just don't know precisely how'.[1]

The next two chapters will look at the organisation of corporate boards in Australia and New Zealand. The focus first is on directors from top Australian (and then New Zealand) companies and their formation of interlocks between company boards and subsequent networks. Then we focus on a more obscure set of underlying ownership relations, revealing patterns of major shareholding that can be contrasted with the interlock networks to show different levels of power.

What is a Corporate Board?

A corporate board is made up of directors. Referring to section 9 of the Australian *Corporations Act* 2001, Topp, James and Nichols point out that a director has:

> a wide ambit. Included within the definition are people: who act in the position of a director, by whatever name called and whether or not validly appointed (*de facto director*); and whose instructions or wishes the directors of the corporation are accustomed to act in accordance with (*shadow director*).[2]

A director is a member of the governing board of a corporation. Typically, the directors are elected for multiple terms at Annual General Meetings (AGMs) of the company's shareholders. Directors are responsible for all ultimate business decisions made by the corporate staff, especially those that legally bind the corporation. Directors operate collectively as a directorate.

Many companies rotate their election of directors so that not all directors are due for election at the AGM in any one year. This makes it difficult for a hostile or complete takeover of the board. Directors are encouraged to have a vested interest in the company through the acceptance of share packages as part of their remuneration. The roles on the board are for a chairperson, a company secretary, and executive, non-executive, alternate or special directors. The Australian Stock Exchange (AXS) recommends that:

> Chairpersons preside over the board and the AGM meetings. Their task is to make sure that the board is well informed and effective, and that the members, have the opportunity to air differences, explore ideas and generate the collective views and wisdom necessary for the board's and the company's proper operation.[3]

Generally, a chairperson is responsible for meetings being conducted competently, ethically, and with effective leadership for the board to review and approve the strategic direction. Other responsibilities include seeing that new board members are well briefed with access to all aspects of AGM procedure and operations and to be the board's representative in dealings with management, ensuring that its views are communicated clearly and accurately. The chairperson should act as the primary counsellor to the chief executive officer (CEO), and represent the views of the board externally. Chairs are also responsible for the selection of the CEO:

> The most difficult task is to choose the right CEO because that choice can make or break a company. Really if you get a brilliant guy, then the company runs brilliantly for the board, but then if you get a chap who doesn't run it and runs it down, the difference is really so tremendous.[4]

The chair should be independent — that is, not combining his/her role with that of CEO in the same individual.[5]

CEOs are sometimes (particularly in American firms) called the Managing Director (MDs). They put into action the strategic direction of the board through the day-to-day management of the company. Clear communication between the Chair and CEO ensures 'that the responsibilities and accountabilities of each are clearly understood'. A CEO's formal service contract will set out his or her duties, responsibilities, rights, conditions of service and termination entitlements.[6]

Executive directors are board members doing the daily operations of the company in accordance with board direction and under the management of the

CEO. They are expected to have some stake in the company other than it being just their place of work. As this executive director said:

> I believe that every director should have a significant stake in the company of which he is a director. To ask a person to be a director, pay them X and say all they have to do is to have some 500 shares — in my view — is criminal. I believe if someone has got to be a director of a company then they have enough interest in that company to say "Look OK you are going to have to buy 20,000 shares. They will say 'Christ — why would I want to do that?' So 'OK unless you want to get that involved don't bother.' And I believe the same with senior executives. Because there are people out there investing their money on the basis that those people are directors or executives of the company.[7]

Non-executive directors are independent directors who are not involved in the daily running of the company. Their legal responsibilities are to act in the bona fide interests of the whole company. They should not be in a contractual relationship with the company or under the influence of the major shareholders.[8] The role of the non-executive is to give advice to the collective board decision-making process. Their independence has four characteristics; the width of their experience assists the board with devising strategy; they are ultimately responsible for monitoring management and the financial results of the company; they must ensure that there are adequate safeguards for the company when there is a conflict of interest between the company and the directors and they must take responsibility for recruiting and remunerating directors. However, the position of non-executives who are multiple directors can be ambiguous as this director indicates:

> The conflict of interest on boards with professional directors is a moral conflict. There has to be. I have been in situations where things have been said purposely because information had to be got to others.[9]

Special directors do not have the rights and powers of a normal director and can therefore not attend board meetings though through their public association, they may be identified in the liability of the company. Overseas directors of local companies usually occupy these roles.[10]

Company secretaries are required to show the board how to comply with the details of company legislation and the articles of association. Action, on the part of the company, can be undertaken by a director or the secretary. They need to ensure compliance with statutory obligations, and matters relating to board meetings, give notice of meetings, prepare the agenda, keep the minutes and file the documents into the board's register.[11]

Major shareholders, though not board members per se, are the primary owners of the company. If there is a large shareholding there may be a board position held by the major shareholder or his or her delegate. This is what a director said about major shareholders being on the board:

> If the major shareholders are represented on the board ... obviously the most influential directors on any board are the ones that represent the most sizable shareholders. In normal circumstances the bigger the shareholder the bigger the influence.[12]

Amongst these directors, the chairperson and the CEO are pivotal to the following centrality analysis because they are at the board's core and are most likely to identify their interests as that company's interest, whereas non-executive directors' involvement is likely to be over a wider spread and through a number of companies.

Board Size

This study found that the number of Australian directors on boards varied little over the twelve-year period 1992 to 2004. The average number on top 30 boards in 2004 was 10.5 members, in 1998 it was 11.4 and in 1992 it was 10.3 (see Table 4.1).

Board membership patterns have varied only slightly overall with a less even spread in 2004 than in 1992. In 1992 there were few large boards with over 10 directors. Largest board sizes peaked in 2004, which could reflect a less stressed, more replete wider economic environment. This larger board size fits comfortably with its place at the later half of a boom cycle within a 40-year period of boom.[13] This is a time of economic comfit.

I interviewed directors in an earlier period of crisis (mid 1980s–1990s) and asked them what the hardest task of the board was? Their most common response was choosing the right strategy in a hostile environment (28 per cent), and then evaluating the CEO (23 per cent), then of equal difficulty was getting the right personnel for the board and the board being made accountable (8 per cent). Maximising profit and organising finances (7 per cent) was a surprisingly low-ranked difficulty, down at the bottom with hiring and firing the CEO (5 per cent) and stopping mergers and takeovers (5 per cent).[14]

Board strategies for survival of the business are crucial in any period but they are particularly important in times of threat when the economy is on the downturn and company's low profits make them vulnerable to takeover bids by more powerful companies. Businesses have little choice but to try to compete and win against bigger, more powerful companies. This is irrespective of how they feel about the fairness of the competition. As this CEO said:

> The reality is, that any business does not have the discretion to 'engage in contrary behaviour' that is, to 'make decisions based on anything other than economic considerations' ... you might not like to close a factory, you might not like to do some of the tax things but if that's what society has agreed are the rules of the game then you are very limited in doing other than playing by the rules of the game.[15]

Table 4.1: Number of Australian Top Board Members 1992, 1998 and 2004

Board members	2004 Frequency	%	1998 Frequency	%	1992 Frequency	%
4	0	0	0	0	1	5
5	0	0	1	4	0	0
6	1	4	1	4	1	5
7	3	12	1	4	1	5
8	3	12	1	4	2	10
9	3	12	2	8	3	14
10	5	19	3	12	3	14
11	2	8	6	24	2	10
12	3	12	3	12	3	14
13	2	8	2	8	3	14
14	1	4	2	8	1	5
15	1	4	2	8	0	0
16	1	4	1	4	1	5
17	1	4	-	-	-	-
Total	274	100	276	100	220	100
Average members per board number	10.5		11.4		10.3	

Source: *Who's Who in Australia* 2004, 1998, 1992.

Business is ruled by the necessity of devising competitive strategies of transformation for centralising and consolidating their corporate power. According to John Scott and Catherine Griff, when an enterprise pursues a strategy of transformation it will try to change its relations to other organisations. The simplest form of strategy is the personal union; when that union is a dyadic interlock.[16] This is an equal relationship between two people sitting on a corporate board. A community of interests (that is, a multilateral strategy) is a loose organisation between several companies that may be informally based on a 'gentlemen's' agreement or more formally structured on the basis of a cartel or price fixing arrangement. The liaison scheme (a bilateral strategy) is consolidated by a 'small capital participation' to solidify the relationship.[17] A holding system exists when there is a mutual exchange of directors and shares across several firms. A joint venture occurs when two enterprises join to form a subsidiary enterprise. A combine is a multilateral strategy for several companies getting together to set up a jointly owned venture where there is a supportive tendency to engage in preferential trading. Mergers occur where two enterprises fuse into one, sometimes preceded by a mutually beneficial arrangement of large inter-organisational joint shareholding exchanges. An amalgamation is a merger where several enterprises have fused into one.

Table 4.2: Strategies of Transformation

Level of integration	Bilateral strategies	Multilateral strategies
Personal relations	Personal union	Community of interest
Capital participation	Liaison scheme	Holding system
Coalition of interests	Joint venture	Combine
Fusion of interests	Merger/takeovers	Amalgamation

The analysis in this chapter focuses on the simplest forms of these relations. In the first instance, we push the personal union past the simple dyadic relationship to an asymmetric interlocking union. Asymmetric refers to a relationship characterised by an imbalance of power, whereby the directional interests of the director flow only one-way. The importance of the asymmetric interlocks is that they help to map the corporate power structures. In the second instance, we look at ownership structures that may or may not develop to formal liaison, but that tell us about the power behind corporate structures.

An Interlock is ...

Interlocks occur when directors sit on their own company board, and on at least one other board.[18] The interlock binds two enterprises through one agent. The agent-director is a multiple director. Not every interlock between boards has the same degree of intensity. The most intense interlock is between a parent company director and a subsidiary company.

This study of the power of interlocks is undertaken in triangulation with other sources (e.g. annual company reports, historic constellations and interviews). This gives a multi-levelled view of corporate power. The first is visible at the level of primarily industrial interlocked directors forming centrality clusters around directors who are class leaders. The second level is at the more shadowy level of ownership by finance capital operating nominee companies. Nominee companies are companies registered by shareholders who do not need to register in the name of their beneficial holder and are thereby able to conceal true ownership. This study starts by looking at the power endemic to this networking of multiple directorship holders.

First, however, I consider the relevant interlock literature to ask: where does the literature hypothesise that power lies within this type of networking?[19]   Primary data from annual company reports is then used to test ideas arising from the theorists and from interviewed directors.[20]

The Network Literature

There are excellent summaries of the interlocking network literature that show why the study is so interesting and significant.[21] These theorists classify perspectives on network interlocks into four groups according to their emphasis on 1. control, 2. collusion, 3. discretion, and 4. social embeddedness (discussed in chapter 3). Two traceable threads underlie these perspectives. The first, emphasising *control* is Weberian, drawn from the work of theorist Max Weber[22] and it aims to provide independent motives for the actions of interlocking directors who control but do not own companies.[23] Weberian-based theorists want us to see the issue of interlocking as one of managers' control and power through their individual agency in the boardroom rather than ownership or class collusion. Power is treated as multifaceted because it resides with many shareholders rather than capitalist owners. The companies that managers control may be characterised as relatively democratically run in ways that are answerable to the wider community, and diversely owned by 'mum and dad' shareholders.[24]

An hypothesis taken from this model is that if ownership is no longer fundamentally significant then managers, unlike owners, are free to be civically responsible and not motivated by economic self-interest.

The second thread to the literature is Marxist, based on Marx's insight into bank domination of industry.[25] These theorists are generally critical of the role of capital and see interlocking boards as a strategy to help secure privilege for the ruling class and further exploit workers and/or consumers. The European-dominated *collusive model* looks at interlocks as structural mechanisms that cement collusion and subsequently help the development of business cartels or monopolies.[26] Hilferding, in his original identification of *Finance Capital* (1910), worked on material provided by Jeidels (1905), to find why 'if you took possession of six large Berlin Banks [it] would mean taking possession of the most important spheres of large scale industry'.[27] He saw bank interlocks as the vital dynamic within this system of collusion. Banks were shown to act to make finance capital dominant in early twentieth century capitalist Germany.[28] According to Hilferding, finance capital is an:

> Ever increasing part of the capital of industry, [it] does not belong to the capitalists who use it. [Industrialists] are able to dispose of capital only through banks, which represent the owners. On the other side, the banks have to invest an ever-increasing part of their capital in industry. [Finance capitalism gives] rise to a desire to establish a permanent supervision of company affairs, which is best done by securing representation on the boards of directors.[29]

Hilferding's abiding contribution is the observation that the most significant development facing capitalism is the concentration of finance capital with bank representatives on industrial company boards supervising company affairs and protecting the ownership of the banks.

An hypothesis that the collusive model offers is that if bank ownership in the top companies is high then this will reflect in dense (highly interconnected and concentrated) patterns of interlocks between banks and industrials.

Tests of the collusive theory have mixed results. Sigmund Grønmo's Norwegian empirical findings give some support to it in that Norway has only low intercorporate networking, with banks 'still hav[ing] a number of interlocks among each other and with other companies', but these companies work hard at creating interlocks during periods of crisis.[30] Roy Barnes and Emily Ritter use their interlocking data from 1962, 1973, 1983 and 1995 to show that corporate network ties in 1995 are less dense and less concentrated with changes occurring and corresponding to a period of dramatic changes in the US financial markets.[31] In contrast, William Carroll and Meindert Fennema's findings support the idea of finance capital networks acting as devices for building hegemony. They use extensive evidence from network studies of interlocking directorates among 176 of the largest corporations in the world economy in 1976 and 1996 to support their case. Their results show that from the 1970s to the 1990s an Atlantic business system developed that created the European Union as a working business entity. [32]

An Australian work testing this collusive model would be the 1937 work of J. N. Rawling, *Who Owns Australia?* Rawling gives an impressive detailed empirical study of the concentration of Australian industry, interlocking directorships, share holdings and corporate subsidies and is able to identify an oligarchy of banks that hold monopoly control over the economy and subsequently have some control over the state.[33] These banks have at their mercy 'manufacturer and retailer, who are not big enough to be in the inner circle, the farmer, and the small business man — many of whom are worse off than the employed worker and the small trader'.[34] Another early text based on a similar premise is Len Fox's *Monopoly* (1940).[35] This text, according to Kuhn, 'covers similar ground to Rawling and the later 1963 work of E. W. Campbell, *The Sixty Rich Families Who Own Australia'*.[36]

The third paradigm is the bank-centred, North American-dominated *discretionary model.* Finance capital's discretion, in controlling the direction of lending, is the key to understanding the role of interlocks within this perspective. Beth Mintz and Michael Schwartz, in *The Power Structure of American Business* (1985), argue that it is the direction of credit through interlocks (and other methods) that is the central function of finance capital. According to this analysis, 'Interlocking directorates are not a source of hegemony but a method for managing discretion. They could not be the source of hegemony because they give access to the apparatus of discretionary decision-making and only indirectly offer the possibility of altering structural constraint ... bank centrality in this context reflects the dominant position of financial institutions in capital-flow decision making'.[37] In contrast to the collusive model, the discretionary model, is a 'hands off' model strategically locating the power of the bank at the decision-making level — who is going to be loaned what and for what.

Mintz and Schwartz go on to argue that banks use interlocks to mediate inter-firm disputes thereby allowing business to approach the state as one actor.[38] This closely parallels Michael Useem's view of an inner circle, which gives coherence and direction to the politics of business through top company CEOs forming networks that influence the state with one voice.[39] Inter-generational support for Useem's work, or that part which argues a strong business unity as a continuing phenomenon, comes from Mizruchi who used the 167 large firms he studied between 1912 and 1935 to come up with supportive evidence for this theory.[40] Scott gives similar support when he writes about companies 'increasingly shaped by the ownership of shares and the allocation of loans and this is now structured largely through an impersonal system of finance capital'.[41] Other international comparative support for the discretionary hypothesis comes from Stokman and others working on a comparative project that shows supportive evidence from the result of interlocks across twelve countries.[42]

An hypothesis arising from this discretionary perspective is that if directional clusters of directors from banks can be assumed to reflect the banks' leverage of credit on the board then the interlocks will reflect powerful credit pathways.

The fourth model, the *social embeddedness* perspective, focuses on the director's social location by providing an awareness of the director's agency within class formation that is missing in much interlock analyses. Interlocks are seen as a mechanism for capitalist class reproduction ('jobs for the boys') and class cohesion ('don't rock the boat; employ your own'). Granovetter suggests that interlocks between companies could influence a wide range of organisational behaviour, such as strategies, structures and performances.[43] Social embeddedness is found within a number of other significant interlock studies within which interlocks are seen as, among other things, communication nodes or information conduit.[44] Useem sees this inter-communication as the most important aspect of interlocks, with companys' interlocking directorates providing the wide scan across companies that they need to give back to boards an 'awareness of its environment'.[45]

Following on from this perspective, Gerald Davis argues that central interlockers are the key carriers[46] of social capital within the class.[47] The most heavily interlocked individuals are a vanguard of the corporate elite and, by implication, its most effective transmitters and its most likely lateral innovators. The political processes in play have an impact on the business networks and dominant class ideology, fashions and enduring myths that are reflected in company behaviour.[48] Dick Byan[49] and Carroll's[50] work shows business networks not just across companies, but across states, and between nation states. The evidence of international business networks involving political processes, both with states and across states, is a concrete link to Marx and Engels,[51] in their theory of capital, always in a chase across the globe.[52]

This social embeddedness perspective suggests a major hypothesis that if the most interlocked individuals act to socially and politically integrate the class and reassure its members of the value of the innovations they propose, then they will form key leadership clusters.

When the director interlocks are correlated with more information about the top five shareholders' ownership of the companies, then the picture gets more complex and also more interesting.

The Methodology

The test of where power lies began by identifying the top 30 corporations according to their revenue. Revenue was chosen as the criteria for inclusion so that financial firms and banks could be included.[53] This first source of information is available to any researcher and can be found in the Australian *Business Review Weekly (BRW)* annually.[54] The Australian (and New Zealand chapter) case studies are both longitudinal, with the shorter Australian case study drawn from 1992, 1998 and 2004 *BRW* data. This twelve-year time period allows some sense of changes occurring in the interlocking directorate network patterns and the centrality method described shows how these patterns can be read.

The second source was interviews of directors undertaken by the author. Most of these 144 male directors and eleven female directors generously gave taped interviews lasting from 30 minutes to four hours. Research ethics require the interviewees and their company to remain anonymous. The director interviewed is only identified by number, and the company names have been changed. In total, over 47 Australian and 108 New Zealand interviews of top 30 company directors were completed from 1987 to 1998. That number does not include the follow-up interviews that took place a number of years later. The work was made possible due to two major grants from the New Zealand Social Sciences Research Foundation and the Australian Research Council.

The third source of data was an analysis of two other publicly available secondary sources: the *Who's Who in Business in Australia* and the *New Zealand Business Who's Who*. These give the directors' own view of who they are and what is important to them in their publicly projected self-image. Another very rich source of top business information is company annual reports, giving descriptions of the performance of the companies and short business biographies of the directors. Most importantly, the annual company reports declare who the top 20 shareholders are and the amount of their shareholdings.

The material from these secondary sources identifies the boards that the directors are on. These boards are then treated to a centrality analysis to find out where company clusters lie; who the core leader is; who the outlying directors are and which company leads; in what direction multiple interlock power flows between boards; and how these patterns of density differ at different times.

Centrality Analysis

Centrality analysis shows us the number of firms that are interlocked, the number of interlocks a firm maintains with each of the firms it is interlocked with and how centered that firm is in relation to other firms. Most importantly, it allows us to trace the directionality (from the most powerful to least powerful) of these interlocks. Interlocks operate at their most basic level to transmit information, which in this context is likely to be that which relates to the operations of a given company. Those who control this information flow are in a position of power because they are able to make faster, more fully informed and strategic decisions.

Centrality analysis is used to find the directional flow of information from boards where directors hold key board roles (as executives or chairpersons) to boards where the same directors will not hold these roles or in exceptional cases where they may have the same role on both boards. To show that information flows at different speeds and at different levels there are three levels of interlocks used; those that have breadth, depth and width.

Directional or asymmetric interlocks (which are interlocks cemented by a director with a key company role, such as chairperson or chief executive) can show us the flow of power relations between companies and the dominance of any one sector in these relations. Power, in this context, means having a key member of your board feeding you information that you can then control. If they are on a number of boards they can give back to their primary board a wide corporate-environmental scan and are better informed of the machinations of inter-firm politics. Directional interlocking directorates are readable as maps of power.

The centrality methodology (outlined below) describes the types of interlocks between the top 30 companies in three different periods (1992, 1998 and 2004). The 1985 method was used by Mintz and Schwartz but modified by Lum and Murray in 1988.[55] Following, the measures, B, D and C refer variously to breadth, depth and centrality of a multiple interlock.

Type of Interlock

Breadth

Breadth measures the immediate span of the board interlocks. The following example begins at Company A and therefore there will be a breadth of four interlocks B, C, D and E, but not F. (For example, A. Stone is a chairperson (remembering that a director is only used, or has directionality, when they are a chairperson or CEO) from Apple Company. She sits on four company boards that are not Apple boards, her board of origin: B = Banana company, C=Corn company, D=Date company and E=Egg Company. But she is not on F=Fig company.

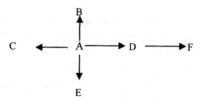

Depth

Depth is the length of the interlock chain. In the following way; when we repeat the first example, A has a depth of 2 interlocks including D+ F only. (For example, Chairperson A. Stone from Apple company (forget she also sits on Banana, Corn and Egg companies) is also on Date company, but on the Date board is Date's CEO, Z. Pip, who happens to be on Fig company board (F) too. Thereby allowing Apple Company to have a depth that goes beyond the reach of their director A. Stone, through to Z. Pip, and onto Fig Company.)

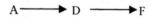

Centrality

Centrality covers the total board interlockers from all multiple directors. Centrality beginning from A is the total of depth and breadth interlocks. A combination of the above two, breadth and depth, would be C, B, D, E and F = 5 connections. (For example, A. Stone from Apple Company is on the board of Apple, Banana, Corn, Egg and Date Company but her companies also having access through the CEO of Date Company, Z. Pip, to Fig Company. So Apple Company through A. Stone and Z. Pip has a directional centrality span of five companies.)

The amount of centrality occurring at any one period amongst the top 30 companies should be different, and this allows us to measure this difference. We will use this centrality measure to look at how the pattern of interlocks of corporate multiple directors work in relation to the wider national economy. That is, in periods of economic crisis (for example, in the 1980s), there could be different patterns from boom times (as in the 1960s and 2000s). If there are noticeable differences, this could be consistent with Mandel's theory of a 40-year economic cycle driven, in an irregular fashion, by the tendency of the rate of profit to fall (that is, money going out of variable capital (labour); and the new technological solutions thus hindering the expansion of profit); the increasing rate of surplus value (that is, where profits are achieved above the average profit, fuelling competition generally). But realisation centres on the monopolistic access to those parts of production such as cheap labour, cheap raw materials, advantages in the distribution network and innovative machinery and the increasing organic composition of capital (the relation of the mass of the means of production to the labour which is required to employ it).[56] These long waves of economic rise and fall bring with them predictable corporate behaviours, mediated by smaller countervailing[57] tendencies of business cycles and class struggle.[58] It should be noted that there are many other cycle theories and theorists beginning with Marx (1864) who wrote of a ten-year business cycle or 'spirals of capital',[59] Kondratieff (1928) who identified an 80-year cycle whose 'basic cause is to be found in the mechanism for the accumulation and diffusion of capital',[60] and Van Gelderen (1913) who spoke of 50-year spring tides of expansion and ebb tides of stagnation and depression.[61] There are also many detractors from the use of cycle theories.[62] Regardless, Mandel's 40-year theory has been chosen for reference because of its seemingly greater explanatory power.

The following Australian multiple interlock material covers the twelve years from 1992 to 2004, approximately a quarter of a 40-year cycle.

Australian Case Studies 1992–2004

What light will Australian interlocking directorates throw on to the 'who holds power in Australia?' question.[63] We have hypothesised that the directional interlocks may show something about control, collusion, social embeddedness, credit lines, informational nodes, leadership and who carries much of this class's social capital.

The background to what was happening on the Australian boards was an Australian economy moving from a period of stress in the early 1990s to considerable growth by the mid-2000s. Figure 4.1 depicts ABS data on Australia's expanding gross domestic product girth from 1992.

Figure 4.1: Australian GDP and Measured Change

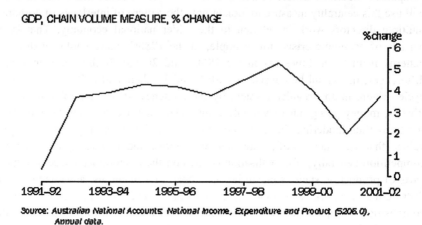

Source: *Australian National Accounts: National Income, Expenditure and Product (5206.0), Annual data.*

Further ABS data show that the industries making the most significant contribution to GDP by 2002 were property and business services, closely followed by manufacturing.[64]

The Comparative Results

This twelve-year period of interlocks under study shows a quarter of a 40-year wave. It begins with the recession periods, reflected in a more heavily interlocked corporate board environment. This eases gradually to fewer interlocks with rising prosperity in 1998 and 2004.

The next section breaks down the centrality analysis to discrete periods to look at who the important players are, the meaning of the board structure and the questions of ownership, control and power that all the data opens up.

The 1992 Australian Interlock Data

The interlocks in 1992 were agitated (see Figure 4.2). This was a business community with directors' heads constantly swivelling like owls to maintain an accurate corporate scan. For example, Kerry Packer moved in on Westpac saying that it was 'big, fat and out of control'.[65] He and Al Dunlap, his CEO, decided to buy $500 million in shares allowing them a strategic stake in the bank, after which, according to Carew, 'Packer rang Westpac Chairman John Uhrig to sound him out about board seats for himself and Dunlap. Uhrig's view was that Westpac ought to foster a good relationship with a shareholder of such significance and encouraged the board to invite Packer and Dunlap to become directors'.[66] Their gratitude was to 'fix the bank's mess'[67] and they wanted to 'get rid of the chairman, Uhrig. Dunlap wrote a letter signed by Packer to the members of the board, questioning Uhrig's ability and calling for his resignation'.[68] However, Packer and Dunlap miscalculated on their power and the loyalty of the directors who did not give majority support to the major shareholder. Disappointed, the Consolidated Press share was sold some months later for $608 million, netting Packer a profit of more than $100 million, with Packer and Dunlap formally resigning from the Westpac board on 14 January 1993.

Table 4.3: Top 30 Company Interlocking Directorates 1992–2004

Company	*1992*			*1998*			*2004*		
	B	D	C	B	D	C	B	D	C
Pacific Dunlop	4	8	11	4	5	8	-	-	-
Telecom/Telstra	3	9	11	0	0	0	1	3	3
ANZ	4	7	10	2	5	6	0	0	0
IEL	2	8	10	-	-	-	-	-	-
BHP	2	9	10	1	4	4	1	1	1
Adsteam	3	7	9	-	-	-	--	-	-
NAB	3	7	9	2	7	8	0	0	0
CRA	3	6	8	-	-	-	-	-	-
CSR	4	5	8	2	6	7	-	-	-
FCL	1	9	8	-	-	-	-	-	-
Qantas	1	9	8	1	9	9	1	1	1
Westpac	1	8	7	-	-	-	0	0	0
AMP	1	7	7	2	7	8	0	0	0
Fosters	1	1	1	3	5	7	-	-	-
Woolworths	0	0	0	0	0	0	1	1	1
Boral	0	0	0	0	0	0	-	-	-
Coles	-	-	-	2	9	10	1	4	4
Lend Lease	-	-	-	-	-	-	3	2	4
CBA	-	-	-	0	0	0	3	2	4
Wesfarmers	-	-	-	-	-	-	1	2	2
Metcash	-	-	-	-	-	-	1	3	3
Brambles	-	-	-	-	-	-	1	1	1
Insurance Australia Group	-	-	-	-	-	-	1	1	1

Key: measurement B= Breadth of interlock, D= Depth of interlock, C=Centrality of interlock. 0=Amongst the top 30 but not interlocked that year.

Early in the 1990s, Australian top directors were heavily interlocked. This was a period of rapid economic regrouping brought about by the turbulence of an economically liberal regime (ironically led by Labor Prime Minister Bob Hawke, and his economically liberal driven Treasurer Paul Keating).

Figure 4.2: 1992 Directional Interlocks in the Top 30 Companies

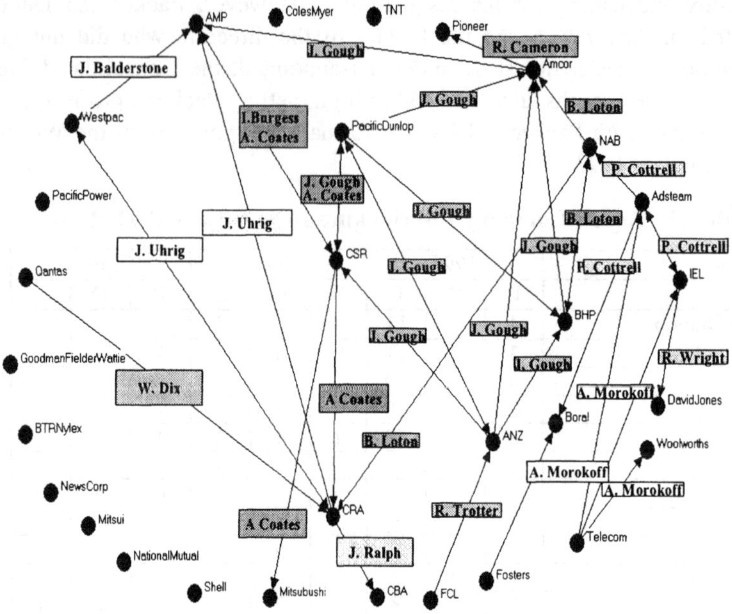

Key:

——————▶   = the direction of the director's power base

◀—————▶   = the director has a power base in two companies

At the bottom left are the non-interlocked companies e.g. TNT

A high 56 per cent of the top 30 companies were interlocked here. Those with highest centrality were Pacific Dunlop (industrial) and Telstra (communications) (see Figure 4.2). The other high interlocks were IEL (industrial), BHP (mining), NAB (banking) Adsteam (industrial marine), CRA (mining), CSR (industrial), FCL (industrial), AMP (insurance) and Qantas (travel). Banks were ranged throughout with the highest bank centrality going to ANZ (10), then NAB (9), Westpac (7) and last the undirectionally interlocked CBA. An indicator of crisis here is the high amount of depth interlocking.[69] Here we see BHP (9) and Qantas (9) with high depth scores. BHP was under threat from takeover at this time, and several years later it merged with a very large South African company, becoming BHP Billiton. The year 1992 shows a defensive corporate environment reconstructing after the disasters of the 1987 sharemarket crash and trying to stave off hostile takeovers in an unstable wider economic environment.

The major interlockers here — such as John Gough — came from productive capital as CEOs but moved on to many other boards, including a significant financial company, in this case one of the top domestic four (the ANZ). These central figures become the political leaders of the ruling class. As one director commented, they had:

> Social skill [that] comes with exposure and success. People who become successful often become more relaxed as a consequence and that can make their personalities seem more open, less fearful. But it is true that the people I have most to do with are pleasant personalities. Confidence is critical.[70]

John B. Gough
Born: 22 August 1928
Qualifications: Diploma, AO OBE, LLD Honours from Melbourne University.
Career: Education Council since 2003, Chair of the Australia and New Zealand Banking Group 1992–95, Director since 1986, Member of the Asia Pacific Advisory Board Sicpa Group 1992–2004, Member of the Advisory Council, General Motors Australia 1988–98, Chair of Pacific Dunlop Ltd 1990–97, Managing Director 1980–87, Deputy Chair of Newcrest Mining Ltd 1990–91, Director CSR Ltd 1989–99, Member Adv. Council AT&T Asia/Pacific 1988, Chair of BHP Gold Mines Ltd 1987–91, Director ICI Aust. Ltd 1986–92, Broken Hill Pty Co. Ltd 1984–98, Amcor Ltd 1983–92; President of the National Gallery Victoria 1995–98, Director Walter and Eliza Hall Institute Medical Residence 1983–2003, Vice-President 1993–2003, Chair of Australia Meat and Livestock Industry. Member of International Council Asia Society since 1988; Chair of the Council Advisory Bureau Industrial Economics 1988–90; Business Council Australia 1984–88; Chair of the Trade Development Council 1981–85; Member of the Australia/China Trade Advisory Group 1981–85; Executive Member of Australia Manufacturing Council 1980–83; Director various international trade missions; Chair of University of Melbourne Business School.
Source: Who's Who in Australia 1992, p. 253, Accessed 12 June 2005.

Figure 4.2 identifies what Useem calls the inner circle.[71] The 1992 business inner circle is Alan Coates (CSR, Brambles and Mitsubishi), John Uhrig (AMP, Westpac, and CRA) and Alex Morokoff (Woolworths, Telecom, IEL, and Adsteam) but they are subject to the key play of director, John Gough (see above).

Contrary to the collusive hypothesis, the 1992 Australian data show a dominance of interlocking among industrial capital rather than among financial capital wanting direct control over industrial capital.

The 1998 Australian Interlock Data

The late 1990s was a period of increasing Australian prosperity based on property and commodity sales but with some significant profit slumps experienced by large companies like BHP (who recorded a loss of $1.5 billion).[72] There was very little interlocking taking place in 1998 (see Table 4.3). This paucity of multiple interlocks between directors reflects the very healthy GDP growth of over 4 per cent already noted and the comfort to be gleaned from the large corporate profits these companies experienced. In cyclical terms, this was a period of rising economic profits.[73]

Figure 4.3 shows that there were ten of the top 30 companies with multiple interlocking directors — that is 33 per cent of the total 1998 sample, which is a lower percentage than in 1992. Those with the highest centrality were Coles Myer (retail) and Pacific Dunlop (industrial), closely followed by Qantas (travel), Amcor (industrial), Fosters (industrial), AMP (insurance), NAB (banking), and CSR (industrial).

The social embeddedness hypothesis helps explain this 1998 pattern of interlocks, in which the most interlocked director, who was certainly an innovator and a key political player, was John Ralph.[74] He was described by his peers as:

> Popular, very easy going ... Yes, they cannot be driving all the time. You want someone that you know can take a reflective position. But they do want to drive, that I can assure you.[75]

Figure 4.3 shows John Ralph at the political centre of the top business network. (Not shown is the fact that Ralph also had many corporate shares — in 1998 he had 160,000 shares in Pacific Dunlop, 14,134 shares in Telstra, 10,602 shares in CBA and 38,500 in Fosters. Substantial as this may seem to someone not in this world, it did not make him a substantial or key shareholder.) Ralph had political, not economic, power in his community. He was described as 'close to the Byzantine workings of government ... a former BCA President ... worked as a link man between the Federal government and the alliance of business groups, the Business Coalition for Tax Reforms'.[76] Ralph was also the person who helped put the concept of 'enterprise bargaining' into the lexicon, and into practice, as the Managing Director at CRA. Enterprise bargaining, second only to individual bargaining, has perhaps been amongst the most disempowering strategies for working men and women since its legislation and implementation by the federal government. In an interview, a director put this achievement in this way:[77]

Figure 4.3: 1998 Interlocking Companies and Their Directors

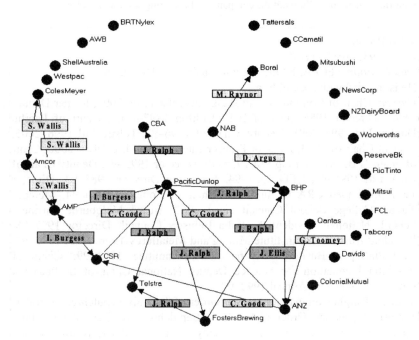

There was a study commission set up by the BCA that worked through a period of about five years [from 1983], from which time it developed the ideas of enterprise bargaining. Enterprise bargaining was, I won't say our greatest success, but it is a really good example. Enterprise bargaining was an anathema when the stake was put in the ground. Now the words are used commonly sometimes to mean something quite different but at least it's in most agendas and things have moved.

Ralph was able to act for his class as both an innovator of new concepts and an exponent of vital ideas, and was a conduit to government in his strategic role as chair of key lobby groups and state committees.

These 1998 centrality figures found in Table 4.3 and illustrated in Figure 4.3 show relatively low bank centrality (NAB 8 and ANZ 6). Contrary to the hypothesis of the collusive and discretionary models, highest centrality is found among retail, travel and some industrials (Coles (retail), Qantas (travel), Pacific Dunlop, AMP (insurance), Fosters (industrial) and CSR (industrial). This may be because the late 1990s were improving economic times and therefore there was no need for bank directors to involve themselves on the boards of industrials:

They don't get involved. If they don't think a company is being run well, in an extreme case they'll tell the chairman or the managing director. But normally they'll express their displeasure by selling out the company and investing somewhere else.[78]

John Ralph
Born: 1932, Broken Hill.
Qualifications: FCPA, FAIM, went to Melbourne University.
He is married with six children.
Career: Chair of Commonwealth Bank Australia 1999–2004, former Deputy Chair, Director 1985–2004 of BHP Billiton 1997–2002, Chair of Pacific Dunlop Ltd 1997–2001, Deputy. Chair of 1996–97, Telstra Ltd 1996–2005, Interim Chair of 2004, Director Pioneer International. Ltd 1995–2000, Chair of Foster's Brewing Group Ltd 1995–99, Director 1993–99, Deputy Chair of CRA Ltd 1994–95, CEO 1987–94, Managing Director 1983–94, Director 1971–95, joined CRA Group 1949, Chair of Comalco 1980–94, Member Xavier College School Council since 2003, Board Melbourne Business School, National President Australia Industry Council. Director 1997–98, President Australasian Institute Mining and Metallurgy 1996, BCA 1992–94, Australia/Japan Business Co-operation Committee 1991–99; Chair of Australia Foundation for Science Deputy National Chair of St Patrick's Cathedral Centenary Appeal 1992–97
Awards: Knight Commander the Star Order of the Holy Sepulchre, Australia-Victoria Equestrian Order of the Holy Sepulchre; Life Fell. AICD 2005, Special Fellow of the Australia Academy of Science. 2004, awarded Grand Cordon of the Order of the Sacred Treasure for Services to Industry 2002, Australasian Institute. Mining and Metallurgy Medal 1998, Key to the City of Melbourne, 1994, Rotary Club Melbourne Vocational Service Award 1992, University Melbourne Graduate School Management Award 1988.
Source: Who's Who in Australia, 2005.

Australian banks did not get involved in interlocking in this late 1990s period because they did not have to. Money flowed easily. Bank practice was dignified, benign and hands off. Bankers were able to continue to practise relative autonomy, which helped their legitimacy by enhancing the popular conception of them as business actors who acted independently, over and above the concerns of individual companies and the concerns of individual members of the public.

The 2004 Australian Interlock Data

In 2004, the economy was maintaining much of the momentum it had developed over the previous decade. According to the ABS, in the calendar year 2004, the growth trend of real gross domestic product (GDP) increased by almost 4 per cent. Most industries made positive contributions to the economy in 2004 to 2005; construction was up 2.2 per cent and finance and insurance up 1.5 per cent. Other major contributors to growth in GDP were manufacturing up 0.7 per cent and ownership of dwellings was up 1.0 per cent.[79]

Australia at this time had again a wealthy, growing, vibrant economy.[80] This excellent economic environment in 2004 was reflected in banks reporting 'very low levels of corporate and personal defaults' with very positive 'performance of the funds management and insurance businesses'.[81] Mandel would say that this is the return to the wealthy part of the 40-year cycle.[82] This relaxed and friendly business environment meant dispersed interlocking patterns amongst relatively trusting and sharing top 30 companies (see Figure 4.4).

Figure 4.4: 2004 Directional Interlocks in the Top 30 Companies

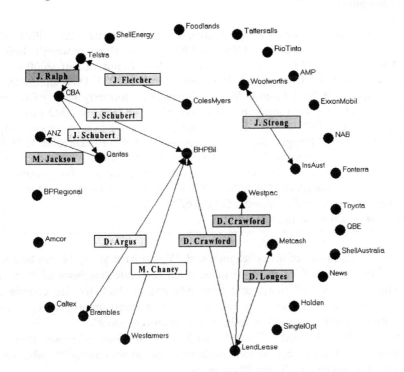

Only eleven of the top 30 companies were interlocked, which is a low 36 per cent of the sample. Those with most centrality (but still with a low centrality of 4) were Lend Lease (industrial), Coles Myer (retail) and CBA (bank).

These centrally interlocked key companies conformed to some of what the *BRW* called the 'New Age industries'.[83] These are communications (Telstra), finance (CBA), insurance (IAG), property (Lend Lease), health and mining and also retail (Coles), transport (Qantas) and Agri-business (Wesfarmers). *BRW* also noted that amongst the top 1000 companies there had been a high level of corporate attrition (87 per cent loss) in the period 1988–2004.[84]

At the political heart of the 2004 inner circle was John Schubert (CBA, Qantas, BHP and Telstra) and to a lesser extent David Crawford (BHP, Westpac and Lend Lease). There was a changing of the guard from John Ralph to John Schubert. Schubert succeeded (not sequentially) Ralph as the chair of the Commonwealth Bank of Australia in 2004 and Schubert, like Ralph, was a past President of the Business Council of Australia (BCA). These men were the political cadre of their class.

John Schubert
Born: 1942
Career: Educated Wesley College, University of Melbourne. Has a PhD in chemical engineering. Began at ESSO in 1969. Entered Commonwealth Bank of Australia in 1991.Chair of CBA since 2004, Deputy Chair 2000–04, Director since 1991, Chair of G2 Therapies Ltd since 2002, Director Qantas Airways Ltd since 2000, Chair of Worley Parsons Ltd (formerly Worley Group Ltd) 2000–04, Director Hanson plc 2000–03, Manager Director CEO Pioneer International Ltd 1993–2000, Chair of Manager Director Esse Australia Ltd 1988–93, Deputy Manager Director Esso Australia 1985–88, Director 1983–85, Executive Assistant to President Exxon Corp. NY 1982–83, Production Division Manager 1981–82, Assistant Treasurer Esso Eastern Inc. Houston Texas 1979–81; President BCA (2001 – 2003), former Vice President, Member Advisory Board Australia Graduate School of Management.
Source: Who's Who in Australia, 2005.

Schubert, of whom one of his colleagues said, 'You'd have to say he can be a bit boring',[85] holds views that 'chant the mainstream corporate catechism of the need for cutting taxes, for efficiency and flexibility and productivity. He complains about the dead hand of regulation and opposes centralised union power, saying organisations need to free workers to be able to contribute more'.[86]

This socially embedded political leadership and structure of power changes again in its significance when we look subterraneously at who owned, or who were the major shareholders, in the top 30 companies.

Shareholding in the Top 30 Companies

When we examine what was happening at the underground level of ownership, an interesting thing happens. To look at how these financial institutions are organised, we use an Ownership Penetration Index (OPI) based on information about the top five shareholders in each of the 30 largest listed companies where the information is available. To calculate the OPI for each shareholding company, the shareholdings in each of the top 30 companies have been averaged. The OPI is a proxy for actual ownership, as a shareholding company's holding in a top 30 company does not contribute towards the OPI if it is not a top five shareholder, and because it weights each top 30 company equally. However, this is a reasonable and practical exclusion to make as the influence of shareholders who are not in the top five shareholders in the company are unlikely to exert much influence. The OPI for each shareholding company takes a value within the theoretical range from zero (where a shareholding company is not a top five shareholder in any top 30 company) to 100 (where a shareholder owns 100 per cent of all top ten companies).

Figure 4.5 shows the Owner Penetration Index (OPI) of the top 30 companies from 1992–2004, based on the material gathered on their top five shareholders.

Calculations on who are the major shareholders (top ten share holding owners) of the top 30 companies in Australia in 1992 show the dominance of AMP (5.33 per cent ownership of the top 30 companies). AMP was a company established in New South Wales in 1849 and demutualised in 1998. In 1992, its revenue was in the top spot, having jumped 159.4 per cent to $16.1 billion in a year, but by 2004 it had suffered its biggest corporate loss of $5,542 million.[87] Next in significance was the National Australia Bank (National Nominees with 2.67 per cent), Westpac (Westpac Nominees 1.5 per cent) and fourth the regional Bank of New South Wales (Bank of NSW Nominees Pty Ltd 0.58 per cent). Hugh Devine, an employee of Westpac, wrote: 'By way of background, Westpac Nominees is a wholly owned subsidiary of Westpac Banking Corporation. Westpac Nominees holds shareholdings on behalf of other parties and, as such, does not own shares in its own right. By the very nature of it being a 'holding' company, the names of its customers (and the shares being held) are not publicly available'.[88]

These large amounts of major share ownership by finance capital are particularly significant because, as O'Lincoln argues, strategic control of a company can be as little as 5 per cent of a company's shares.[89] Finance capital, by this evidence, had a very dominant ownership position in relation to the top 30 companies in Australia in 1992. The key owners of the major companies were not the little shareholders (the 54 per cent of 'mum and dad 'Australian shareholders of whom 42 per cent have portfolios of $10,000 or less, or the workers who may have employee funds tied up in the company), but the large shareholders who take the form of bank nominee companies, mutual insurance or superannuation funds, and occasionally individuals.[90] These finance capitalists are the key to this web of power.

Figure 4.5 Owner Penetration Index of Australia's Top 30 Companies

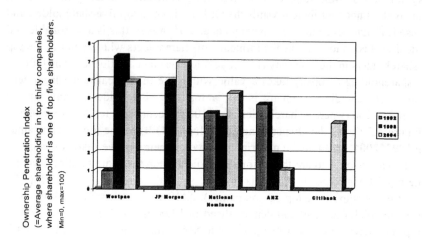

Note: [91] 1.   2004 There were ten (from 30) companies with top 20-investment information in their Annual Report.

2.   1998 There were eleven (from 30) companies with top 20-investment information in their Annual Report.

As the managerial control model indicates, the distinction between ownership, management and board membership is important. But top managers earn substantial remuneration (chapter 3) that locates them in the ruling class. They make key executive decisions about the running of companies and are answerable to a (maybe interlocked) board of directors who are in turn answerable to the major shareholders. But although managers, directors and owners may be one and the same, the evidence above shows that in the top 30 companies, they were not. Managers often have a very healthy sized shareholding; for example, John Gough had 11,889 shares in BHP, 806,249 in Pacific Dunlop, and 26,838 in CSR. However, this did not give Gough large shareholder status in his or any other major company. The central point here is that although a lot of the directors have company shares, collectively manage, direct corporate strategy and gather corporate intelligence, ultimately their most important task was to protect the political and economic interests of their major shareholders. Their power was secondary to that of the top shareholders who were most often financial organisations, usually banks (usually operating through nominee companies) and investment fundholders.

Both AMP and John Gough, the key 1992 company and the key 1992 interlocker, had lost their centrality by 1998. This change in central players reflected both the changing political needs of the class and the penetration of foreign financial capital competing successfully with domestic capital.

1998 Shareholdings in the Top 30 Companies

In 1998, the extremely concentrated bank capital ownership showed no correspondence to political patterns of director interlocks. Information found in the top 30's annual company reports show that when we look at who has the largest amount of shares in all the top 30 companies, we find Westpac in the dominant position with seven per cent of the unweighted average of the top 30 companies, followed by Chase Manhattan Bank at 6 per cent, then National Nominees at 4 per cent, ANZ at 2 per cent and Permanent Nominees Pty Ltd at 1 per cent.

Chase Manhattan Bank began in America as Bank of the Manhattan Company and was founded in 1799 in the US by Aaron Burr. In the 1950s, the Rockefeller family exercised strong influence over it. In December 2000, the merger of The Chase Manhattan Corporation and J.P. Morgan and Co. was completed and the name they took was J.P. Morgan Chase and Co. (also referred to as J.P.Morgan Chase). J.P. Morgan Chase and Co., as US capital's top entry into the Australian market, represented a very significant change in the 2004 data.[92]

Shareholdings of the Top 30 Companies in 2004

Stressing the decision-making power of major shareholders, a director said, 'Obviously the most influential directors on any board are the ones that represent the most sizable shareholders'.[93]

According to John Ralph, the retiring CBA chairperson, in 2004, Australian banking was highly competitive because there were 51 banking groups operating, even though these were dominated by the four Australian-owned major national banks (CBA, NAB, Westpac and ANZ).[94] There were thirteen foreign-owned banks operating in Australia through a locally incorporated subsidiary. An additional 24 banks operated through a foreign bank branch. While many foreign banks operating in Australia initially focused their activities on the provision of banking services to the Australian clients of their overseas parent bank, most had diversified their operations by 2004. Five foreign banks were represented in Australia by both a locally incorporated subsidiary and a branch. International fund managers and global investment banks were also increasing their presence in Australia. This trend of foreign finance capital entry into Australasia showed in the changing ownership patterns with the new central role of American bank J.P. Morgan followed by the three Australian owned national banks — Westpac, ANZ and NAB (i.e. National Nominees).

Comparative 1992–2004 data (Figure 4.5) show J.P. Morgan as competitively ousting the four major Australian owned banks in its bid to establish control over Australasian corporate ownership. Berle and Mean's argument is now lost. Ownership, in the form of finance capital's nominee investment, is globally concentrating into ever-smaller circles. Paul Sweezy in 1939 saw eight significant groups. In the first was this investment bank — J.P. Morgan and Co. and its alliance with the First National Bank as the most significant.[95] At the time, Sweezy's own father, Everett B. Sweezy, was the 'vice president of the First National Bank of New York ... a close partner of J.P. Morgan and Company'.[96]

Many theorists have continued to under-estimate the power of owners, including Sweezy who wrote *Monopoly Capital* and who criticised his own earlier work for 'not having placed enough emphasis on the growth of the financial sector'.[97]

What does the Australian Interlocking Material Mean?

This work takes the growth of the financial sector seriously.[98] The first most significant point about this evidence (referring to the managerial thesis differentiating control from ownership) is that, although financial capital does not appear to control business through any centrality exercised through interlocking directorates, this is smoke and mirrors, for real power lies in major shareholdings. Ownership patterns show the recent central penetration of US capital into Australian top business. The new centralising pivot is the very old family controlled J.P. Morgan bank. However, other financial capital (see Figure 4.5) also acts as the largest shareholders in most of these top 30 firms. These most powerful financial institutions seldom put their directors on industrial or any boards because they do not have to; large finance capital ownership gives them hegemonic control with no necessary board presence.

But (and this relates to the second collusive hypothesis) this bank ownership does not mean dense bank interlocking, because these concealed relations of power are not formalised in board membership. Australian boards even appear to favour board members who are not major shareholders or do not represent the major finance capital shareholders. For example, in 1992 the CRA chief executive officer, John Ralph, was on the Commonwealth Bank Board but the company's major shareholders were Bankers Trust, Chase Manhattan and Westpac Nominees. Because of their ubiquity, large finance capitalists are able to maintain their invisibility and contingently their dominance. For example, a banker director explains the inputting of the bank into a company as being not through the board:

> A good banker will feed information to a company all the time, particularly if it is lending money to the company. It will see it as their duty to help that company to be successful without prejudicing its other portfolios of customers. Because the more

successful that company is then the bank is much more assured of getting the money back.[99]

The discretionary hypothesis about indirect control by manipulation of finance capital on top companies was closer to the findings. When a director was asked if it meant that banks control through credit, he answered, 'Yes, they control credit.' Pressed further, 'So they make discretionary decisions about who they are going to lend money to?' He replied, 'Yes, they do all that and so indirectly they can have some influence on ... [board decisions]'.[100]

The evidential material has shown that the larger economic environment affects what occurs within the interlocking networks. In the changing twelve-year period of this study, the interlocks went from dense interlocking in a period of economic stress in the early 1990s to loose and progressively fewer interlocks in the early 2000s when there was a return to a period of healthy economic growth. With the top 1000 companies accounting for 51 per cent of the total national revenue, the top 100 companies had revenue of $656,418 million in 2004 (up from $566,292 million in 2003) and the top 30 (as seen here) have 64 per cent of the top 100 companies' revenue.[101] Taken in total this supports Mandel's hypothesis that is, unlike those of the collusive or cohesive models, the density of director interlocks reflects the cyclical economic environment and the degree of corporate security within this.[102]

The social embeddedness hypothesis, that the most interlocked individuals will integrate the class and be the innovators and the class cadre, is also supported. The central political cadre is John Gough (1992), John Ralph (1998) and John Schubert (2004). They are all heavily interlocked on both industrial and finance capital boards, though primarily the latter. All are past Presidents of the BCA, and strong in their commitment to economic liberal thinking — support for individual contracting, low tariffs, low corporate tax rates, privatisation and ideas that are compatible with competitive advantages generally.[103] These measures are necessary to discipline labour, to get more productivity and in return give workers insecurity of tenure, lower real wages and poorer working conditions.[104] As the work of John Higley et al. suggests, the nature of the interlocks runs parallel to fractional power in the lobby groups; specifically the BCA.[105]

Conclusion

The major empirical difference between the situations in 1992 and 2004 was the increasing penetration of finance capital from the US. Whilst the top 30 companies were still primarily Australian based, their major shareholding shifted dramatically towards becoming offshore. Although only a small degree of overseas penetration was revealed by the data considered here, the OPI allows us to measure and then point to its growing significance.[106]

Still, the degree of international finance capital penetration into Australia continues to remain smaller than the bulk of capital investment by Australian capitalists in Australia.[107] What the data has shown is that generally finance capitalists remain happy to see industrial capital's directors running industrial boards and in some cases also chairing the bank boards (e.g. Ralph, Schubert and Gough). Financiers are particularly relaxed in periods of boom when there is a profit surfeit for all business. This is not because globalisation (the penetration of overseas capital) is in the process of disintegrating finance capital in Australia (as suggested by Carroll and Alexander) but rather the opposite.[108] Financial capital in Australia is only a part of the circuit of capitalist production but it is a dominant part that indirectly controls productive capital at different degrees of intensity depending on exogenous economic factors involved in the business cycle and the long economic waves.

Is financial capital a coalition or fusion of interests in Australia? This relates back to the question asked by the Scott and Griff work.[109] The answer is a careful 'maybe', because new penetration of US financial institutions does not support a centrality transformation by anything other than a global circuit of capital. There are no joint ventures, combines, mergers or amalgamations taking place at this level — yet. However, when we look at the next chapter we can see how top Australian financial capital can fuse their interests together by forming a new company called the New Zealand Central Securities Depositary to penetrate the relatively newly opened New Zealand market.

Notes

[1]   Cornell, A. (2005), 'In the Belly of the Beast', *The Australian Financial Review Magazine*, p. 59.
[2]   Topp, A. & James, T., Nichols, P. (2004), 'To Whom do Directors' Duties Apply'? March, [Accessed 1 December, 2005] http://www.findlaw.com.au/ articles/default.asp?task=read&id=11714&site=LE.
[3]   ASX (2003), *Principles of Good Corporate Governance and Best Practice Recommendation* Government Coporate Council, v.1.1 March, [Accessed 15 December, 2005] http://www.asx.com.au/about/pdf/ ASXRecommendations.pdf.
[3]   Murray, G. (1990), *New Zealand Capitalism,* PHD, Auckland, Auckland University.
[4]   Murray, G. (1990), Respondent 18, p. 152.
[5]   ASX (2003), 2.3, 8.1.
[6]   ASX (2003), 1.1.
[7]   Murray, G. (1990), Respondent 101, p. 166.
[8]   Northey, J. (1981), *Introduction to Law,* 9th Edition, Wellington, Butterworths.
[9]   Murray, G. (1990), Respondent 101, p. 193.
[10]   Northey, J. (1981), in Murray, G. (1990), p. 147.
[11]   Northey, J. (1981), in Murray, G. (1990), p. 149.
[12]   Murray, G. (1990), p. 150. Respondent 53.
[13]   See Mandel, E. (1972), *Late Capitalism*, London, New Left Books.
[14]   Murray, G. (1990), p. 151.

[15] Fletcher, H. (1988), quoted in Murray, G. (1990), p. 202.

[16] Scott, J. & Griff, C. (1984), *Directors of Industry, the British corporate network 1904–1976*, Cambridge, Polity Press, p. 21.

[17] Scott, J. & Griff, C. (1984), p. 21.

[18] This definition is from Scott, J. & Griff, C. (1984), p. 21.

[19] From Murray, G. (2001), 'Interlocking Directorates: What do they tell us about Corporate Power in Australia?' *Journal of Australian Political Economy*, June, n. 47, pp. 5–27.

[20] The quotes are from two projects; first (1987–1990), *New Zealand Corporate Power* funded by NZSSRF and second (1993–1997), *Economic Power in Australia* funded by ARC included in the project was Dr Malcolm Alexander and Dr John Houghton.

[21] Examples are Scott, J. (1985), 'Theoretical Frameworks and Research Design', (in) Scott *et al, Networks of Corporate Power*, pp. 1–19, Cambridge, Polity Press. Glasberg, D. (1987), The Ties that Bind? Case Studies in the Significance of Corporate Board Interlocks with Financial Institutions, *Sociological Perspectives*, v. 30, n.1 pp. 19–48; Mizruchi, M. (1996), 'What Do Interlocks Do? An analysis, Critique and Assessment of Research on Interlocking Directorates', *Annual Review of Sociology*, v.22, pp. 271–302.

[22] See Weber, M. (1922), *Economy and Society*, G. Roth & C. Wittich, New York, Free Press, p. 13.

[23] Berle and Means (1932), *The Modern Corporation and Private Property*, New York, Macmillan.

[24] Mum and dad shareholder is a generic term referring to inexperienced shareholders.

[25] See Marx, K. (1956), *Capital*, v.2 1880 Moscow, Progress publishers p. 79.

[26] See Baran, P. & Sweezy, P. (1968), *Monopoly Capital: an essay on the American Economic and Social Order*, New York, Monthly Review Press.

[27] Hilferding, R. (1981), *Finance Capital*, London Routledge Keagan & Paul, (1910 first printed reprinted) p. 368.

[28] Lenin, V. (1916), *Imperialism the Highest Stage of Capitalism*, Collected Works, n. 22, 45 v.2 Moscow, Progressive Publishers, 1964 original publication, Fennema, M. & Schijf, H. (1979), 'Analyzing Interlocking Directorates: Theory and Method', *Social Networks*, v. 1. N. 1, pp. 297–332.

[29] Hilferding, R. (1981), p. 225.

[30] Grønmo, S. (1995a), 'Structural Change during Deregulation and Crisis; the position of Banks in the Norwegian Intercorporate Network', *International Social Networks Conference*, London, July. Grønmo, S. (1995b), 'Assessing the Centrality of Banks in Intercorporate Networks', *Research on Banking, Capital and Society*, Report No 63 Oslo, Research Council of Norway.

[31] Barnes, R. & Ritter, E. (2001), 'Networks of Corporate Interlocking 1962–1995', *Critical Sociology*, 1 July, v.27, n.2, pp. 192–220.

[32] Carroll, W. & Fennema, M. (2002), 'Is There a Transnational Business Community?' *International Sociology*, September, v.17, i.3, p. 393 (27).

[33] Rawling, J.N. (1937), *Who Owns Australia?* Sydney, Modern Publishers in Kuhn, R. (1996), Kuhn, R. (1996), 'Class Analysis and the left in Australian history' in R. Kuhn & T. O'Lincoln (ed.s) *Class and Class conflict in Australia*, Longman, Melbourne, pp. 145–62.

[34] Rawling, J. N. (1937).

[35] Fox, L. (1940), *Monopoly*, Research Department, Sydney, Left Book Club.

[36] Kuhn, R. (1996), pp. 145–62.

[37] Mintz, B. & Schwartz M. (1985), *The Power Structure of American Business*, Chicago, University of Chicago Press, p. 250.

[38] According to Mizruchi, M. (1996), pp. 271–302.

[39] Useem, M. (1984), *The Inner Circle*, Oxford, Oxford Press.

[40] Mizruchi, M. (1982), *The American Corporate Network*, Beverly Hills, Sage.

[41] Scott, J. (1996), *Corporate Business and Capitalist Classes*, Oxford, Oxford University Press, p. 15.

[42] Stokman, F. & Zeigler, R, Scott, J. (1985), *Networks of Corporate Power*, pp. 1–19, Cambridge, Polity Press.

[43] Granovetter, M. (1985), 'Economic Action and Social Structure: the Problem of Embeddedness' *American Journal of Sociology*, n. 91, pp. 481–510.

[44] See Scott, J. & Griff, C. (1983); Useem, M. (1984); Mizruchi, M. (1996), pp. 271–302.

[45] Useem, M. (1984).

[46] Davis, G. (1991), 'Agents without Principles? The Spread of the Poison Pill through the Intercorporate Network', *Administrative Science Quarterly*, n. 36, pp. 583–613.

[47] Social capital is a concept associated with Bourdieu, P. (1973), 'Cultural Reproduction and Social Reproduction' (ed.) Brown, R. *Knowledge, Education and Social Change*, London, Tavistock, pp. 71–112.

[48] See Cyert, R. & March, J. (1963), *A Behavioural Theory of the Firm*, Englewood Cliffs, N. J, Prentice Hall; Goshal, S. & Bartlett, C. (1990), 'The Multinational Corporation as an Inter organisational Network', *Academy of Management Review*, 15 (3) pp. 603–25.

[49] Bryan, D. (1996), *The Chase Across the Globe: International Accumulation and the Contradictions for Nation States*, Boulder, Westview Press.

[50] Carroll, W. (2004), *Corporate Power in a Globalizing World*. Toronto, Oxford University Press.

[51] Marx, K. & Engels, F. (1975), *The Communist Manifesto*, 1848 in the Collected Works of Karl Marx and Fredrich Engels, London, Lawrence and Wishart.

[52] See also Bedggood, D. *Rich and Poor in New Zealand*, Wellington, Allen & Unwin, Cronin, B. (2001), *The Politics of New Zealand Business Internationalisation 1972–1996*, v. 1 & v. 2. Auckland University, PHD Thesis, p. 51.

[53] Following Scott, J. (1985), p. 15.

[54] *Business Review Weekly 1000*, (1992), p.76, 23 October; *Business Review Weekly 1000*, (1998), n.16, p.120, *Business Review Weekly 1000*, (2004), 11–17 November, p.88. *Individual Annual Reports* (2004, 1998, 1992).

[55] Mintz, B. & Schwartz, M. (1985), pp. 261–277; Lum, R. & Murray, G. (1988), *Centralisation in top New Zealand Business 1966–1986*, Department of Sociology, Auckland University.

[56] Mandel, E. (1972), p. 27 based on Marx, K. (1977).

[57] Mandel, E. (1972), p. 49.

[58] Marshall, M. (1987), *Long Waves of Regional Development*, Houndsmile, Macmillan, based on Mandel, E. (1972).

[59] Marx, K. (1983), *Capital*, v.1, p. 588.

[60] Kontratieff, N. (1984), *The Long Wave*, New York, Richardson & Synder, p. 104.

[61] Freeman, C. (1984), *Long Waves in the World Economy*, London, Frances Pinter.

[62] Among whom are theAustralian Bureau of Statistics [ABS] (1992), *Feature Article — Leading Indicators Two Decades*, n. 1350, These authors conclude 'it was generally not possible to gain any information on the amplitude of the business cycle from the individual indicators tested.'

[63] According to Ville, S. & Fleming, G. (1999), p. 2.

[64] All of this statistical data unless noted is from Australian Bureau of Statistics (2004), *Measuring Australia's Economy*.

[65] Carew, E. (2006), 'Strongarm tactics backfire badly in tilt at Westpac' *The Weekend Australian Financial Review*, January 2, p. 19.

[66] Carew, E. (2006), p. 19.

[67] Carew, E. (2006), p. 19.

[68] Carew, E. (2006), p. 19.

[69] Mandel, E. (1972).

[70] Murray, G. (1993–1997), Respondent 73.

71 Useem, M. (1984).
72 *Business Review Weekly* (2004*)*, '200 Rich List', p. 50.
73 Mandel, E. (1972).
74 Davis, G. (1991), pp. 583–613.
75 Murray G, (1993–1997), Respondent 73.
76 Gluyas, R. (1999), 'Utopian Agenda', *The Australian*, 22 January, p. 32.
77 Murray, G. (1993–1997), Respondent 70.
78 Murray, G. (1990), Respondent 94, p. 277.
79 Australian Bureau of Statistics (2004), *Measuring Australia's Economy Section 1. Measuring Economic Activity.*
80 Australian Bureau of Statistics (2004), *Measuring Australia's Economy Section 1. Measuring Economic Activity.*
81 Ralph, J. (2004), *CBA Annual Report*, p. 1.
82 Mandel, E. (1972).
83 *Business Review Weekly* (2004), '200 Rich List', p. 46.
84 *Business Review Weekly* (2004), '200 Rich List' p. 48.
85 Hooper, N. (2006), 'Schubert's Restrained Melody', *The Weekend Financial Review*, 11-12 February, p. 22.
86 Hooper, N. (2006), p. 22.
87 *Business Review Weekly* (2004), '200 Rich List', pp. 48, 61.
88 Devine, H. (2000), *Westpac*, 16 June.
89 O'Lincoln, T. (1996), *Wealth, Ownership and Power, the Ruling Class* (ed.s) R. Kuhn & O'Lincoln, T. *Class and Class Conflict in Australia,* Melbourne, Longmans; Larner, R. (1970), *Management Control and Large Corporations*, New York, Dunellen; Burch, P. (1972), *The Managerial Revolution Reassessed*, Massachussetts, Lexington Books; Scott, J. & Hughes, P. (1976), 'Ownership and Control in a Satellite Economy', A discussion from Scottish Data, *Sociology* 10.
90 ASX (2000), *Survey*, p. 1.
91 Source is the *Annual Reports* (2004, 1999, 1992).
92 Annual Report J.P. Morgan (2005), Natapoff. S. (2004), *The American Prospect*, March, v 15 i3 p. 16 (2).
93 Murray, G. (1990), Respondent 53, p. 149.
94 Ralph, J. (2004) *CBA Annual Report,* pp. 1–12.
95 Foster, J. B. (2004), 'The Commitment of an Intellectual: Paul M. Sweezy' (1910–2004) *Monthly Review*, p. 5.
96 Foster, J. B. (2004), p. 4.
97 Foster, J. B. (2004), p. 22.
98 Foster, J. B. (2004), p. 22.
99 Murray, G. (1990) Respondent 94, p. 262.
100 Murray, G. (1990), Respondent 18, p. 276.
101 *Business Review Weekly* (2004), 'Rich 200 List' p. 46, pp. 88–9.
102 Mandel, E. (1972), pp. 130–32.
103 Porter, M. (1990), *The Competitive Advantage of Nations,* London, Mcmillan.
104 Bryan, D. & Rafferty, M. (1999), *The Global Economy in Australia: Global Integration and National Economic Policy*, St Leonards, Allen and Unwin.
105 Higley, J. & Deacon, D., Smart, D. (1979), *Elites in Australia*, Boston, Routledge.
106 van der Pijl, K. (1998), *Transnational Classes and International Relations,* London & New York, Routledge.
107 Bryan, D. & Rafferty, M. (1999).
108 Carroll, B. & Alexander, M. (1999), 'Finance Capital and Capitalist Class Integration in the 1990s: Networks of Interlocking Directorships in the Canada and Australia,' *The Canadian Review of Sociology and Anthropology*, August, v.36, i.3, pp. 331–50.
109 Scott, J. & Griff, C. (1984), p. 21.

Chapter 5

The New Zealand Interlocks of Power

New Zealand has been described as a mixed economy.[1] This is an economy that is no longer based on one specialist industry — agriculture — and it works from free market principles. But as we have seen in chapter two, this has not always been the case. Although the last British imperial forces left New Zealand in 1870, they left New Zealanders with a commitment to produce what the British market wanted. The highly fertile soil and arable land continued to provide food and the raw material for clothing for the British urbanised working populations until at least the late 1960s. In 1966 when this part of the story of the top 30 company interlocking directorates begins, there is only a small labour force of one million people. New Zealand is still operating within an agriculturally dominated postcolonial framework; however, during this period — after the New Zealand Labour Party and Norman Kirk were elected in 1972 — New Zealand was forced to accept the withdrawal of 'mother England'. In 1973 Britain joined the European Economic Community or EEC. That same year, oil prices were raised so high that the worst terms of trade for 30 years were created.[2] The economy was forced to diversify. What follows in this chapter are data slices taken from New Zealand corporate history in 1966, 1976, 1986 and 2004 to explore and to try to understand the long-term corporate trends over (an almost) 40-year Mandelian cycle 1966 to 2004.[3]

The New Zealand Corporate Board

The New Zealand company board is similar to, but often smaller than, its Australian equivalent. The general meeting of the shareholders (AGM), like the Australian AGM, elects the directors of public corporations either at a general meeting or through a ballot or poll. Appointment procedures are laid out in the Articles of Association (these are the company rules). They provide for a rotating retirement of directors with a retiring director free to stand for re-election. Although the appointment of directors at the AGM is often seen as a formality, this is not always the case. In 1976, a chairperson and large family shareholder, Alex Patterson, was 'caught with his proxies down'.[4] Patterson was in favour of a centralised board management but two other directors the Goodman brothers, Pat and Peter, were not. Patterson went to the AGM unaware that the Goodman brothers had organised the proxy votes against his re-election to chairperson and the AGM stood him down. The conspirators were then able to buy enough shares to control the company and stop Patterson getting back into control. Their top 30 companies moved on to eventually become Goodman Fielder Watties after merging with the Australian company, Fielders, and the New Zealand Company, Watties. In 1993, Goodman Fielder Watties sold Watties to the American food giant, H.J. Heinz.

The Changing Board Size

The board size often reflects the ownership structure of the company:

> Smaller companies that are owned by the proprietors can be driven in a private way. Someone like a Judge or Newlands or Hawkins can drive his own corporation. It is in the nature of the size of the operation. As it gets larger like NZFP or the BNZ then you have a different balance altogether.[5]

The following data shows the changing size of the New Zealand public company boards and how they have altered in a 38-year period, 1966–2004. This material is from four discrete secondary sources — *Broadlands* 1987, *The National Business Review* 1976, *Equity Investment Register* 1966 and *Management New Zealand Magazine* 1998, 2004.

Table 5.1: Size of Board of Directors

No. of Board Members	1966	1976	1986	1998	2004
	N=1528	N=1616	N=1180	N=151	N= 168
1	0.3	0.8	0.4	0	0
2	0.3	0	0	0	0
3	5.0	4.7	1.6	0	0
4	12.9	6.7	11.0	0	5.0
5	25.7	15.0	19.6	6.0	5.0
6	21.1	18.2	18.4	12.0	0
7	11.6	16.6	15.9	6.0	25.0
8	10.2	17.0	12.2	18	40.0
9	7.6	9.1	9.0	24	5.0
10	3.6	5.9	6.5	18.0	10.0
11	1.3	3.2	2.9	6.0	0
12	0.3	1.2	0.8	0	5.0
13	0.3	0.4	0.8	12.0	0
14	-	0.4	0.8	0	5.0
15	-	0.4	0.8	0	0
16+		0.8	-	0	0
Total	100	100	100	100	100
Average	6	7	6	8.9	8.1

Note: In 1966, 1976, and 1986 the number is of all listed New Zealand companies whereas in 1998 and 2004 these are just the top 30 companies.

In the 38 years from 1966 to 2004, the average size of New Zealand company boards appears to be uniformly between six and nine directors. The small size in the 1980s would seem to be because this was a point of economic stress in the swider environment. The sharemarket had a major collapse in 1987. There were mergers and takeovers going on with the newly opened deregulated economic liberal economy, therefore directors and companies were not as comfortable as they had been in an economy that had formerly protected local capital. As this director said in 1987:

> I think the director standard … is in a pretty poor state of affairs. But it's getting better. It's changing dramatically. It no longer when someone retires at sixty-five that his colleagues would see that he gets a few board seats amongst the team.[6]

The Comparative Centrality Results

The corporate centrality results over the period 1966 to 2004 show that there has been no one continuous New Zealand company acting as a central interlocker, 'leader' or 'innovator' spanning the whole 38-year period. The closest to this has been the reformed back to basics industrial, Fletcher Building, which temporarily disappeared in the 1980s when it was busy moving off shore to Canada and Chile among other countries. When this off shore expansion and some diversification failed it then returned its focus to New Zealand and redeveloped its original company, Fletchers into Fletcher Building.

Figure 5.2 shows the very successful rise of cooperatives — Fonterra (the New Zealand Dairy Company), PPCS and Richmond — as a collective strategy of small land capital against global agribusiness. Small domestic land capital has historically been disadvantaged by economic, political and social trends of urbanisation slipping them down to levels when they needed and received subsidies. This rise indicates a return in the 1990s to doing what New Zealand does best — growing and exporting things from the rich, well watered soil.

Where there is a group of companies in a row (e.g. Fletcher, Tasman Pulp and Paper), this is because the one company has taken over or merged into an entity, therefore the two sets of figures become one. In this way, also, a number of companies go out of existence. The methodology used to describe the interlocks between the top 30 companies in the four different periods is as follows and is based on the centrality analysis described in chapter four.

When we look below at the centrality of director interlocks amongst the top 30 companies in 1966, 1976, 1986 and 2004, a cyclical 40-year boom–bust–boom pattern emerges with the earliest and latest periods of high profits being the least interlocked with the 1986 crisis period being the time of densest interlocking.

Table 5.2: Comparing Top New Zealand Companies 1966–2004

Company	1966			1976			1986			1998			2004		
	B	D	C	B	D	C	B	D	C	B	D	C	B	D	C
Fletcher Bld.	3	2	4	3	1	3	-	-	-	1	1	1	1	1	1
Tasman P. & P.	1	1	1	0	0	0	-	-	-	-	-	-	-	-	-
Wright Stephenson	1	1	1	-	-	-	-	-	-	-	-	-	-	-	-
Brierley	-	-	-	-	-	-	6	1	6	2	2	3	-	-	-
Farmers Coop	2	1	2	-	-	-	-	-	-	-	-	-	-	-	-
New Zealand Refineries.	1	2	2	-	-	-	-	-	-	-	-	-	-	-	-
N.Z. Insurance	1	1	1	1	1	1	-	-	-	-	-	-	-	-	-
South British Ins.	0	0	0												
N.Z.F. P.	0	0	0	-	-	-	1	2	2	-	-	-	-	-	-
Carter Holt Harvey							2	3	4						
Hellabys	1	1	1	2	2	3	-	-	-	-	-	-	-	-	-
Watties	0	0	0	0	0	0	2	3	4	-	-	-	-	-	-
Goodman Fielders	-	-	-	-	-	-	3	5	7	-	-	-	-	-	-
Lion Nathan	-	-	-	-	-	-	-	-	-	-	-	-	-	-	-
NZ Breweries	3	3	5	3	1	1	-	1	3	-	-	-	-	-	-
Progressive	-	-	-	-	-	-	1	1	1	-	-	-	-	-	-
Cable Price Downer	2	2	2	-	-	-	-	-	-	-	-	-	-	-	-
Feltex	-	-	-	-	-	-	1	1	1	-	-	-	-	-	-
McConnell Dowell	-	-	-	-	-	-	3	3	5	-	-	-	-	-	-
Owens	-	-	-	-	-	-	-	-	-	-	-	-	-	-	-
Ceramco	-	-	-	-	-	-	1	1	1	-	-	-	-	-	-
NZ Dairy Board Fonterra	-	-	-	-	-	-	-	-	-	2	3	4	0	0	0
NZ Dairy Board Group of Companies	-	-	-	-	-	-	-	-	-	1	2	2	0	0	0
Air NZ	-	-	-	-	-	-	-	-	-	1	1	1	2	2	3
Fernz	-	-	-	-	-	-	-	-	-	1	1	1	-	-	-
DB Group	-	-	-	-	-	-	-	-	-	2	2	3	-	-	-
Foodstuffs NZ	-	-	-	-	-	-	-	-	-	1	1	1	-	-	-
Independent News	-	-	-	-	-	-	-	-	-	1	1	1	-	-	-
Richmond	-	-	-	-	-	-	-	-	-	-	-	-	2	1	2
Warehouse Group	-	-	-	-	-	-	-	-	-	-	-	-	1	1	1
Telecom	-	-	-	-	-	-	-	-	-	1	2	2	1	2	2
Fisher & Paykel	-	-	-	-	-	-	-	-	-	2	3	4	0	0	0

Sources: 1. 1966 *Equity Investments*. 2. *National Business Review Rich List* (1976), *Guide to Comparative Performance of New Zealand Companies*, and *NBR Investors Services Publications*. 3. *Buttle and Wilson Share Registry* (1986), 4. *Management* (1998), 'Top 200 NZ Companies', December, p. 76. 5. *Management*, (2004), *Management* (2004) 'Top 200 NZ Companies', *Management* December, p. 62.

Period One, 1966–1975: An Orphaned Settler Colony

In the 1960s when this 40-year cycle began, the capitalist class fraction dominant in the settler colony was agrarian, supported primarily throughout this time by a conservative National Party government.[7] This National Party government was led first by Sir Keith Holyoake (September 1957–December 1957 and December 1960–February 1972), and then briefly by Sir John Marshall (February 1972–December 1972). Although both men were conservatives, they governed by what seems, in retrospect, to be a very Keynesian policy framework that used protective tariffs, income stabilisation, export management, state housing, processing of raw materials and food products which moved the country toward a period of dependent industrialisation.[8] Following the Second World War, the leading accumulation strategy employed had been state-led industrial import substitution with low level technology, low labour productivity and the withholding of reinvestment that went back as profits to the core (mostly Britain).

The pattern of 1966 interlocks that follows (see figure 5.1) is scattered because it was a highly protected economy where competition and fear of hostile takeovers was very low. As in the Australian data, the interlocks were directional because they were used only where the director was a chairperson or an executive. The higher the director's centrality, the more potential power they had to enhance their personal advantage and the advantage of their company.

Of the top 30 New Zealand companies in 1966 there were only nine companies that had asymmetric multiple directorates, that is, a low 30 per cent of the sample. The directors involved in these relationships are noted.

This picture of interlocks is quite sparse. Centrality was focused in three main corporations — New Zealand Breweries, Cable Price Downer and Fletchers. All three were industrial capital enterprises. There is little evidence here of any depth other than in Fletchers and that goes to only two other companies.

In Figure 5.1, the top 30 companies that are not interlocked are to be found around the outer circle of the interlocked companies. Figure 5.1 shows that the 1966 interlocks had low density. This is particularly evident in comparison to the other four New Zealand periods to be seen later in this chapter. This low network density reflects a low business anxiety associated with the impending loss of British investment and a new move away from land capital toward more urban-based industrial capital. Cronin's work suggests farmers, comprador merchants, British and American financiers were forming dominant class alliances.[9] The diversity of firms from which the 1966 interlocking directorates come from supports this. The companies include domestic industrial capital (e.g. Fletchers, Tasman Pulp and Paper, Hellabys, Alex Harvey, New Zealand Refrigeration), comprador merchants (e.g. Dominion Breweries, New Zealand Breweries, New Zealand Refineries), overseas finance capital (South British Insurance, Cable Price Downer) and agrarian-land capital (Farmers Cooperative, Wright Stephenson). The three key clusters were national industrial capital, overseas industrial capital and land capital. Land capital was least interlocked.

Figure 5.1: 1966 NZ Top 30 Companies and Their Interlocking Directors

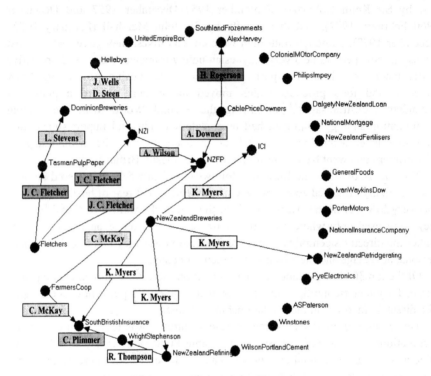

Financial capital had few multiple interlocks for there were few finance capital companies in the top 30 companies in 1966, apart from South British Insurance. Possible reasons for this could include that some large companies had their own finance company (e.g. Fletchers had MARAC) and that in 1966, New Zealand banks did not employ a hands-on approach. A director interviewed in 1986 explained why banks were not prominent on company boards:

In New Zealand they don't seek to have any influence — banks and insurance companies — they don't have people on boards and they don't seek to influence boards.

Interviewer: Does this mean that banks don't have any control over decisions about how capital is to be spent?

No, they deliberately keep out of it, the banks and the insurance companies, primarily because they act for different companies. Bigger companies these days have four or five banks — all the major trading banks — as their bankers and they might see several insurance companies, life assurance companies, looking after their pension funds and other different things, so the banks and the insurance companies stay strictly neutral.

Interviewer: This is different from bank–corporate relationships in America?

Yes they do over there. In Germany in particular, banks do have a big influence. In Germany the banks own a lot of the shareholding in public companies. Many have directors on the board. In many cases the banker is chairman. Not so much in the US certainly in some parts of Europe and Germany in particular.

Interviewer: Is that changing in New Zealand?

No, it's not changing in New Zealand. You ask the AMP or National Mutual and they will say the same — they don't get involved.[10]

This interviewee saying that 'banks and the insurance companies stay strictly neutral' gives no support for the collusive hypothesis and only a little indirect support for the discretionary hypothesis that through indirect methods banks interact with their corporate clients.

In this period, import substitution existed ostensibly to protect jobs but also importantly, resulted in the protection of local capital against foreign competition. (For example, Sir Tom Clark, founder and major shareholder of the company Ceramco exerted a profitable monopoly on New Zealand ceramic production; all New Zealanders ate from one of five bad designs that embossed all sets of plates, cups and saucers. This system permitted placing huge excises on bringing ceramics into the country.) Consumer goods became unattractive, antiquated and expensive. This protective industry process enhanced family dynasties. The Myers, Hellabys and Fletchers families, for example, did well at this time.

Fletchers

Fletchers, in 1983 became Fletcher Challenge and then in 2001 Fletcher Building. They were a key New Zealand family business dynasty. The official history of the Fletcher family puts their beginning at 1909 when James Fletcher, a 23-year-old Scot, arrived in New Zealand with a few 'pounds in his pocket' and carpentry skills that he used to found a building company which in 1916 became Fletcher Brothers.[11]

According to Jesson, this official Fletcher 'Annual Report' version of the rags to riches myth, is not as good as the real story of continuous privilege.[12] James Fletcher came from a prosperous Scottish background, migrated to New Zealand and married more money in the form of Charlotte Cameron. In 1919, James floated Fletcher Construction with the assistance of his two brothers Andrew and John and their cousin James Smith. The Fletchers were then able to take advantage of the post war expansion and development in the building industry. The real boost to the Fletcher family fortunes came when Sir James C. Fletcher aligned his fortunes and personal friendship with the Labour Party and in particular two Labour Prime Ministers, Peter Fraser (1940–49), and Walter Nash (1957–60). In 1942, he was made Commissioner of Defence Construction. This gave Fletcher wartime power over the entire construction industry. He was given responsibility for setting up the Ministry of Works and was instrumental in organising state housing for homeless New Zealanders. Fletcher's company built all the New Zealand state houses. By 1955, James junior persuaded the New Zealand government that not only should Fletchers build a huge pulp and paper factory at Kawerau, but also it should own part of it.[13] Jesson argues that in the early 1940s and 1950s, 'there was no visible distinction between the state and (this) private enterprise'.[14] James C. Fletcher denies Labour links were the basis of their fortune and says that the company under-estimated the costs of building; 'we nearly lost our shirts'.[15] But by 1981, a peak was reached when grandson, Hugh, organised the amalgamation of Fletcher Holdings, Tasman Pulp and Paper and Challenge Corporation to form Fletcher Challenge Corporation that then became New Zealand's biggest company, representing almost a tenth of the New Zealand sharemarket.[16]

This period of fading land capital and rising industrial capital around family dynasties was followed by a period characterised as 'state led encouragement of international competitiveness through incentives and a gradual and planned reduction of import protection, culminating in the Closer Economic Relations with Australia or CER'.[17] CER in full is the Australia–New Zealand Closer Economic Relations Trade Agreement that was signed in Canberra on 28 March 1983. Its objectives, according to the Australian Department of Foreign Affairs, were to:
1. Strengthen the broader relationship between New Zealand and Australia
2. To develop closer economic relations between the Member States through a mutually beneficial expansion of free trade between New Zealand and Australia
3. To eliminate barriers to trade between New Zealand and Australia in a gradual and progressive manner under an agreed timetable and with a minimum of disruption
4. To develop trade between New Zealand and Australia under conditions of fair competition.[18]

Period Two, 1976–1984: 'Think Big'

In the period 1976–1984, the country continued to be largely led by the National Party under the leadership of Prime Minister Robert Muldoon and his 'think big' governing strategy. This strategy was a state-led heavy industrialisation regime whereby the growth of the nation hinged upon building up domestic energy resources and advanced technology. There was a shift away from agrarian accumulation strategies toward industrial production with its urban population drift. The reason for these shifting patterns was the changing political and economic needs of the core (specifically Britain) but also because the large agrarian landowners' profits were waning as the original fertility of the soil was being spent and so their hands were forced to diversify into industry.

There were four companies with directional interlocks involved out of a possible 30 (that is, a very small 13 per cent). Fletchers and New Zealand Breweries were the corporate giants here with Fletchers having the top (but still low) centrality ratings (centrality 3). Sir James Fletcher is the key to the network with Sir Kenneth Myer as his only rival. Sir Kenneth Myer was head of the Myer family dynasty whose company was New Zealand Breweries (centrality 3) they later became Lion Nathan. The striking feature of Figure 5.2 is the sparseness of the interlocking.

Figure 5.2: 1976 NZ Top 30 Companies and Their Interlocking Directors

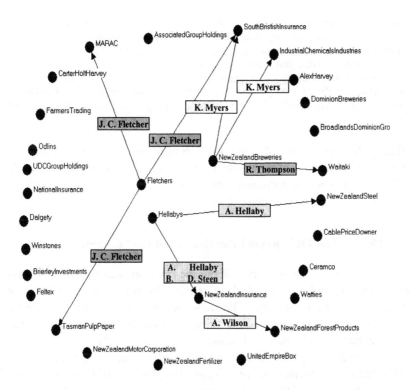

The 1976 business environment made the top director feel relaxed and harmonious where they were metaphorically enjoying the full blaze of the economic summer. Capital was obviously not under threat here and even though there was a global oil crisis and domestic rationing, this did not manifest in the New Zealand ruling class anxiously forming defensive interlocks. Interestingly, the interlocks that were formed no longer featured any agrarian-land capital but instead came from an industrial capital base. New Zealand political business leadership was changing.

British financial capital was still in New Zealand in the form of South British Insurance but its days were numbered. As Cronin writes, in 1972–1988 overseas earnings are 'particularly significant for South British Insurance and NZI ... [but they] fall significantly from 1981 and dramatically from 1987 with the merger and then collapse of these insurance firms'.[19] New mergers were in the offing — for example, Fletchers and Tasman Pulp and Paper merged in 1981. Features such as growing inflation and growing union militancy began to unsettle the ruling class. As a top director said:

> Industrial relations wasn't looking good. Employers generally weren't looking good... it was really the general wage orders that would come out and you would find that the companies would start to break the award by some trick and then it would lead to more pressure and we were just leading to a break down. It was probably the worst of regulation that created the atmosphere...unions waiting for a year for a hearing... because I remember that things were starting to move into the first stages of inflation — prices moving very rapidly. The unions were dropping behind and suffering badly for it.[20]

During this period, New Zealand was becoming reacquainted with the global market where 'merchant, commercial and financial fractions become less significant as they are reconstituted with industrial capital in the form of finance capital, expanding beyond the domestic market'.[21]

Period Three, 1984–1997: Rapid Liberalisation of the Economy

Rapid liberalisation of the economy became the key feature of the 1984–87 period, when finance capital in New Zealand reached its zenith in its political and economic power over the state. This very pleasurable time for New Zealand finance capitalists was serendipitously being experienced by finance capitalists in other countries at this time.[22] Following the 1984 election of the Labour government under the prime ministership of David Lange, and the installation of his IMF-influenced finance minister Roger Douglas, a rapid series of liberal economic reforms were introduced. Finance capital dominated the New Zealand business community and provided liberal economic policy to the government through their state lobby group, the New Zealand Business Roundtable (NZBR).

At first this liberal economic push was not held to be entirely desirable by all of the top 30 company directors. Capital fractions emerged strongly on the issue. Non-financiers expressed doubts about economic liberalism as policy, both for their company and for the New Zealand public with the potential problems associated with the removal of the safety net. In a newspaper article, top industrial capital director, Sir Laurence Stevens, the ex-President of the Manufacturers Association said:

> We are right to re-structure and to stop doing some of the things that we were doing but at the moment I am fearful we might be going too far in the other direction... I am not talking about undue protection. We do not want to return to that but we need an environment where industry decisions are not measured solely in terms of the imported landed goods... No manufacturer can adjust his costs as quickly as the exchange rate can move... I do not think that the advisers to government are aware of the harm they are doing in pursuing this economic purity theory.[23]

In the immediately following period this sentiment changed quite rapidly. The 1986 map of the top companies' interlocks was dense and defensive (see figure 5.3.) The general impression of the period, 1984 to 1986, was one of frenetic interlocking. This was a period when the high rises' mirror glass was metaphorically red so that the internecine blood letting inside could continue undetected by the outside world. The results of this fevered corporate activity only became fully apparent after the stock market crash in 1987 when some companies had to go public with their problems including a lack of cash liquidity (Waitaki), bad debts (BNZ Finance) and over gearing (Newmans through NZFP).

The asymmetric interlocks of 1986 formed a pattern far removed from the sparse interlocking of 1976 and 1966 when the old protected industries cosily existing side by side within a tariff-insulated economy. Figure 5.3 shows a diversity of multiple interlocks. This unease about what to do next and how to deal with a fast changing business world was echoed in the words of this director:

> The next most difficult thing is to shake off practices and procedures of the past and to take an entirely new approach because boards in New Zealand have not been accustomed to what is happening. The change from a controlled regulated environment to an unregulated one is difficult for boards to entirely shift their way of thinking to and to persuade management to do the same. That is the current difficulty. To change your whole approach is a difficult thing to do. Easy for the bright young guys, fellows in their twenties, they are not bowed down by the traditions and practices of the past.[24]

Figure 5.3: 1986 NZ Top 30 Companies and Their Interlocking Directors

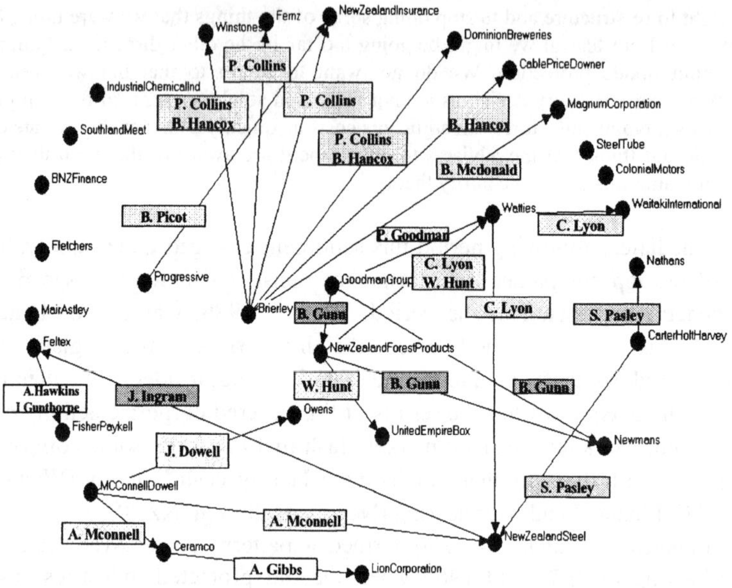

Winstones　Femz　NewZealandInsurance
DominionBreweries
P. Collins
CablePriceDowner
IndustrialChemicalInd
P. Collins　　**P. Collins**　MagnumCorporation
SouthlandMeat　**B. Hancox**　　　　　**B. Hancox**
SteelTube
P. Collins
BNZFinance　　**B. Hancox**　　ColonialMotors
B. Mcdonald
Fletchers　　**B. Picot**　　　　Watties　　Waitakilnternational
C. Lyon
P. Goodman
Progressive　　　　GoodmanGroup　**C. Lyon**　　Nathans
MairAstley　　　　　　**W. Hunt**
Brierley　**B. Gunn**　　**C. Lyon**　**S. Pasley**
Feltex　　　　　　　　　　　　CarterHoltHarvey
NewZealandForestProducts
A. Hawkins
I. Gunthorpe　**J. Ingram**　**W. Hunt**　**B. Gunn**　**B. Gunn**
FisherPaykell　　　Owens
UnitedEmpireBox　　Newmans
J. Dowell
MCConnellDowell　　　　　　　**S. Pasley**
A. Mconnell　　**A. Mconnell**
Ceramco　　　　NewZealandSteel
A. Gibbs　　LionCorporation

Brierley is the key to the multiple interlocking. The company built its base on asset stripping formerly import-protected companies such as Ceramco, Aulsebrooks, Gear Meats, Winstones, Dominion Breweries and Whitcoulls. No asset rich company was safe from the stealth of a Brierley takeover. Brierley, the company, was founded in 1961 by Ronald Brierley (later Sir Ronald). The company was known as a corporate raider but this was also characteristic of Brierley the man, who is quoted as saying, 'I suppose that it is fair to say that I have always been a wheeler-dealer rather than a manager'.[25] Although it took Brierley nine years to have his company listed on the New Zealand Stock Exchange, by the 1970s he had become one of 'those canny capitalists who had worked out new ways to manipulate the elaborate controls of the welfare state'.[26] In the 1980s, Brierley the company took off with the state's help after it made Ron Brierley the chair of the state-owned Bank of New Zealand (BNZ).

Brierley had on its board two very enthusiastic economic liberals — Sir Roger Douglas (after his retirement from government) and Bob Matthew. Bob Matthew was concurrently chair of New Zealand's Brierley Investments and vice chair of the New Zealand Business Roundtable (NZBR). Finance capital dominated the NZBR because it was able to articulate economic liberal policy expertly for the state.

The significance of this power base will become more obvious when we focus on the New Zealand Business Roundtable (chapter six).

Period Four, 1998–2003: Constrained Economic Liberalism

By the end of the 1990s, the economic liberalism that had been associated with politicians such as Roger Douglas, Richard Prebble and the economic liberal prime ministers Michael Moore (4 September to 2 November 1990), Jim Bolger (1990 to 1996), and Jenny Shipley (1997 to 1999, had run its course. A form of social democracy replaced economic liberalism, and a social democrat, Helen Clark, became prime minister on 10 December 1999.

With the cycle having turned, 1998 was not a heavily interlocked period. There are eleven companies involved in these asymmetric interlocks or 36 per cent of the top 30 companies. There were three clusters, two of which were industrial capital. The third was around the key director, Selwyn Cushing, a central Brierley director who was interlocked with Air New Zealand (travel) and ECNZ (a former state enterprise). This is shown in Figure 5.4 with a low to middle range of top director interlocking in 1998. These interlocks were more relaxed and comfortable than they had been in 1986 before the stock market crash. They were no longer defending themselves against the rapacious financial capitalist Brierley, although Brierley was still a background player. The central interlocking directors were Colin Maiden from the industrial capital boards, and Roderick Deane.

Dr Roderick Sheldon Deane
Qualifications: PhD 1967, B.Com (Hons) 1964, FCA 1988, FCIS 1987, FCIM 1991, FNZIM 1992.
Biographical Details: Born 8 April, 1941. Educated at Victoria University and awarded a postgraduate scholarship 1960–64.
Career: Held a Part-time Lecturership in Economics at Victoria University 1964–78, Deputy Governor of the Reserve Bank 1963–74, 1976–86. Chief Economist and Head of the Economic Department 1976–82, Deputy Governor of the Reserve Bank, Alternate Executive Director of the IMF, 1974–1976, CEO Electricity Corporation of NZ 1987–92. Some company directorships — ANZ Bank, AMP 1990–92, State Services Commission 1986–87.
Publications include *Foreign Investment in New Zealand Manufacturing* (1970), *Policy and the NZ Financial System* (1979), and *Financial Policy Reform* (1986). He is an executive Council Member of the Institute of Policy Studies.
Clubs/ Societies: Member of the New Zealand Business Roundtable
Source: New Zealand Who's Who Aotearoa (1996), *Fletcher Building* Annual Report (2004), p. 8.

Figure 5.4: 1998 NZ Top 30 Companies and Their Interlocking Directors

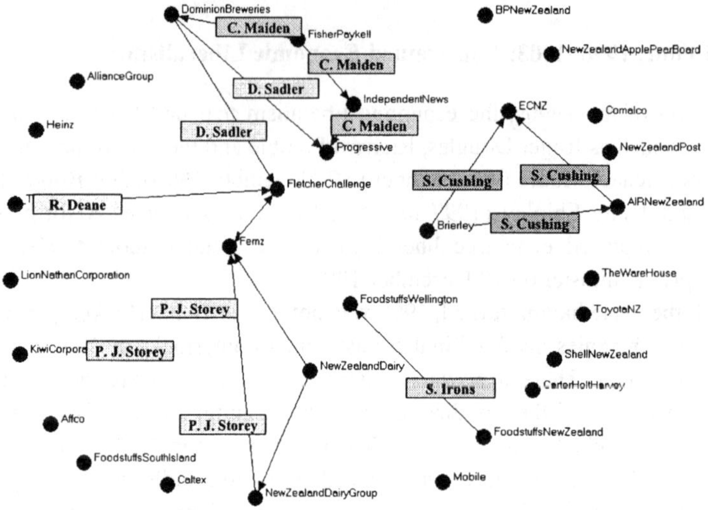

Finance Capital

Roderick Deane was the key multiple interlocker for finance capital, although ironically he was only on two boards here and neither of them were finance capital.

According to Jesson, Deane was the economic liberal muse who pulled finance minister Sir Roger Douglas's strings. Deane was a:

> trustee of the libertarian right-wing think tank, the Centre for Independent Studies. This is consistent with his ideas on monetary policy, which have been monetarist since the 1970s. In the interests of controlling inflation, he has believed it necessary to restrict the growth of money supply. In order to achieve that, it is necessary to allow interest rates to move freely. This is all part of a coherent package of policies that includes financial deregulation and the floating of the dollar: it is these policies more than anything else that established the character of the fourth Labor government as a government of hard-line monetarism.[27]

Carroll and Carson's work shows that New Zealand and Australia were not alone in the way their economic liberal state policy was informed by corporate and think tank interests. Globally the networks of 'policy boards and the world's major corporations form an important communication structure' for the expansion of the ideas that further their class interests.[28]

Industrial Capital

Professor Colin Maiden was the key interlocking director representing the interests of industrial capital. As former vice chancellor of Auckland University he was also, in a different sense, a traditional establishment figure.

By 1998, there remained little active participation of the old industrial capital family dynasty members in the reconstitution of their companies — Fletchers (becoming Fletcher Building) and Myer (Lion Nathan). Easton argues these founder (capital) companies had grown up in the regulated pre-1984 environment, and ... [that] world in which Fletcher Challenge was conceived was very different from that in which it died, because by 1999 the FCL directors resolved to dismantle the failing FCL share structure and by 2001 Fletcher Building had become a stand alone publicly listed company on only the ASX. Conglomerates in the Fletcher Challenge mould were going back to basics.[29]

Land Capital and the Emergence of Cooperatives

Cooperatives began in 1871 when New Zealand's first collectively grower-owned cheese company was formed on the Otago Peninsula. They have continued very successfully into the early twenty-first century. Ian Reid, the chief executive officer of the New Zealand Cooperatives Association, defines cooperatives (also known as coops) as 'a collection of individuals or businesses that decide to operate together for advantage'.[30]

In this period, land capital had to defensively become globally competitive by forming itself collectively into a corporate body. This they did but their success became a source of anxiety and challenge for other larger New Zealand capitalist fractions. Roger Kerr (from the NZBR) wrote about cooperatives: 'When we look at the agricultural supply cooperatives ... the benefits that they are alleged to offer in terms of allowing farmer control to be maintained seem to be vastly overrated' and he frowned on 'the current proposal to form a single large cooperative ... a poor solution to the dairy industry's problems'.[31] However, the huge success of Fonterra (now no longer the New Zealand Dairy Cooperative) continues to contradict Kerr. Cooperatives' success varies, but Fonterra's *Annual Report* claims them to be the world's largest exporter of dairy products, exporting 95 per cent of their production.

The NZBR directors were very disappointed. A financial capitalist and NZBR member expressed this in an interview:

> The main area still to be deregulated now in New Zealand is the producer boards, which are these monopoly outfits that the farmers have ... These organisations are products of the highly regulated last 30 years or so. In my view they are not doing the farmers any good and not doing the New Zealand economy any good and it would be excellent if they can be deregulated. And the New Zealand Roundtable has been working very hard to educate the farmers and the politicians about the advantages from deregulating

agricultural exports. This focus on the producer boards has been one of the NZBR prime agenda items.[32]

Farmers, whilst continuing to make huge profits from their company, sensibly reject the NZBR logic.

Period Five, 2004 —2006: Land Capital Regrouping

A major characteristic of capital in New Zealand in 2004 was the return of the importance of land capital (e.g. Fonterra, Richmond and PPCS) with New Zealand again becoming a world leader in sheep and beef production despite trade barriers put in place by other free markets like the US and Australia. According to the cooperative Alliance Company's 2004 *Annual Report*, in 2003 some 85 per cent of New Zealand meat, representing nearly three-quarters of a million tonnes of processed product, went to 70 overseas markets. Notably, a significant amount of this meat was used by McDonalds in the USA.[33]

There was very little asymmetric interlocking occurring in 2004. The cooperatively owned meat processor, Richmond, Air New Zealand and Telecom were the most central companies.

These figures of low interlocking would indicate a period of economic growth and a lack of internecine warfare among the capitalist fractions. The year 2004 looked like a period of corporate harmony.

Interestingly, this dominant land capital was not reappearing in its former dynastic or large run-holder guise. Rather, land capital was appearing as a series of cooperative movements, with farmers organising collectively against overseas investment, domestic finance capital (in the form of NZBR attacks) and global agribusiness. Land and merchant capital was regrouping collectively as farmer co-operatives (e.g. Fonterra, Alliance, PPCS and AFFCO) or as retail collectives (e.g. Foodstuffs). There were growing numbers of these cooperatives now registered on the New Zealand Stock exchange.

A different aspect of change was the growth of overseas ownership in local (formerly) New Zealand companies. Ten of the top 30 companies were majority foreign owned (including Telecom, Foodlands NZ, Carter Holt Harvey, Mobil Oil, BP NZ, Caltex, Vodafone, British America Tobacco, Heinz and ANZCO). These companies did not have interlocked New Zealand directors because they did not have large local networks and their meetings were often held in places other than in New Zealand — maybe at the companies' headquarters in the US, UK or elsewhere.[34]

Figure 5.5: 2004 NZ Top 30 Companies and Their Interlocking Directors

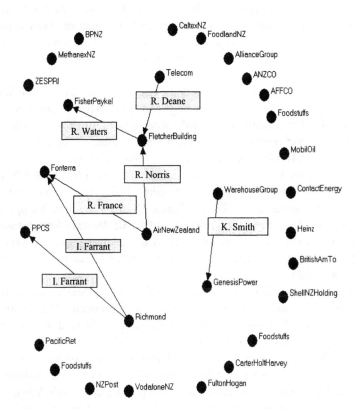

Combined with the above factors, the 2004 interlocking directorate network (see Figure 5.5) shows a relaxed political organisation of top directors basking in a good economic climate, supported by the building boom financed by Asian loans and the fecundity of the New Zealand soil. A chief recipient of this boom has been the reinvented FCL, Fletcher Building, now without any Fletchers as executives and with a new CEO, R.G. Waters.

Land Capital

Cooperatives, which grew to dominate this economic period, vary in their viability but using their own words their unique qualities can be shown:

1. Fonterra, the largest of the farmer cooperatives, was formed in October 2001. This is 'co-operatively owned by more than 11,600 dairy farmers [and is] one of the top ten dairy companies in the world ... responsible for more than a third of international dairy trade'.[35] Fonterra is now a multinational dairy company

that is owned by thirteen thousand New Zealand dairy farmers. Their global supply chain encompasses shareholders' farms in New Zealand through to customers and consumers in one hundred and 40 countries. They collect over thirteen million litres of milk a year, manufacture and market over two million tonnes of dairy products annually, making them a world leader in large-scale milk procurement, processing and management.[36]

2. PPCS in 2004 is a producer's cooperative that grows and exports lamb, venison and beef products. The company began in 1947 when some New Zealand farmers decided against traditional, meat-exporting channels and instead established direct relationships with their end customers. The company exports to approximately 60 countries, employs 4,300 workers at the peak of the season, owns twelve processing facilities and is owned by about 9,000 farmer suppliers. Their head office is in Dunedin. The company has international offices and markets in the United States, United Kingdom, Europe and the Middle East. In a hostile takeover in 2005, the largest New Zealand meat processor, PPCS, completed 'a seven-year takeover battle for rival meat company, Richmond. Legally, the two companies became a single entity on 31 January 2005'.[37]

3. Alliance notes in 2004 that it is one of New Zealand's largest producer cooperatives, exporting 95 per cent of its meat products. The company was established in 1948 by a group of farmers who formed the process and marketing company for the dispersal of meat and co-products to international markets. They have five thousand staff and an annual turnover in excess of $1 million [with] approximately seven million lamb, one million sheep, 140,000 cattle and 80,000 venison annually processed through Alliance's eight plants — seven in the South Island of New Zealand and one in the North Island. Alliance exports over twelve hundred separate products to more than 65 countries. They produce chilled, fresh and frozen meat cuts, wool, pelts, hides, leather and other animal related products.[38]

4. Foodstuffs are a retail cooperative that has trading operations under the Pak'n'Save, Write Price, New World, and Four Square banners. This Co-operative Society Ltd jointly accounts for over 65 per cent of the grocery turnover in the southern half of the North Island. Each individual store is owner-operated by a cooperative member. At the end of July 2004, there were 45 New World supermarkets throughout the lower North Island, nine Pak'n'Save food warehouses, seven Write Price food barns, 92 Four Square/Four Square Discount stores and eighteen non-advertising member stores.[39]

This is not a definitive list of all cooperatives — even those top ones shown are not new, but they are very innovative and very economically significant. And they are now happily (if ironically) becoming — as in the Fonterra and PPCS cases — multinational companies them-selves.

Shareholdings in the Top 30 New Zealand Companies

By examining the top five shareholders in 1999, we can see that 37 per cent of ten companies from the top 30 companies (those who list their shareholders in their annual company report) were predominantly owned by a single nominee company — the custodial depository of the Reserve Bank of New Zealand (or RBNZ) called The New Zealand Central Securities Depository (or NZCSD) (see Figure 5.6 below).[40] The NZCSD is a nominee holding company for an array of finance capital, primarily Australian banks, including the National Australia Bank, AMP, ANZ and other miscellaneous overseas finance capital companies such as Citibank, Tracker and Trustee Executors. This concentration of capital represented by the NZCSD is large, considering an earlier point made by O'Lincoln that 5 per cent shareholder ownership of a company can give strategic corporate control.[41]

This finance capital control/ownership of New Zealand's top companies is symptomatic of a wider regionalism happening to New Zealand since the Australia–New Zealand Closer Economic Relations Trade Agreement in 1983, and the free trade of goods achieved in 1990. According to Robinson, foreign bank ownership is ubiquitous in New Zealand as 90 per cent of the country's banking assets are foreign owned and 70 per cent of that ownership is by Australian banks.[42]

The New Zealand managers of these Australian owned banks are autonomous in their day-to-day running of the banks, but the Australian parents make the big decisions. 'Australia is the conduit for New Zealanders' money to go to the rest of the world'.[43] The Commonwealth Bank of Australia owns the ASB Bank, Australian and New Zealand Banking Group Ltd own the National Bank of NZ and the Bank of New Zealand.

The comparable ownership data for 2004 show some change away from the dominance of the NZCSD to a growth in shares held singly by National Nominees (Australia National Bank NZ branch), Westpac and ANZ. Banks still dominate top Australian finance capital. Most important is the recent penetration of US capital into Australia and New Zealand, in the form of J.P. Morgan Bank and Citibank through the NZCSD.

Figure 5.6: Owner Penetration Index of New Zealand's Top 30 Companies

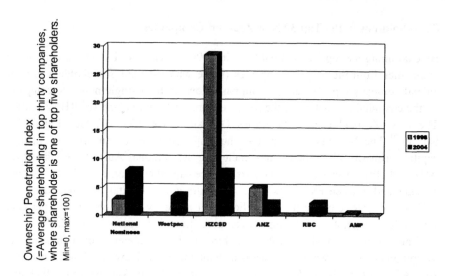

1. In 2004 there were 10 (from 30) companies with top 20 investment information in their Annual Report.

2. In 1998 there were 11 (from 30) companies with top 20 investment information in their Annual Report.

To recap, the Ownership Penetration Index (OPI) has been created based on information about the top five shareholders in each of the ten largest listed companies. To calculate the OPI for each shareholding company, their shareholdings in each of the top ten companies was averaged. The OPI is a proxy for actual ownership, as a shareholding company's holding in a top ten company does not contribute towards the OPI if it is not a top five shareholder, and because it weights each top ten company equally.

Network Limitations

Criticisms of this sort of research on interlocking directorates fall into at least five groups. The first critics are the directors themselves:

> The only reason that I accepted this interview, because I am so damn busy that I haven't got the time, is because I am so sick of reading rubbish that comes out of universities about conspiracy theories: The idea that the whole country is run by a whole lot of people who sit round on each other's boards playing. I felt that you deserved a bit of exposure to reality and of course the reality is that we are all competitors in the real world out there. We fight like hell with each other, all the time, and the chances of

getting any two competitors even if they sat around a room all the time to actually agree is remote because they are always trying to beat each other. [44]

This is a valid point for it is easy to get carried away with network theories and forget that these men (sic) are warring fractions of competing brothers joined only against labour.

The second group of critics agrees that it is acceptable to quantify corporate interlocks, but they argue that this mapping does not tell you anything about the behavioral motives of the actors.[45] Mizruchi argues that interlocks may not reveal a great deal about individual director's motives but they can predict much that is interesting in strategic firms' allegiances, choices and information flows, and thereby help create a picture of rich and complex board relations.[46]

A third group of critics rejects the quantitative method outright, charging that it is an unsuitable mechanism for understanding the richness and diversity of business behavior. Criticisms are answered here by triangulating the data with interviews and other primary sources, such as ownership data. This New Zealand case study highlights the centrality of industrial capital in the recruitment of the key political leaders, with their family dynasties in the 1966 and 1976 data and Roderick Deane the economic liberal leader. The sparseness of the centrality of inter-locking directorates in 2004 shows the return to the power of land owning capital, in a new cooperative form.

A fourth criticism of the lack of substantial analytic insight involved with just looking at interlocking directors when searching for power in the network is highlighted by this research. You have to look beyond the interlocking directorship level of political power to the level of ownership to see who has economic clout. Ownership of companies is still the key to understanding what is happening. This is what a director said about this:

> If the major shareholders are represented on the board then it means everything to do with the election of directors but not in the sense of the AGM [but] in the sense of the selection of new directors when vacancies become available. Obviously the most influential directors on any board are the ones that represent the most sizable shareholders. In normal circumstances the bigger the shareholding the bigger the influence. [47]

A fifth criticism of the limitation of interlocking findings is that they neglect the links to their global parents or what is happening amongst global transnationals. This is true too for national companies are often tied to unacknowledged global links. Both Carroll[48] and Fennema's work shows this with Fennema using a sample of 176 major industrial and banks, where there 'exists a cohesive international network of interlocking directorates [but at the same time it] should be considered primarily a communication network rather than a network of domination and control'.[49] For domination and control of either national or international interlocking networks you have to look at the ownership structures below the surface. That is why research quantifying the number of outsiders (non-executives) and the board's size as indicators of finance capital's hegemony and then arguing that the degree of global penetration of finance capital is only 'evident' in Australia, is only part of the story.[50] The evidence here points to a much heavier involvement of finance capital than this, because it goes beyond the political and communication levels of the board interlocks to focus on the level of ownership as a more significant indicator of power relations. Ownership figures are still most pivotal and by just looking at the largest stakeholders in the top 30 companies as is done here, it can be shown that over a period of ten years there is some penetration of 'new' finance capital into positions of prominence in Australia. For example, in both Australia and New Zealand, there is evidence of the growing US-based banks Chase Manhattan (later JP Morgan) and Citicorp in the top 30 companies — something that would not be picked up by just looking at the interlocks.[51]

Conclusion: Corporate Networks in Australia and New Zealand

These findings, in both chapters four and five, are of economic and political significance because they differentiate two levels of power — economic and political. On the level of economic ownership, finance capital (used in its most catholic sense as money capital immediately outside of production, not as the collusive model does, by conflating industrial and financial capital symbiotically) remains dominant in its stake holding of the top 30 Australian and New Zealand companies. This challenges the original control model because, although the type of finance company may change by name and country of origin, it remains that finance capital is the largest stakeholder. It has ultimate control through ownership and influence on board decisions.

Australasia in 2004 appears to be approaching the end of what Mandel calls a 40-year economic cycle begun in the 1960s.[52] At the beginning of the cycle in New Zealand in the 1960s there was high economic growth and prosperity with the slow death of colonial capital.

Cooperatively organised land capital in New Zealand is a very interesting national response to global capitalism. The old landholding dynasties are not being reborn but being added to by a growing collectivity of farmers with a variety of products — wool, meat, kiwifruit — and collective ownership structures to organise them. This cooperative and collective initiative of originally embattled farmers has proved very profitable for them.

In both countries, financial capital is acting to centralise wealth. Like a giant vacuum cleaner, it is sucking up competition and spreading its ownership. Its strategies of transformations, using the Scott and Griff idea,[53] include the fusing of nominee companies to form one — the New Zealand Central Securities Depository. This eased them into a regionalism that was not yet global but it is becoming increasingly so. Most capital exchange is still within Australia and New Zealand because industrial capital has until relatively recently been tied to the local (later national) circuits of capital whereas, in contrast, finance capital circulates more freely and globally. As will be developed in chapter six, economic liberalism and the integrated, state-supported circuit of finance capital has set the Australian and New Zealand stage.[54]

Notes

[1] The material for this overview is from Bateman, D. (2003), *New Zealand Official Yearbook*, Wellington, Government Printer, p. 383.

[2] Bateman, D. (2003), p. 22.

[3] Mandel, E. (1972), *Late Capitalism*, London, New Left Books.

[4] Delahunty, J. (1986), 'Pat the Knife', *Public Eyes*, n.4, October, p. 4.

[5] Murray, G. (1990), *New Zealand Corporate Capitalism*, Respondent 88, p. 143.

[6] Murray, G. (1990), Respondent 53, p. 151.

[7] Armstrong W. & Bradbury, J. (1983), 'Industrialisation and Class Structure in Australia, New Zealand and Canada 1870–1980', in Wheelwright, F. & Buckley, K. *Essay in Political Economy of Australian Capitalism*, Frenchs Forest, Australian and New Zealand Book Company, p. 30.

[8] Cronin, B. (2001), *The Politics of New Zealand Business Internationalisation 1972–1996*, v. 1 & v. 2. Auckland University, PHD Thesis, p. 117.

[9] Cronin, B. (2001).

[10] Murray, G. (1990), Respondent 18, p. 277.

[11] The details are found on the fletcherbuilding.co.nz [Accessed 4 July 2005].

[12] Jesson, B. (1980), *The Fletcher Challenge, Wealth and Power in New Zealand*, published by the author, South Auckland, P. O. Box 8, pp. 4–8.

[13] Easton, B. (2004), 'Who's Hugh?' *Listener*, November 17, p. 24.

[14] Jesson, B. (1980), p. 12.

[15] *National Business Review* Rich List (1996), p. 17.

[16] Easton, B. (2004), p. 24.

[17] Cronin, B. (2001), p. 1.

[18] Department of Foreign Affairs Canberra (1995), No. 2 New Zealand ANCERTA — trade http://www.dfat.gov.au/geo/new_zealand/anz_cer/anzcerta1.pdf.

[19] Cronin, B. (2001), p. 228.

[20] Murray, G. (1990), Respondent 9, p. 234.

[21] Cronin, B. (2001), p. 111.

[22] Grønmo, S. (1995a), 'Structural Change during Deregulation and Crisis; the Position of Banks in the Norwegian Intercorporate Network', *International Social Networks Conference*, London, July, p. 19.

[23] Stevens, L. (1988), *New Zealand Herald*, 4 August, s.3, p. 3.

[24] Murray, G. (1990), Respondent 18, p. 146.

[25] Eldred-Grigg, S. (1997), *The Rich: A New Zealand History*, Auckland, Penguin Books.

[26] Eldred-Grigg, S. (1997).

[27] Jesson, B. (1989), *Fragments of Labour, The Story behind the Labour Government*, Auckland, Penguin.

[28] Carroll, W. & Carson, C. (2003), 'The Network of Global Corporations and Elite Policy Groups: a Structure for Transnational Capitalist Class Formation', *Global Networks*, v.3, n.1, pp. 29–57.

[29] Easton, B. (2004), p. 24.

[30] Reid, I. quoted in Kerr, R. (1999), *Cooperatives versus Corporates New Zealand agribusiness and food congress*, Christchurch, p. 3.

[31] Kerr, R. (1999), p. 15.

[32] Murray, G. (1993-1996), *Economic Power in Australia*, ARC Funded Interviews, Respondent 97.

[33] Alliance Annual Report, (2004), http://www.alliance.co.nz/PDF/Alliance%202004%20Report.pdf and http://www.businessmentor.org.nz/patrons/detail.php?de=141&cat=36.

[34] Pers com Erakovic, L. (2004); Erakovic, L. & Goel, S. (2004), 'Building Effective Board-Management Relations: Evidence and prescriptions from New Zealand', *University of Auckland Business Review*, 6, 1, pp. 20–37.

[35] *Fonterra* Annual Report (2005), online http://www.fonterra.com/content/aboutfonterra/factsandfigures/default.jsp.

[36] *Fonterra* Annual Report (2004), http://www.fonterra.com/content/shareholderfinancial/resultsreports/default.jsp*http://www.fonterra*, p. 1.

[37] New Zealand Herald (2005), 'PPCS posts $17.46m half-year profit' 28 March [Accessed 12 December], http://www.nzherald.co.nz/organisation/story.cfm?o_id=176&objectid=10122756.

[38] *Alliance* Annual Report 2004, http://www.alliance.co.nz/PDF/Alliance%202004%20Report.pdf and http://www.businessmentor.org.nz/patrons/detail.php?de=141&cat=36.

[39] *Foodstuffs* Annual Report 2005, http://www.foodstuffs.co.nz/OurCompany/AnnualReports/.

[40] As noted in the top 30 companies Annual Reports.

[41] O'Lincoln, T. (1996), 'Wealth, Ownership and Power, the Ruling Class', (ed.s) R. Kuhn & O'Lincoln, T. *Class and Class Conflict in Australia*, Melbourne, Longmans.

[42] Robinson, S. (1998), 'Calling Home: As Globalization erases National Borders, Control of the New Zealand Economy is Shifting Across the Tasman', *Time International*, Nov. 9, pp. 58–60.

[43] Robinson, S. (1998), pp. 58–60.

[44] Murray, G. (1990), Respondent 14, p. 272.

[45] Fligstein, N. & Brantley, P. (1992), 'Bank Control, Owner Control or Organizational Dynamics: Who Controls the Large Modern Corporation?' *American Journal of Sociology*, n. 98, pp. 280–307.

[46] Mizruchi, M. (1996), pp. 271–302.

[47] Murray, G. (1990), Respondent 53, p. 150.

[48] See also the pathbreaking work of Carroll, W. (2006) 'Mapping Global Corporate Power: a Longitudinal Network Analysis of Elite Social Organization', Durban, ISA Congress.

[49] Fennema, M. (1982), *International Networks of Banks and Industry*. Boston, MA, Martinus Nijhoff.

[50] Carroll, B. & Alexander, M. (1999), 'Finance Capital and Capitalist Class Integration in the 1990s: Networks of Interlocking Directorships in the Canada and Australia,' *The Canadian Review of Sociology and Anthropology*, August, v.36, i.3, pp. 331–50.

[51] Carroll, B. & Alexander, M. (1999), pp. 331–50.

[52] Mandel, E. (1972).

[53] Scott, J. & Griff, C. (1984), *Directors of Industry, the British corporate network 1904–1976*, Cambridge, Polity Press, p. 21.

[54] van der Pijl, K. (1998).

Chapter 6

Think Tanks, Corporate Collectivity and the Reproduction of Ruling Ideas

How important are those who control the production and reproduction of ideas? And how important is that control in ensuring that all classes are educated into agreeing with the overarching need for society to be organised around individual profit within a free market? And why do we consider the liberal paradigm to be *common sense* in Australia and New Zealand? These are the questions this chapter looks at; beginning by defining the economic liberal idea and then examining the development of the economic liberal paradigm from the seventeenth century and moving briefly to its modern genesis.

What is Liberal Economic Ideology?

Economic liberalism is typically a set of ideas aimed at establishing the supremacy of the market and the superiority of private interests over public interests and public decision-making. Subsequently, it involves commitment to policies that reduce public expenditure and promote *flexible* labour practices through the removal of labour market regulations and by cutting social welfare, deregulating financial markets and privatising public assets. Frank Stilwell suggests that underlying economic liberalism are four fundamental assumptions. These are individualism (the individual is the basic unit of society), hedonism (individuals are driven by self interest), rationality (the pursuit of self interest takes a deliberate form) and inertia (people are basically lazy unless motivated by the prospect of personal gain).[1] Fred Argy adds the insight that economic liberals' commitment to a *fair go*, plays out as 'equal treatment for everyone without discrimination on the base of race, ethnicity, gender, and sexual preference'.[2] This undertaking to treat everyone the same does not embrace an understanding that there are disadvantaged groups that start a hobbled race and that they may need help to be on par at the beginning of the race, nor that the rewards for winning and penalties for losing are unequal.

Although economic liberal ideas are the ruling ideas because the ruling class has the power and the means to sustain them, they do not necessarily remain unquestioned and are sometimes open to hostility when they are unable to deliver the benefits they claim to be able to deliver within a volatile and unpredictable market.[3] In an attempt to make their popular appeal more palatable, economic liberals often lace their ideas with social conservatism.[4]

How do economic liberals describe themselves? John Roskam, managing director of the think tank, the Institute for Public Affairs (IPA), and quintessentially economic liberal, prefers the self describing moniker 'free market or liberal or conservative or some combination of the three. Right-wing is fascist and there is nothing fascist about liberalism or conservatism or the free market. Call us radical free market, call us radical anti-Kyoto, call us radical choice, call us radical anti-government, call us radical small government, call us all those sorts of things, but none of that is right-wing'.[5]

Economic liberalism, evolving over the lifetime of capitalism from the sixteenth century, has this central idea: how can we convince those who work for their living that they are self-interested individuals who have an important role in the only self-sustaining economic game in town, and that their essential commitment to that idea and its practice ensures rewards will trickle down to them? At its antithesis is the radical idea that, by acting collectively, those who work for their livings can leverage the wealthy to share more of the rewards that workers work hard for. These are beliefs held by some social democrats and some Marxist theorists within a capitalist system. The debates that unfold are set out in the context of what the ruling economic liberal ideas are, who the economic liberals are,[6] how these ideas are reproduced, what their critique is and who the major critics are.[7] Pictorially, this follows this broad theoretical framework:

Figure 6.1: Competing Ideas for Workplace Policy Creation

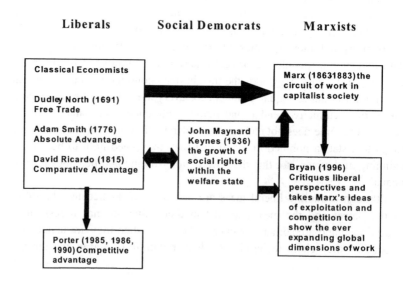

The social liberals — Thomas Hobbes (1588–1679), John Locke (1632–1704), David Hume (1711–1776), John Stuart Mill (1806–1873) and others — have contributed to the economic liberal argument with varied amounts of insight and humanism. At the high humanist end is John Stuart Mill who argues almost a socialist position when he said 'that the pattern of income distribution was essentially a political choice, not determined by any economic 'laws' of the sort that shaped the production of economic wealth'.[8] At the lowest end, lacking humanism is eugenicist, Thomas Malthus (1766–1834), who advocates the unabated immiseration of the working class to contain their tendency to excessive breeding.[9] Social liberal neglect here is done not on the basis of lack of interest but for tightness of focus.

In chapter one, we began the debate by describing Marxist work which has to be understood antithetically in relation to the work of these economic liberals. Marx had a deep respect for some of their economic insight, but an even deeper contempt for their use of these ideas to further the interests of the bourgeoisie:

> The ideas of the ruling class are in every epoch the ruling ideas, i.e. the class which is the ruling material force of society is, at the same time, its ruling intellectual force. The class which has the means of material production at its disposal has control at the same time over the means of mental production so that, generally speaking, the ideas of those who lack the means of mental production are subject to it'.[10]

This chapter will look at this idea in relation to what happens to ideas in Australia and New Zealand.

Liberal Ideologies that Further Provide the Basis for Corporate Ideology

The earliest economic liberal theorists were the economists Dudley North, Adam Smith and David Ricardo. Classical economic liberalism makes sense in its historical context, for when it emerged in the seventeenth century it was a response by the middle classes to what they saw as meddlesome aristocratic interference into bourgeois affairs. Economic liberalism was the antithesis of the bourgeoisie to mercantilism, in a dialectical sense.[11] Dialectical refers here to a process of moving from a thesis to its opposite antithesis and onward to a yet unknown synthesis or compromise position.

Mercantilism — the Origins

Mercantilism is an economic term based on the Latin word *mercari* meaning to run a trade and from *merx* meaning 'goods'.[12] Mercantilism developed in the fifteenth century with the growth of three-masted, heavily armed sailing ships capable of carrying substantial crews and cargoes over long ocean distances. These new European ships pushed forward both international commerce and naval warfare, spreading out across the globe in search of profits and plunder. The mercantile system was sustained by the belief expressed by Thomas Mun (1571–1641) that the way for a nation to maintain a favorable balance of exports versus imports was 'to sell more to strangers yearly than we consume of theirs in value',[13] and that a nation's prosperity relied on its acquisition and supply of gold and silver. This theory of bullionism was that precious metals equal wealth. The role of the state is to actively discourage imports and encourage exports through the most stringent use of tariffs. Mercantilism justified the plunder — often through pirating — of other countries, not only for their gold and silver but also slaves for labour. A key feature of this merchant stage of capitalism is that it provided not only the markets but also the wealth that bankrolled the industrial revolution as it began in the eighteenth century.[14]

Mercantilists such as Mun were often active in trade. They wrote to legitimate their own and their sovereign's wealth, and to identify aristocratic and state interest as one and the same thing. Full-fledged mercantilism used protectionism in the form of excise and customs duties to inhibit imports and encourage domestic growth. But increasingly mercantilist plundering became recognised as an inefficient way of satisfying the needs of the emerging capitalism. Capitalism was born in a small world economy where old and new colonies were increasingly recognised as a way of providing the mother country with raw materials, labour and expanding markets. At the same time, wool manufacturing was replacing cottage industries in England and the European demand for wool increased the growth of foreign trade to satisfy the need. New markets grew with increased English and foreign demand. Wool production signaled the beginning of capitalism, the beginning of a money economy and the very beginnings of capital's globalisation.

Free Trade and the Small State — Dudley North

Anti-mercantilist writing began not with Adam Smith, but with Dudley North (1691) in his book, *Discourses upon Trade*.[15] Against the central tenets of mercantilism, North argued that free trade and non-government intervention were the prerequisites of good business 'since it is impossible to force men to deal in any prescrib'd manner'.[16] North formulated the first ideas of free trade and the small state, ideas that were incorrectly credited to originate with Adam Smith. What they did share equally was a crusading zeal against mercantilism and, therefore, for production not plunder; for trade and for the unfettered market; and for the development of emerging industrial capitalism.

Harry Magdoff argues that, although industrial capitalism developed at different times in different countries and its features were not identical, it does share underlying laws of motion, demanding a degree of balance between investment, consumption, and finance.[17] These dynamics are what Smith sought to explain, exploit, manipulate and promote.[18]

Absolute Advantage — Adam Smith

Adam Smith (1723–1790), in his five-part work *An Inquiry into the Nature of the Wealth of Nations* (1776), made at least two original contributions to a theory of how the wealth of nations is developed on the basis of free trade. First is what became known as the theory of *absolute advantage*, meaning the ability to produce a product or service more cheaply than it is produced elsewhere by using fewer labour hours, specialist skills or more advanced tools. This theory developed from his second major contribution to the literature, his theory of the *division of labour*, that is, it is most efficient to assign specific, partial tasks, to enable completion of one task. Rather than each individual producer producing an entire product or service, workers specialised in doing a part of the operation.

This was the beginning of assembly line production, a method of speeding production and enhancing profit that became (and is still) a standard method of capitalist production. These ideas led many years later to Taylorism with its related time and motion studies designed to speed work and enhance profit (from Frederick Taylor (1856–1915), who wrote *The Principles of Scientific Management* 1911) and then onward to Fordism (mass production utilising a factory line that involves large numbers of workers each performing a narrowly defined and standardised set of tasks). Michel Aglietta identifies Fordism as capitalism's most intensive accumulation regime that revolutionised ruling class social power without improving workers' conditions or improving their ability to consume.[19]

Smith advocates the benefits of this method: workers on assembly lines developing greater dexterity, with no time lost between operations and in-depth association with one task enabling them to develop advanced tools for the task in hand. This division of labour was not just for within the factory, but also between enterprises in the same branches of production. For example, different factories specialising in different parts of wool production with some merchants obtaining the wool, some dye the wool and others as carriers etc.

Smith saw an absolute advantage occurring when labour productivity rose. Then the nation could make products that it excels in producing cheaply. In England, its advanced technology (the spinning jenny) gave them an advantage in the production of wool. Thus an absolute advantage leads to the development of the wealth of the nation based on the labour of citizens rather than plunder or one-way trade.

Smith recognised working class man not just as a commodity for producing value but also as a theoretical construct within a social hierarchy. Three classes had been previously identified by physiocrat François Quesnay in his work *Analyse du Tableau Economique* (1766): the landowners, producers (farmers) and people in commerce (the sterile class). Smith, following Quesnay, added wage labourers or workers as a class category. For Smith, there were two ways that wealth could be made: through a rise in individual worker productivity; and when the number of productive workers increased as a ratio to population. This was the beginning of the *labour theory of value*, improved upon by David Ricardo.

Comparative Advantage — David Ricardo

Smith was the economist of early industrial capitalism, whereas his follower David Ricardo (1772–1823) was the economist of the Industrial Revolution and the machine. Ricardo's commitment to Smith was clear in his work *On the Principles of Political Economy and Taxation (*1817). In this work Ricardo sought to show capitalism as the best means to liberate people from the economic oligarchy of the privileged land-owning class (a belief shared by Smith). In his opinion, the surest way to achieve the greatest amount of individual human happiness was to liberate the productive forces from the landowners (the aristocracy and the monarch).

Ricardo's key contribution to debate on work and globalisation was the idea of *comparative advantage* — that is, that the gains from specialist work flow into specialised trade allowing an economy to achieve superiority in a product.[20] This builds on Smith's idea of absolute advantage, though Ricardo is arguing for a country's specialisation in key goods that it can produce most advantageously. If a country is relatively better at producing wool than wheat (although it may be presently exporting both wool and wheat) and even if they are not the best producer of wool, they will gain from specialising in just that product. They can then have a profitable exchange with their neighbours, who in return have different, but complementary specialties. For example, England can exchange its cheaply produced wool with France's cheaply produced wheat. Even though one may not have an absolute advantage in either, they can exploit their relative advantage. Ricardo believed that every country has a relative or comparative advantage in something. Specialisation allows each country to make (and subsequently consume), goods beyond the limit of their own production.

Writing in the 1990s, Dick Bryan finds at least two major problems with this *comparative advantage* strategy.[21] The first is that it naively assumes a level playing field amongst the players whereas corporate players in real life have very different strengths and weaknesses. The second is that it never delivers the desired results for the countries with some of the best natural resources globally, such as Australia and the US, both of which have large current account deficits.[22]

With economic growth slowing towards the end of the twentieth century, capital has had to look for alternative strategies. Economic liberals evolved a strategy that rejected the John Maynard Keynes inspired revolution of the 1950s to the 1980s and followed the 1930s work of Joseph Schumpeter to become 'competitive advantage'.[23]

Competitive Advantage — Michael Porter

Littler defines *competitive advantage* as securing a differentiation of your organisation and its products 'in some way in order to gain preference by all or part of the market.[24] This may result in a higher market share and or [higher] margins than competitors. In general, *competitive advantage* will be obtained through offering higher customer value'.[25] The literature tends to divide into the advocacy of two sources of *competitive advantage* — assets (accumulated endowments of the company) and capabilities (deeply embedded into organisational routines).[26] Zysman and Tyson[27] coined the name *competitive advantage* in the context of American industry policy, but today it is usually associated with the work of American Michael Porter.[28]

In Porter's work, *The Competitive Advantage of Nations,*[29] he follows Schumpeter closely when he suggests that innovation drives and sustains competition.[30] In Porter's diamond typology of natural advantage, he argues that four major components make up a company's natural advantage. These components are:

1. *factor conditions* — that is, the ability of the nation to continually upgrade, create, and deploy its factors of production, particularly labour, successfully. This is more important than any reliance on a natural endowment;

2. *demand conditions* — these relate to the amount of competition and health the company first displays in the domestic market. Firms that survive the home market are likely to have developed a fine competitive edge;

3. *related and supporting industries* — relationships with these must be close, cooperative and involve constant information interaction with suppliers. This is essential for an end-product that is attractive and appropriate to the needs of the customers;

4. *firm strategy structure and rivalry* — the conditions in the firm in its home nation necessary to make or break the international competitiveness of the company.

The justification for the strategy of *competitive advantage* is its potential to 'fix' the high current account deficit of Western nations and its potential to standardise low cost labour.[31] This compulsion to drive down the costs of labour is the key link to economic liberalism.

In sum, the primary difference between the liberal theories is that:

1. *Absolute advantage* builds on wealth creation for a nation state based on the efficacy of labour, not trade as with Mercantilism. Labour becomes specialised in the production of one product through the division of labour. Companies likewise become organised around the division of labour producing better products cooperatively than they could as individuals or individual enterprises.

2. *Comparative advantage* is the further exploitation of labour and its mechanisation, but it entails product differentiation between countries.

Companies work out what productive advantage they have and then they organise their trade around this advantage.

3. *Competitive advantage* implies the standardisation of the lowest costs of the factors of production (particularly labour) so that companies can establish a competitive advantage in a global market place.

Economic liberalism is the advocacy of the interests of the market above all else, whereby a states intervention in:

> Economic planning, conducted independently on a national scale, [is] bound in the aggregate effect to be harmful even from a purely economic point of view and, in addition to produce serious international friction.[32]

Hayek's belief, expressed here, was that economic policies like those belonging to John Maynard Keynes and Keynesian economists could not be compatible with individual freedom and therefore should be lumped together with all other forms of perceived authoritarianism including Nazism, Fascism and Communism.

Keynes' Program of Liberal Social Democracy

John Maynard Keynes (1883–1946), an interventionist social democrat, argued that orthodox liberal economics exacerbated economic crisis, increasing instability within the capitalist business cycle in the long term. He challenged their orthodoxies, such as the prevailing belief that capital formation governs the rate of savings (e.g. Von Hayek).[33] Instead, he suggested that investment or capital formation governs income accumulation. The full utilisation of the capital goods industry and full employment stimulate the output of consumer goods. He argued that the greater the propensity of society to consume, the greater the stimulation to increased primary investment. Crisis occurs because of 'doubts arising about the reliability of the prospective yield' or because 'current costs of production are thought to be higher than they will be later on'.[34] In other words change occurs due to psychological factors associated with expectation. The downturn of the economy brings about a decline in investment, which has a multiplier effect, spreading as a malaise through the private sector and depressing employment. Consumption decreases and income falls. As capital stock and surplus stock are consumed then the efficiency of capital begins to rise again and stimulate further investment. This is the business cycle. The obvious policy prescription to counter this is to prime the pump of demand, particularly in the down phase of the recession. This means fiscal and monetary manipulation of the market to keep up spending and achieve full employment.

This advocacy of radical intervention into the market by priming demand helped promote the development of the welfare state and the social wage for workers. The idea of the welfare state was not original to Keynes but built on Count Otto von Bismark's (1815–98) welfare state model, promoting limited workers' welfare with the added benefit for the state of keeping the German economy operating at maximum efficiency whilst staving-off radical socialist alternatives.

These Keynesian ideas were abhorrent to the economic liberals, particularly Friedrich von Hayek. Von Hayek began his anti-Keynesian activism in 1938 when he ran a conference to try to reverse what he saw as a trend toward socialist, collectivist and totalitarian ideas.[35] This gathering proved very popular with Milton Friedman and Austrian School members including Ludwig Von Mises and Karl Popper. Interrupted by the Second World War, the second conference was held in Switzerland in 1947 at Mont Pelerin. What became biannual meetings took the name of their second meeting place, hence they became the Mont Pelerin Society (MPS). According to historian Richard Cockett, this organisation became the ideological heart of economic liberalism for many countries including Australia.[36] Their collective brilliance lay in their energetic and wide dissemination of economic liberal information. As this Australian BCA director said:

> The genesis of [BCA] work comes from much work done through the Centre for Independent Studies (CIS) and the Institute of Public Affairs (IPA), the H.R Nicholls Society and the Mont Pelerin Society. They all made important contributions to providing an intellectual framework and support basis for community attitudes to start to change. Once those changes were there then the BCA and the Chambers of Commerce all changed their positions as well.[37]

The opening question concerned how we came to accept these economic liberal ideas as received wisdom or common sense. One of the answers is through the extremely effective marketing of think tanks many begun by this economic liberal hard core.

What is a Think Tank?

There is no accepted definition of what a think tank is, although there is an identifiable consensus amongst think tank writers and think tank members that they are predominantly non-partisan, public-spirited, fragmented and charitable bodies.[38] This picture of think tanks is that they are not 'involved in the implementation and administration of government policies ... [though they do] desire to inform the policy process'[39] and they are 'intellectually independent ... [with] research agendas ... determined within the institution rather than by outside bodies ... [with] most think tanks striv[ing] for a diversity of funding to help preserve their intellectual integrity'.[40] And they are selflessly 'characterised by public spirit ... they do not represent vested interest in society but they conduct research for the sake of building a body of knowledge, raising public awareness of issues and improving policy'.[41]

However, this value-free façade is cracking when some members of think tanks admit to their partisan nature. The vice-president of the American Rockford

Institute (a think tank) wrote 'my point is that there is no such thing as a disinterested think tanker. Somebody always builds the tank, and it's usually not Santa Claus or the Tooth Fairy [and] unfortunately, many of these folk are often interested in satisfying the requirements of whoever pays the tab, whether it be a government, a business, an association, or an interest group'.[42] Therefore, those most likely to have the money to be able to pay are the ruling class. Others agree, writing 'more explicit pro-business propaganda is provided by various right-wing think tanks, working for the Liberal Party, funded by the major corporations and high flying CEOs such as Hugh Morgan and the now disgraced Rodney Adler'.[43] Such think tanks are described as 'crucial to the struggle for hegemony of a particular class'.[44] They may like to think they act as individuals in circumstances of their own choosing but they are dependent on business patronage for their personal and class survival. Historian James A. Smith goes further in his analysis of the role of think tanks by seeing their long-term impact as having less to do with reproducing the ideas that sustain the ruling class but rather in 'helping to shape a conservative policy elite. Think tanks of the Right did not make a revolution; rather, they prepared the revolutionary cadres who ascended to power'.[45]

Australian Think Tanks

Australian think tanks are, according to Beder, 'generally partisan, politically or ideologically motivated', and practise the art of 'directed conclusions', tailoring their studies to suit their clients' or donors' demands.[46] Beder goes on to suggest that 'in recent times a number of think tanks have become more openly ideological. These conservative think tanks aim to influence government and set the agenda in a variety of policy arenas'.[47] For think tanks to be effective, they must 'insinuate themselves into the networks of people who are influential in particular policy areas. They do this by organising conferences, seminars and workshops, and by producing books, briefing papers, journals and media releases. They liaise with bureaucrats, consultants, interest groups and lobbyists. They seek to provide advice directly to the government officials in policy networks and to government agencies and committees'.[48]

Australian think tanks using economic liberal theory have been around since the Australian Institute of International Affairs was established in 1924. The next was the Institute of Political Affairs (IPA) established in 1942 by the Victorian Chamber of Manufacturers to 'combat socialism'. It was used extensively by the United Australia Party (UAP) under Robert Menzies to unite right factions against the Labor Party and form the Liberal Party of Australia.[49] The IPA publishes the work of liberals such as 'Friedrich von Hayek (whom the IPA brought out to Australia in the 1970s) and Milton Friedman; Nick Greiner, former premier of NSW; Gary Sturgess, former Director-General of the NSW Cabinet Office under Greiner' and the media baron Rupert Murdoch.[50] Its council has included Rupert

Murdoch as well as other conservative business leaders. Like many of the US conservative think tanks, the IPA has good connections in the media via right-wing commentators with regular columns in major newspapers. It also has good political connections. Their staff members include former senior public officials and former politicians. John Stone, a former Secretary of the Treasury, is a consultant to the IPA and Dame Leonie Kramer, Chancellor of the University of Sydney, has headed one of the IPA's units. [51]

Think tanks have proliferated in Australia within the last twenty years. In the 1990s, think tanks became an industry with the number of estimated think tanks in Australia estimated at between 83[52] and 90.[53] Bruce Herd's sample of 83 think tanks shows only five that he credits with being commonly known as 'wet' tanks (that is, politically left). Marsh estimates that Australian think tanks have a collective budget of $130 million; they employ 1,600 people, publish 900 reports and discussion papers, holding almost 600 conferences and symposia each year. Corporate contribution and personal wealth are the biggest source of funding to the budgets of think tanks. Another aspect identified by Beder is the Australian think tanks trend to follow, and to maintain close links with, English as well as American model–think tanks.

Table 6.1 gives some examples of think tanks, their political focus, their budget sources, key staff members and comments as to how they came about. An important lacuna here is some missing information about the funding of think tanks. This is, according to John Roskam, the 38-year-old head of the Institute of Public Affairs (IPA) and a former adviser to state and federal Liberal Party ministers, because we (the public) cannot handle this information. 'It's not for us to reveal our supporters … Whether we like it or not, the Australian democracy is not so sophisticated that companies can reveal they support free-market think tanks, because as soon as they do they will be attacked'.[54] When further asked whether this meant that the justification for secrecy was on the grounds that the Australian electorate was immature, Roskam replied, 'Yes, absolutely'.[55]

Table 6.1: The Main Australian Think Tanks

Name	Political Focus	Budget & Funding Sources	Key staff and members	Comments
The H.R. Nicholls Society www.hrnicholls.com.au	'The Society's ambition is to bring about urgently needed reform in our industrial relations attitudes and institutions'.	Unknown	Ray Evans (CEO)	Founded in 1986 with 40 interested members Founding members chair John Stone & Peter Costello, Barry Purvis, Ray Evans

Institute of Public Affairs (IPA) www.ipa. org.au	In 1942 aimed to 'combat socialism'. Advocates Free Market economics, anti-big government and anti-Kyoto.	2005 revenue $1 million from private sources plus a $50,000 grant from Howard govt (2004); Donors: WMC, Philip Morris, BHP Billiton, & Visyboard.	J. Roskam (CEO) 7 staff 500 members Board includes Alan Stockdale (former Victorian treasurer)	Founded in 1942; Melbourne based. Organised by the Victorian Chamber of Manufacturers; set up in other states after 1943. Publications in 12,000 schools, 475 companies and for 2,000 individuals.
Centre for Independent Studies (CIS) www.cis. org.au	Advocates of the small state; Economic liberal.	2005 Revenue $2 million; Donors include McDonalds Australia, Philip Morris, Dame E. Murdoch, Fairfax.	Greg Lindsay (CEO) 11 staff; 1,800 members. Board members include R. Champion de Crespigny and NAB & BCA head Michael Chaney.	Founded in 1976; Sydney based. Has a philosophy of individual freedom, responsibility and choice. Influences the Howard government on welfare. Lindsay influenced by F. Von Hayek and M. Friedman.
Tasman Institute www.tas man. com.au	Free market economics. The Institute's objectives are to provide research, advice and strategies on…economic restructuring and reform in Australia, New Zealand and the region.	Budget $1 million; privately funded with 21 corporate sponsors. *Sources*: Melbourne University	Professor Michael Porter (CEO); Amy Auster, resident economist, was Vice President in J. P. Morgan, New York.	Founded in 1990 by Sydney. Baillieu Myer AC and Sir Roger Douglas. Tasman Institute is an affiliated institution of University of Melbourne and was formed from the Centre of Policy Studies, Monash University.
The Australia Institute www.tai. org.au	Progressive aims to counter conservative rivals	Revenue $450,000 Bulk of funding from the Kantor family.	Dr Clive Hamilton is CEO. Board members: S. Burrow, ACTU President & M. Crooks, Victorian Women's Trust.	Founded in 1994, Canberra based. Outspoken about climate change and a range of other environmental, economic and social issues.
The Lowy Institute for International Policy www.lowyin stitute.org	Promoted as non-partisan. Aims to generate new ideas and dialogues on international developments.	2005 revenue is $5 million Draws on a $30 million commitment from F. Lowy.	Allan Gyngell CEO (advisor to PM Paul Keating) Directors: Frank Lowy, Ian McFarlane (Reserve Bank) and Prof. R. Garnaut.	Founded in 2003 by Frank Lowy to celebrate his 50th year in Australia. Sydney based.

Sources: Da Silva, W. (1996), 'The New Social Focus', *The Australian Financial Review Magazine*, June, pp. 18–28. Nira World Directory of Think Tanks (1996), http://www.nira.go.jp/ice/tt-info/nwdtt96/1050.html. Gluyas, R. (1999), 'Utopian Agendas', *The Australian*, 22 January, pp. 32.

With the exception of The Australia Institute and possibly the Lowy Institute, these think tanks share an economic liberal philosophy, but with different degrees of intensity and enthusiasm.

Australian Think Tank Ideology

Think tanks have been very successfully associated with the rise of economic liberalism in state policy and deserve the edge of triumphalism that has crept into their writing. Beder suggests that successful think tank marketing of the economic liberal ideology in Australia has 'enabled the conservative, corporate agenda of deregulation, privatisation and an unconstrained market to be dressed up as ... virtue'.[56] Success has not made think tanks stand still, as they keep moving further to claim what is traditionally conservative ground. Dr Mike Nahan, ex-head of the IPA, wrote 'In the past, because our overwhelming focus was on economics, social issues were not our major focus ... The debate has moved on. These are areas that the left thought they had sown up'.[57] The very economic liberal CIS shares this conservative catch-up strategy. CEO Greg Lindsay, credits the Centre's considerable economic liberal victories as being due to its 'advocacy of welfare change [which his centre has been pushing] in the area since 1987, examining how single mothers — once their children get older — can move from welfare into the workforce. It has also looked at how people with disabilities can be encouraged into some form of paid work.[58]

The IPA's push under CEO Roskam is for the Howard government's radical changes to labour market regulation, through its 2005 'Work Choices' legislation, to be taken further. He argues that 'the Government's new industrial relations laws don't go anywhere near far enough ... The institute advocates an economy where no one is referred to as an 'employee' but rather as an 'enterprise worker' — an individualistic business unit'.[59]

Another key think tank is the H.R. Nicholls Society. This society was formed by four people (see Figure 6.2), one of whom was Peter Costello, Barrister at Law, and at the time of writing, Federal Treasurer. This society's focus is the abolition or reduction of the role of the trade unions by putting workers onto individual contracts and the abolition of labour regulations including the minimum wage. Their stated aim is to 'support the reform of Australian industrial relations with the aim of promoting the rule of law in respect of employers and employee organisations alike, the right of individuals to freely contract for the supply and engagement of their labour by mutual agreement, and the necessity for labour relations to be conducted in such a way as to promote economic development in Australia'.[60] They are credited with influencing (but not to their full satisfaction) the 'Work Choices' legislation, the Workplace Relations Amendment Bill 2005. This Bill gives 'effect to the federal government's agenda to actively promote the individualisation of employment relations'.[61] The society's ultimate aim is to dismantle the AIRC and replace formal IR regulation with a regime entirely based on common law employment contracts. At the 2005 annual general meeting of the H.R. Nicholls Society, CEO Ray Evans, in response to what he claims is conservative Prime Minister John Howard's claim that the introduction of the IR 'Work Choices' legislation was the most far reaching 'labour market legislation since the 1904 *Conciliation and Arbitration Act*', said:

> The Work Choices legislation shows that Prime Minister John Howard has failed to fulfill his 1983 promise to turn H.B. Higgins 'on his head' and that he continues to accept the Marxist dogmas that inspired the labour movement in the late 19th Century.[62]

He said that he had to put on the record the Society's 'deep disappointment at the failure of the Howard Government to legislate change that would drive economic prosperity for Australia.' He added that 'the Work Choices legislation with minor exceptions, supports regulation and disparages freedom' and the common law.

The H.R. Nicholls Society think tank ideologues write these things not because they are capitalist (many are not) or even ruling class (many are not), but because they unquestionably believe this hegemonic discourse. Why, when it might not be in their interests? Because, like the rest of us, think thank members have been socialised and educated into this type of thinking. How? By, amongst other things, the use of extremely successful think tank marketing techniques.

Techniques

Evan Thornley, an internet entrepreneur who has recently returned from the US, suggests that Institute of Public Affairs and Centre for Independent Studies have 'lifted from the American think tanks terms such as "elites" ... and "political correctness"'.[63] They were completely imported. The key think tanks here are just like the main ones in the US: they are really ad and PR agencies who are in the business of word branding. They make a pitch on behalf of the brand, and they do it relentlessly so that eventually the word or the term they are pitching assumes a new meaning and is accepted.[64] According to Ewin Hannan and Shaun Carney, the ultimate goal of think tanks is 'to push an idea, or repudiate someone else's idea, so hard and for so long that it enters general public debate: down-shifting, political correctness, the out-of-touch elites, welfare to work, school vouchers' are apparently all a product of this push. 'When the idea that has become a term becomes a word that enters the general vocabulary — used by talkback radio callers, taxi drivers and politicians — the think tank has done a little bit more to advance its agenda'.[65]

Influence

How does a think tank go about its business of influence? According to the Australian Michael Porter (no relation) at the Tasman Institute, to be effective, well-funded think tankers network with people who influence policy-making. To do this they work by 'organising conferences, seminars and workshops, and by producing books, briefing papers, journals and media releases. They liaise with bureaucrats, consultants, interest groups and lobbyists. They seek to provide advice directly to government officials in policy networks and to government agencies and committees'.[66] How effective is this? Two officers of the NSW Labor Council summed up the influence of thank tanks when they wrote 'the H.R. Nicholls Society is winning the intellectual and political debate'.[67]

Porter also claims to have 'worked for a number of government entities and private clients, having played a key role in the Victorian reforms of the early 1990s'.[68] The Tasman Institute's Project Victoria study argued for 'the large scale sell off of state assets and a new right orientation (for) the public service, [and] served as a manifesto for the revolution brought about by Premier Jeff Kennett and treasurer Alan Stockdale'.[69]

Noted as Australia's most influential think tank, the CIS and its CEO Greg Lindsay define the Centre's role as seeking to:[70]

> influence the general ideas environment ... but as I went on I realized that there was more to achieving change than dreaming up what a Liberal Party future might be. For instance ... If you felt that shopping hours should be deregulated, it was not just a matter of putting it on to paper and feeling confident that your brilliant statement would win the day.[71]

The CIS had to actively lobby and network with others to bring about change. Networking links on the CIS website include 27 other international think tanks and sixteen others that include the New Zealand Business Roundtable.[72] In the 1980s Lindsay met with a key think tank force in the person of Lord Anthony Fisher, 'the ex chicken farmer' and then head of the British Institute of Economic Affairs (IEA).[73] Lindsay is reported to have discussed with Fisher the opening of a replica of the IEA in Australia and Fisher 'wished me luck'.[74] In 1978, Lindsay went to his first Mont Pelerin Society meeting in Hong Kong where he was introduced to Milton Friedman and the Public Choice advocate, James Buchanan.

Roskam from the IPA said his organisation had links with a number of local and overseas groups, including 'good relations with the Washington-based American Enterprise Institute, home to some of the driving forces behind the neo-conservative movement in the US'.[75] Roskam sits on the H.R. Nicholls Society board and attends Lavoisier Group forums; this group claims climate change is 'nothing to worry about'.[76]

Claiming not to be a think tank, though privately funded, the Sydney Institute has every appearance of one as it operates as 'facilitators of debate'.[77] Gerard Henderson, its managing director, was chief of staff to John Howard from 1984 to 1986. He has written a history of the Liberals and he exercises a great deal of influence through his weekly columns in *The Sydney Morning Herald* and *The West Australian*, appearances on ABC TV's *Insiders* and a weekly spot on ABC Radio National's breakfast program. The Sydney Institute papers are published as *The Sydney Papers*. The Institute also publishes *The Sydney Institute Quarterly*, which includes a media watch section.[78]

Funding

Peter Botsman, ex director of the left-leaning Evatt Foundation, claims that 'the Centre for Independent Studies is the best in the country by far when it comes to resources, capacity and the ability to get the cabinet and the shadow cabinet into the same room'.[79] On the left, the leading think tank is the Australia Institute 'but to compare that with the Centre for Independent Studies is like saying there is a casino with all the international high rollers over there and there is a game of tiddlywinks being played over here ... The problem for all think tanks on the left is that the finances are always very precarious. Clive Hamilton has done a lot with very limited resources. But on the left or the centre-left when you're strapped for cash ... if you make one wrong decision you lose your money, whereas the Centre for Independent Studies and the Sydney Institute can make five or six mistakes a year and it doesn't matter'.[80]

Finding out what that funding is, as both a key to understanding what think tanks are talking about and what their resources are, is not easy because it is not transparent. However, when pressed by Hannan and Carney, IPA's Roskam confirmed the identity of past donors included the tobacco industry, Dick Pratt's Visyboard, Telstra, Western Mining and BHP Billiton. Coincidently, the IPA has argued claims about passive smoking are not based on science and an institute staffer wrote an article two years ago supporting smokers' rights.[81]

The Sydney-based CIS raised $2 million from private donors in the past year. The Centre's funding is 'a matter between the individuals or the organisations that give to us, and us, and it's a private thing, It's nobody else's business' says founder, Greg Lindsay.[82] The bulk of funding for think tanks comes from corporations. Director Lindsay of the CIS is on record saying that he got his big financial break from Hugh Morgan, the CEO of Western Mining. 'Morgan had a financial 'whip around' amongst mates for seed money for the CIS. He raised $200,000 that was to be spent by the CIS over five years'.[83] Financial supporters of the Centre's projects include Dame Elisabeth Murdoch, J.O. Fairfax and McDonald's Australia, while BHP, Shell, ICI and Western Mining are among companies that provided funds when the centre started in 1976. Its current subscriber base includes 70 companies and 1200 individuals.[84]

The government is another rich source of funds for think tanks. The Menzies Foundation, the Liberal Party pro-market think tank, reportedly received a $100,000 Liberal government grant in 1997. This meant the Liberal Party could 'undertake this 'intellectual' branch of their work without eating into their funds that they can use for other work'.[85] According to Michelle Grattan this was money stripped by the government from the Evatt Foundation, a more left-leaning think tank, and redirected to revive the moribund Menzies Centre.[86] The Menzies Centre was opened in 1994 with David Clark as the chairperson of the board. Clark was also the chair of the Macquarie Bank. Other board members of note were former Premier of New South Wales Nick Greiner, and Professor John Rose of Melbourne University.

University Links

Universities have a number of think tanks within their ambit that at various times have played key roles in policy debates. Professor Peter Dixon, formerly employed by the IMF in 1973, runs the Centre for Policy Studies. CPS was influencing state policy from 1975. Other notable think tank university initiatives were Flinders University's National Institute of Labour Studies (NILS) that in the late 1980s and early 1990s provided academic legitimacy to the BCA's industrial relations reform agenda. Since the departure of Dick Blandy, Judith Sloan and, more recently, Mark Wooden, NILS has returned to its original role of being a 'labour studies' research institute without ideological alignment.[87] The Tasman Institute is operated from the University of Melbourne, they by sub-section 18(3) of the *Melbourne University Act* 1958, have power over the institute.

Lobby Groups

Lobby groups, as distinct from think tanks, exist purely to pressure the state on the rightness of their corporate, or group of corporations', interest. This may require corporate lobbying or sustained advocacy on state members or politicians if the required policy-maker does not see that the corporation's interest is also the state's interest. Lobby groups have CEOs and presidents whose job it is to produce attractive literature that convinces those to whom they are advocating change and also unites their members with an understanding of their core interests. Like think tanks, these lobby groups have ideological positions that vary in their political strength. Table 6.2 gives some examples of lobby groups, their political focus, their budget sources, key staff members and comments on their formation.

Table 6.2: Australian Lobby Groups

Name	Political Focus	Budget Sources	Key staff & members	Comments
Business Council of Australia (BCA) www.bca.com.au	Economic liberal	$4.9 million; Sources: members	CEO Ms Katie Lahey, President Michael Chaney 2005-2007, 101 members top CEOs 14 staff.	Result of a merger of AIDA and Business Round Table (BRT). 100 members.
Australian Chamber of Commerce and Industry (ACCI) www.acci.asn.au	'A free enterprise economy in conjunction with a liberal democratic political system'	-	President Peter O'Brien Deputy President Tony Howarth	ACCI history dates back to 1826 in Sydney. ACCI is a 1990s mix of three groups: Associated Chambers of Commerce of Australia 1901, Federal Council of the Chambers of Manufacturers 1903 and Central Council of Employers 1904.
Australian Industry Group (AIG) www.aigroup.asn.au	Provides comprehensive advice and assistance to members to help them run their businesses more effectively and to become more competitive at a domestic and international level.	-	National President John Ingram, CEO Heather Ridout.	AI Group began in 1998 merging MTIA and the Australian Chamber of Manufactures (ACM). AIG represents 10,000 in manufacturing, construction, automotive, telecommunications, IT & call centres, transport, labour hire and other industries.
Australian Mines & Metals Association (AMMA) www.amma.org.au	A strong advocate of individual contracts and labour deregulation	-	MD and CEO Tony Palmer	AMMA provides support services to members, submissions, representations and lobbying to governments and industrial tribunals at State and federal level; consultancy services, training services: practically orientated and workshops.
New Zealand Business Roundtable (NZBR) www.nzbr.org.nz	Extreme economic liberalism	members pay $40,000. Annual income of $2,000,000 p. a.	CEO Roger Kerr, 60 members and four associate members February 1999. Chairperson Bob Mathew	Began in 1976 to counter the perceived strength of unions. NZBRT in 1980s became domiciled in Wellington with CEO R. Kerr. Their political arm is ACT winning 6 per cent of the vote (1999).

Sources: Da Silva, W. (1996), 'The New Social Focus', *The Australian Financial Review Magazine*, June, pp. 18–28. Nira World Directory of Think Tanks (1996), http://www.nira.go.jp/ice/tt-info/nwdtt96/1050.html. Agendas', Gluyas, R. (1999), *The Australian*, 22 January, pp. 32. Thomsen-Moore, L. (2005), Katie Lahey's Passion for Business, *Management Today*, July, p. 3, BCA http://www.bca.com.au, AIG http://www.aigroup.asn.au.

From the list of lobby group examples above, the most central to this corporate story are the Business Council of Australia (BCA) and the New Zealand Business Roundtable (NZBR).

Business Links — the Business Council of Australia (BCA)

The functions of the top lobby groups are multifarious but one often overlooked is cementing power for the ruling class. Lobby groups like the BCA provide the idea to managers that they are the capitalists, even though according to Poulantzas, 'supervisors and managers take part in productive labour, but in a position of ideological domination. This domination is the most important aspect of their work: the function of capitalists has been delegated to them. While higher managers act as if they were capitalists, the lower ones are exploited as subalterns'.[88]

But these are not dupes. According to others, such as the BCA's CEO Katie Lahey, these are 'very smart people. They don't get to be in those positions unless they are smart and possess the vision and strategy to take their businesses forward'.[89] She describes her job as having a 'public policy focus'.[90] BCA members are the CEOs from the top 100 Australian companies listed on their website. There is also an executive board of nine and a secretariat of six.[91] In 1997 the BCA had a reported budget of $4.9 million and their members' companies covered the working lives of more than 1.1 million people.

The BCA was the result of the marriage between the old pro-tariff Australian Industry Development Association and the pro-free market Business Roundtable.[92] Prime Minister Bob Hawke and the Labor Party of 1983 wanted a tri-partite corporatist relationship between big business, the state and the unions. However, in 1983 there were always enough 'New Right' BCA members to ensure that it did not become a captive member of the Accord'.[93] What was achieved was a bipartite corporatist arrangement between the state and unions and a degree of closeness with big business that lasted for the next thirteen years; it was ended by the coalition Prime Minister John Howard whose driving interest was rather 'a close association in various guises with the activities of the Business Council'.[94]

The key BCA agenda item is industrial relations reform. Ex-president Hugh Morgan said 'my view is that the BCA play[s] a vital role in key debates ... about labour market reform ... the continued pursuit of labour market reforms, where much progress has been made, will remain on our agenda'.[95] The conservative social agenda, to make this economic liberalism more palatable, is an articulated concern for ageing. Their stated concern is for the depletion of skills and future budget deficits with higher taxes and fewer people to pay them.

The BCA is not without critics. John Hyde, Emeritus Fellow of the IPA, thinks that the BCA's real problem is that its Australian membership is 'unpatriotic and they are always prepared to put their own interests ahead of the national interest', for the BCA has sometimes 'lobbied against the national interest', citing its support for the textile and car industry.[96]

Australian State–Business Ties

Katie Lahey suggests there is a 22-year-old closeness between the BCA and the Coalition government that reaches beyond the BCA to other economic liberal think tanks.[97] For example, the CIS's CEO, Greg Lindsay, was asked about being a 'firm favorite' of John Howard. He replied: 'If we are a firm favorite, that's nice.' Also, the IPA, Melbourne's most prominent think tank, apparently regularly acts as a policy ambit setter for the federal government. John Roskam, its CEO, says part of the IPA's role is to 'push the boundaries of debate so political parties can move in that direction. By not moving as far, politicians are seen as pragmatic and considered'.[98]

This closeness to economic liberal think tanks is not new. According to the retiring Keating government Minister of Finance, John Dawkins:

> such was the intimacy of the relationship [between the ALP government and the BCA] that it has been useful on occasions to have the BCA appear to be a critic of the government's performance. It suited the government to have the endorsement of the BCA when it needed it, but to be able to create some distance on other occasions.[99]

Dawkins continued to say that the role of the BCA was a:

> Policy pacesetter and as critic of the government's progress had assisted the government to maintain the support of its own constituency on reform ... After the 1983 election, the ACTU was converted to the central elements of a pro-business agenda and through its enhanced central power was able to engage the entire union movement in support.[100]

Block's point that the ruling class do not rule because they do not have to is relevant here. Whatever the political persuasion of the state politicians, the ruling class manage it so that their interests continue to be seen as the interests of all. The ruling class members know that members of the state, both politicians and bureaucrats, sufficiently identify with capitalist class interests because they share these interests.[101]

The situation of think tank influence and business lobby group power is similar, if not stronger, in New Zealand. An abiding question is why?

New Zealand Business Roundtable (NZBR)

New Zealand Business Roundtable (NZBR) is a lobby group consisting of a collection of 60 invited top company directors and four associate members. These are invited individuals with a 'special interest in public affairs'.[102] The membership has always been predominantly white and male with exceptions being Roseanne

Meo, an associate member, and Lesley Mason from Mobil Oil, a full member.[103] Roger Kerr identifies the inner core of NZBR as Sir Ron Trotter, Roderick Deane, Bob Mathew, Ralph Norris and himself. Michael Porter refers to this closed and exclusive nature of the NZBR membership as a strength and the basis of its great success because it has 'an inbuilt quality control. They can keep out the wimps'.[104]

The NZBR was described as 'the most powerful [of the] driving forces of free market economic reforms transforming New Zealand'.[105] It seeks to influence fellow businesspeople, the state and the New Zealand public with its economic liberal perspective on a very wide variety of topics. In just one university library there were listed over 120 books and other publications authored or published by the NZBR.[106] The NZBR is economically influential because it represents companies from 80 per cent of the market capitalisation on the New Zealand Stock Exchange[107] and represents companies accounting for 10 per cent of all goods and services produced in New Zealand.[108]

This wide ambit was not the NZBR's original intention, according to an older member there at its inception.[109] According to a director who was there the NZBR began in 1976 when a group of industrialists met to try to intervene in the state's handling of industrial relations:

> They called a meeting with business and trade unions right at the very beginning and they used Ron Trotter [CEO of FCL at the time] as the chairman. It had only just got underway and a government minister was invited ... It was started by Ken Jarvis who was frustrated by what was happening on the industrial relations scene ... Industrial relations was at a very low ebb. Employers generally weren't looking good. Employer's Associations generally had no support from the CEOs, they were not participants — our fault that they didn't meet. The setting up of the Roundtable was an indication that they really wanted to be specifically behind the Employer's Federation ... The NZBR was a response to economic changes happening. But it has become in the last five years a very much bigger forum or visionary organisation.[110]

However, Roger Kerr's idea of the origin of the NZBR is different. The NZBR 'started up as a loose coalition of chief executives meeting informally and on a regular basis ... around 1980'.[111] According to Kerr, the NZBR was modelled on US and Australian lobby organisations of a similar type and ambit. The first permanent office of the NZBR was established in the Fletcher Challenge building in Wellington in 1986. It comprised four persons: Kerr as CEO, a policy analyst and two administrative staff. By 1990, membership had grown to 40. They met for half a day five times a year and the tasks of members involved reading and commenting on draft reports, attending ad hoc committee meetings on specific topics, 'taking part in occasional meetings with ministers and opposition members, and perhaps undertaking a speaking engagement or two'.[112]

Funding

Members of the NZBR face an annual membership fee of $40,000 per member. The Roundtable has an operating budget of $2 million to be spent on research commissioning, publications, distribution, travel and the expenses of the regular visiting guests.

New Zealand State–Business Ties

The NZBR has no direct institutional links to the state other than Roger Kerr's membership on the Victoria University Council.[113] However, the relationship between the NZBR and the state was always close. Managh wrote in 1989 that 'when Manurewa MP Roger Douglas wore the Finance mantle his relationship with the Roundtable was rumored to be so close you couldn't slide a Treasury paper between them'.[114] The political orientation of the NZBR literature is economic liberalism at its driest.[115] NZBR's success in supplying the ideas and the policy to introduce their interests into New Zealand's legislation is impressive. The ultimate NZBR achievement was the *Employment Contracts Act* 1991 introduced by a National Party government to abolish the award system, diminish unions and promote individual contracts. (This was replaced by the *Employment Relations Act* 1999 which restored the impetus to collectively bargain.) Apart from this major weakening of the union structure in New Zealand, they have also influenced micro-economic changes in fiscal strategy, social and state expenditure. Table 6.3 shows key issues in relation to the action recommended by the NZBR and the action taken by the state, indicating the increased reluctance by the state to knee jerk react to NZBR recommendations as it did in the 1980s.

A reason why the economic liberals have been so efficient in getting their ideas enacted so quickly may have had something to do with the New Zealand parliament's uni cameral status. They did have an undue number of successes as this NZBR director-member said in a 1992 interview:

> I would say that over ninety per cent of any decent policies that have come out of the government in the last seven years have had a hell of a lot to do with the intellectual contribution of the Roundtable. It is the least self-interested body that I am involved with. It has been captured by the intellectual processes of Roger Kerr and he has done a wonderful job of keeping self interest out of the project and controlling conflicts of self interested institutions.[116]

Table 6.3: The State's Response to Initiatives from the NZBR

Area	NZBR Recommendation	Government Action
Industrial Action	• Nullify awards • Dismantle arbitration system • Most statutory minimum wages abolished • Contracts only guarantee of pay equity • Employers able to dismiss workers 'at will'	• *Employment Contracts Act*, 1991 abolishing awards. • *Employment Court and Tribunal* replaces the Arbitration Court 1987 • *Labour Relations Act* 1987 limits strike action • *Employment Relations Act* 1999 introduces more pro-labour regulation, albeit limited.
Producer Boards	• Disband all statutory functions and protection of producer boards	• No action taken.
Fiscal Strategy	• Privatise all state assets • Introduce flat taxes • Deregulate banking and financial sector	• 19 major state assets sold to NZBR members (see below) • 1984 A residual welfare state • 1987 (Goods & Services tax) GST 10 per cent; 1989 increased to 12.5 per cent • 1984 Financial deregulation begins
State Social Expenditure	• Minimise the safety net. Govt. must reduce its economic role in welfare • Time limits on sickness for the under 25s • Reducing ACC* and DPB* levels to that of the unemployment benefit • Using charities to provide emergency benefits to beneficiaries	• All benefits reduced from 1987 • Value of unemployment and related benefits reduced by between 3 and 25 per cent • Education severely cut from 1987

Note: *ACC= Accident Compensation, *DPB = Domestic Pension Benefit
Source of policy positions: NZCTU (1999), pp. 11–12, Green, D. (1996), From Welfare State to Civil Society, Wellington, New Zealand Business Roundtable, Wellington, New Zealand. Harris, P. and Twiname, L. (1998), First Knights an Investigation of the New Zealand Business Roundtable, Wellington, Howling at the Moon.

NZBR members had good reason to feel satisfied over the effect of their lobby on the state, particularly in support of privatisation of state assets; this has made some of them very wealthy. Nineteen major state owned assets were sold (through whole or partial ownership) to NZBR members; including Petrocorp (1988, bought by Fletcher Challenge director and NZBR member, Sir Ron Trotter), New Zealand Steel (1988, sold to Allan Hawkins, Equiticorp), New Zealand Liquid Fuel Investment (1990, sold to Fletcher Challenge), Housing Corp (1991, sold to ANZ bank directors, Sir Ron Trotter and Sir Roderick Deane), New Zealand Post (1989, sold to ANZ), Telecom (1990, sold to Freightways directors, and Fay Richwhite), BNZ (1988, sold to directors Michael Fay and David Richwhite), New Zealand Railways (1991, sold to Michael Fay and David Richwhite), the Rural Bank (1989, sold to Fletcher Challenge), Forest Corp (1991, sold to Fletcher Challenge and Brierleys director, Bruce Hancox), Synfuels (1990, sold to Fletcher Challenge), Air New Zealand (1989, sold to Brierleys).[117] Gaynor (1999) argues that:

1. By the end of the 1990s New Zealand state assets had been resold for an estimated value of $35.7 million, $16.6 million above their original sale price. In 1999 their sale process was almost complete because the Government's remaining commercial assets had a book value of only $4.6 million.
2. The privatisation program was a huge windfall for overseas investors. Just over seventy-nine per cent, or $13.1 million, of the increase in value has gone to offshore interests. At the top of these overseas interests is a combined group of overseas institutions that have made a net gain of $3.8 million. Overseas capital is well represented in the NZBR membership.[118]
3. Wealthy New Zealand investors have also made huge profits. The outcome of these share sales has been a net gain to domestic investors of $1.9 million. Sir Michael Fay and David Richwhite have realised a total gain of $410 million. This is made up of Telecom ($274 million), Bank of New Zealand ($41 million) and Tranz Rail ($95 million). Alan Gibbs and Trevor Farmer realised a larger profit from their Telecom investment because they sold their shares at a higher price than the Fay–Richwhite interests.[119]

The repercussions of privatisation have not been so well received by the public, for not only have they experienced it as financial losses but also the loss of essential facilities. Take the example of Mercury Energy. When it was privatised 'local authorities resisted ... [but] the government forced on Mercury Energy a structure whereby it was owned by a community trust but control rested with one of the country's largest law firms which had exceptionally close relationships with many of the private corporations ... It took on a prominent corporate raider and union basher from Australia, Wayne Gilbert, as its chief executive'.[120] The privatised company failed to renew the old infrastructure and 'from February to May 1998, the entire central business district of Auckland — the main business centre of New Zealand — was completely blacked out by a failure of the main power feeds'.[121]

Outside of the New Zealand capitalist class itself, the response to the NZBR has not been positive. Clifton writes of the NZBR going into 'Gothic public odium' for moving from bad micro-economic fundamentalism to an even worse conservative focus on the family.[122] Class struggles over 'truth' have arisen with union activists saying that 'the best way of beating it is to ensure the election to power of parties which will pursue alternative policies to those the Roundtable supports'.[123]

Conclusion

The answer to this chapter's opening question — how important is the role of those who control the production and reproduction of ideas? — is that it is crucial. The key role of think tanks and their subset, business lobby groups, is to identify business needs and to market these needs as the public good and subsequently just common sense. They change our language in the process, so that key economic liberal words and phrases, such as enterprise bargaining, political correctness, out-of-touch-elites, downsizing and individual contracts, are accepted into the lexicon and into the popular culture and thereby making key ruling class 'truths' everyone's truth. Argy suggests that a consequence of this 'commonsense' acceptance of economic liberal ideas is government policy that widens the opportunity gap between Australians and that the 'distribution of wealth, already very skewed, is becoming increasingly more concentrated ... with a growing 'under-class' of Australians (and New Zealanders) facing the prospect that their lifetime earnings and quality of life will fall steadily behind the 'over-class' of upper and middle managers, professionals and technocrats. They are increasingly becoming isolated — in terms of employment, income, location, school choice, health care, social attitudes and way of life'.[124] Meanwhile, in an attempt to further re-assert economic liberal common sense a government minister dismissed criticism of 'Work Choices' legislation by 151 academics, with 'a group of academics is no substitute for commonsense proposals'.[125]

Another key finding of this chapter on economic liberal ideas is how few these ideas are, and how internally and historically consistent their marketing has been. These key ideas about the superiority of the free market or private interests over public interests and public decision-making, were originally designed to thwart the feudal aristocracy, but now are used to consolidate ruling class power over us. The ideas are used in think tanks, by lobby groups, by economically 'dry' politicians and subsequently by the general public. Consequentially, there has followed a commitment to reduce public expenditure, promote flexible labour practices through the removal of labour market regulations, cut social welfare, deregulate financial markets and privatise public assets.[126] The strength of the dominant economic liberal ideology reflects the strength of that part of the ruling class that it most represents, finance capital.[127]

Notes

[1] Stilwell, F. (2002), *Political Economy, the Contest of Economic Ideas*, Melbourne, Oxford Press, p. 71.

[2] Argy, F. (2003), 'Achieving Equality of Opportunity', [Accessed 29 December, 2005] http://evatt.labor.net.au/publications/papers/96.html.

[3] Byan, D. (2000), 'The Rush to Regulate: the Shift in Australia from the Rule of Markets to the rule of Capital' *Australian Journal of Social Issues*, November, v.35 i.4 p. 333.

[4] Cahill, D. (2004), 'Contesting Hegemony: the Radical Neo Liberal Movement and the Ruling Class in Australia', N. Hollier, *Ruling Australia: the Power, Privilege and*

Politics of the New Ruling Class, Melbourne, Australian Scholarly Publishers pp. 87–105.

5   Hannan, E & Carney, S. (2005), 'Thinkers of influence', 10 December, [Accessed 29 December, 2005] http://www.theage.com.au/news/national/thinkers-of-influence/2005/12/09/1134086810518.html.

6   North, D. (1691), *Discourses Upon Trade,* quoted in Rubin, I. (1929), *A History of Economic Thought,* New York, Pluto Press, p.63; Smith, A. (1776), *An Inquiry into the Nature and Causes of the Wealth of Nations,* London, J. Dent; Ricardo, D. (1817), *On the Principles of Political Economy and Taxation,* (1957), London, Dent; Porter, M. (1990), *The Competitive Advantage of Nations,* London, Mcmillan.

7   That is Marx, K. & Engels, F. (1977), *The Communist Manifesto,* in the Collected works of Karl Marx and Fredrich Engels, Moscow, Progress Publishers; Bryan, D. (1996), *The Chase Across the Globe: International Accumulation and the Contradictions for Nation States,* Boulder, Westview Press.

8   Stilwell, F. (2002b), 'Why Bother about Economic Inequality?' Australia's e-journal of social and political debate Monday, 15 July. http://www.onlineopinion.com.au/view .asp ? article=1866.

9   Malthus, T. (1798), 'An Essay on the Principle of Population, as it affects the Future Improvement of Society, with Remarks on the Speculations of Mr Godwin, M. Condorcet and Other Writers', London, J. Johnson; enlarged to be (1803), *An Essay on the Principle of Population; or a View of its past and present Effects on Human Happiness; with an Inquiry into our Prospects respecting the Removal or Mitigation of the Evils which it occasions,* 2 v. London, J. Johnson.

10   Marx, K. (1977), 'German Ideology', *The Selected Works,* Moscow, Progress Publishers, p. 47.

11   Rubin, I. (1929), *A History of Economic Thought,* New York, Pluto Press.

12   The origins of various economic terms http://www.louisville.edu/~bmhawo01 econpage /meanings.html.

13   Mun, T (1952), *English Treasure by Forreign Trade,* 1664. Reprinted in *Early English Tracts on Commerce,* ed. by J. R. Mc-Culloch. Cambridge, U.K., Economic History Society, p. 125.

14   Magdoff, H. (2003), *Capitalism as a world economy* (Review Of The Month) (Interview) by Huck Gutman, *Monthly Review,* September, v.55 i.4, p. 1 (13).

15   Rubin, I. (1929).

16   North, D. (1691), p. 63.

17   Magdoff, H. (2003), p. 1.

18   Smith, A. (1776).

19   Aglietta, M. (1979), *A Theory of Capitalist Regulation: the US Experience,* London, Verso.

20   Samuelson, P. (1969), 'The Way of the Economist' in P. Samuelson, (ed.) *International Economic Relations: Proceedings of the Third Congress of the International Economic Association,* pp. 1–11, London, Macmillan.

21   Bryan, D. (1995b), 'International Competitiveness: National and Class Agencies', *Journal of Political Economy,* 35, pp. 1–23.

22   See *Australian Financial Review,* 2004,'Economic Thermeter', 4 June, p. 57.

23   Schumpeter, J. (1934), *Theory of Economic Development,* Cambridge, Harvard University Press.

24   Littler, D. (1998), 'Competitive Advantage' (ed.s) C. Cooper & C. Argyris *et al, The Concise Blackwell's Encyclopaedia of Management,* Oxford, Blackwells.

25   Littler, D. (1998).

26   Dierickx, I. & Cool. K. (1989), Asset stock and Accumulation and Sustainability, *Management Science,* n. 35, pp. 1504–11.

27 Zysman, J. & Tyson, L. (1983). *American Industry in International Competition: Government Policies and Corporate Strategies*, (ed.s) Ithaca, Cornell University Press.

28 Porter, M. (1986), *Competition in Global Industries*, Boston, Harvard Business School Press, 2. Porter, M. (1985), *Competitive Advantage: Creating and Sustaining Superior Performance*, New York, The Free Press, 3. Porter, M. (1990), *The Competitive Advantage of Nations*, London, Mcmillan.

29 Porter, M. (1990).

30 Schumpeter, J. (1934).

31 Bryan, D. (1995b) 'International Competitiveness: National and Class Agencies' *Journal of Political Economy*, v35 pp.1–23.

32 Von Hayek, F. (1944), *The Road to Serfdom*, The University of Chicago Press, p. 240.

33 Von Hayek, F. (1933), *Monetary Theory and the Trade Cycle*, New York.

34 Keynes, J. M. (1967), *The General Theory of Employment, Interest and Money*. 1936, London, Macmillan, pp. 321–22.

35 Cockett, R. (1994), *Thinking the UnThinkable, Think Tanks and the Economic Counter Revolution 1931-1983*, London, Harper Collins, pp. 9–12.

36 Cockett, R. (1994), pp. 100–21.

37 Murray, G. (1993-7), *Economic Power in Australia*, ARC funded Project, Respondent 57.

38 See Stone, D. (1996), 'From the Margins of Politics', *Western European Politics*, v. 19, n. 4, October, pp. 676–92; Stone, D. (1996), '*Capturing the Political Imagination: Think tanks and the Policy Process'*, London, Frank Cass; Denham, J. (1993), 'The Ideas Brokers: the Impact of Think Tanks on British Government', *Public Administrator*, v. 71, Winter, pp. 491–506, James, S. (1993), 'The Ideas Brokers: the Impact of Think Tanks on British Government', *Public Administrator*, v. 71, Winter, pp. 491–506; Worpole, K. (1998), 'Think Tanks Consultancies and Urban Policy in the UK', *International Journal of Urban and Regional Research*, v. 22, n.1, pp. 147–55.

39 See Stone, D. (1996a), pp. 676–92; Stone, D. (1996b); Denham, J. (1993), pp. 491–506; Worpole, K. (1998), 147–55.

40 See Stone, D. (1996a), pp. 676–92 & (1996b), Denham, J. (1993), Worpole, K. (1998), pp. 147–55.

41 See Stone, D. (1996a), pp. 676–92; Stone, D. (1996b), Denham J. (1993) pp. 491–506, Worpole, K. (1998), pp. 147–55.

42 The Vice President of the Rockford Institute Executive, Warder M. *(*1994), 'The Role of Think-Tanks in Shaping Public Policy; our Society is well Served by Thinkers', *Vital Speeches of the Day*, 1 May, v.60 n.14 p. 434(4).

43 Hollier, N. (2004), Hollier, N. (2004), *Ruling Australia*: Power, *Privilege and Politics of the New Ruling Class*, Melbourne, Australian Scholarly Publishing, p xvii.

44 Cahill, D. (2004), 'Contesting Hegemony: the Radical Neo Liberal Movement and the Ruling Class in Australia', in N. Hollier *Ruling Australia: the Power, Privilege and Politics of the New Ruling Class*, Melbourne, Australian Scholarly Publishers, p. 89.

45 Smith, J.A. (1991), *The Idea Brokers: Think Tanks and the Rise of the New Policy Elite*, New York, Free Press.

46 Beder, S. (1999), 'Fronting the Environment, the Intellectual Sorcery of Think Tanks,' *Arena Magazine*, June, p. 30.

47 Beder, S. (1999), p. 30.

48 Beder, S. (1999), p. 30.

49 Crisp, F. (1970), *Australasian National Government*, Melbourne, Longman Cheshire.

50 Beder, S. (1999), p. 30.

51 Beder, S. (1999), p. 30.

52 Herd, B. (1999), *The Left's Failure to Counter Economic Rationalism in Australia: Classical Economists Legacy to Government, Bureaucracy, Think Tank and the Union Movement*, incomplete Doctorate of Philosophy, Griffith University.

53 Marsh, I. (1994), The Development and Impact of Australia's 'Think tanks', *Australian Journal of Management*, December, pp. 177–200.

54 Hannan, E & Carney, S. (2005), p. 1.

55 Hannan, E & Carney, S. (2005), p. 6.

56 Beder, S. (1999), p. 30.

57 Nahan, M. in Da Silva, (1996), 'The New Social Focus', *The Australian Financial Review Magazine*, June, pp. 18–28.

58 Hannan, E & Carney, S. (2005), p. 3.

59 Hannan, E & Carney, S. (2005), p. 4.

60 HR Nicholls Society (2004), website, http://www.hrnicholls.com.au/work.html.

61 Peetz, D. (2006), *Brave New Workplace*, Sydney, Allen and Unwin, p. ix.

62 HR Nicholls Society (2004), *Presidents Report to the AGM*, http://www.hrnicholls.com.au/work.html.

63 Thornley, E. quoted by Hannan, E & Carney, S. (2005), p. 1.

64 Hannan, E & Carney, S. (2005), pp. 1–2.

65 Hannan, E & Carney, S. (2005), p. 4.

66 Beder, S. (1999), p. 30.

67 HR Nicholls Society (2004), website.

68 Tasman Institute Homepage http://www.tasman.com.au/about.htm#amy.

69 Da Silva, W. (1996), p. 6.

70 Hannan, E & Carney, S. (2005), p. 3.

71 Lindsay, G. (1996), 'Greg Lindsay Speaks Out about the Early CIS', interviewed by Andrew Norton, Editor of *Policy*, interview first appeared in Winter, *Policy*.

72 *CIS website* http://www.cis.org.au/.

73 Cockett, R. (1994), pp. 122–58.

74 Lindsay, G. (1996).

75 Hannan, E & Carney, S (2005), p. 5.

76 Hannan, E & Carney, S (2005), p. 5.

77 Hannan, E & Carney, S (2005), p. 4.

78 Hannan, E & Carney, S (2005), p. 6.

79 Hannan, E & Carney, S (2005), p. 4.

80 Hannan, E & Carney, S (2005), p. 4.

81 Hannan, E & Carney, S (2005), p. 5.

82 Hannan, E & Carney, S (2005), p. 3.

83 Da Silva, W. (1996).

84 Hannan, E & Carney, S (2005), p. 5. p. 3.

85 Grattan, M. (1997), 'The Dirty Trail of a Think Tank Grant', *Australian Financial Review*, 21 April, pp. 25–31.

86 Grattan, M. (1997), pp. 25–31.

87 Pers com Peetz, D. (2005).

88 Poulantzas, N. (1972), 'The Problems of the Capitalist State' (in) *Ideology and Social Science*, R. Blackburn, (ed.) New York, Random Press.

89 Thomsen-Moore, L. (2005), 'Katie Lahey's Passion for Business', p. 5.

90 Thomsen-Moore, L. (2005), p. 5.

91 BCA website http://www.bca.com.au/content.asp?staticID=about.

92 Hywood, G. (1997), 'BCA Needs New Energy', Editorial, *Australian Financial Review*, 13 February, p. 14.

93 Hywood, G. (1997), p. 14.

94 Thomsen-Moore, L. (2005), p. 5.

95 Morgan, H. (2003), *The Rule of Law, the Corporation and Australia's Future*, 1 December, Melbourne, Business Council Australia.

96 Penberthy, J. (1996), 'Absent Friends Knock Nervously on Howard's Door', *Australian Financial Review*, 18 March, pp. 1/14.

97   Thomsen-Moore, L. (2005), p. 3.
98   Hannan, E & Carney, S (2005), p. 5. p. 3.
99   Williams, P. & Ellis, S. (1994), 'Dawkins Kisses and Tells All on the BCA', *Australian Financial Review*, pp. 1/18.
100 Williams, P. & Ellis, S. (1994), pp. 1/18.
101 Block, F. (1987), 'Revising State Theory', *Essays in Politics and Postindustrialism*, Temple University Press, Utah.
102 NZCTU (1999), 'A Trade Unionists Guide to the New Zealand Business Roundtable', June ISBN 0-909011-17-6. p. 5.
103 NZCTU (1999), p. 8.
104 Penberthy, J. (1996), p. 5.
105 Ninness, G. (1992), 'Round the Table: the New Zealand Business Roundtable and Who are They?' *Sunday Star*, 1 March, pp. D. 1/3.
106 NZCTU (1999).
107 Kerr, R. (1990). 'The New Zealand Roundtable Roles and Goals', Auckland Rotary Club Speech, Auckland, 12 November.
108 Cullinane, T. (1995), *The Business Roundtable in 1995,* The Spectrum Club, Rotorua, New Zealand, 12 June.
109 Murray, G. (1990), Respondent 9, p. 234.
110 Murray, G. (1990), Respondent 9, p. 234.
111 Kerr, R. (1990), 'The New Zealand Roundtable Roles and Goals' p. 1.
112 Kerr, R. (1990), p. 3.
113 NZCTU (1999), p. 7.
114 Managh, C. (1989), 'Knights Driver sticks to Issue', *Sunday Star*, s. A, 12 February, p. 11.
115 Kerr, R. (1999), Cooperatives versus Corporates *New Zealand agribusiness and Food Congress*, Christchurch, 2, (1997a), Producer Board Acts Reform Brierley, *Submission by the New Zealand Roundtable*, [Accessed 3 July, 2005] http://ww.nzbr. org.nz/ documents/speeche...es-97/producer-boards-act.doc.htm, (1997b), Seven Deadly Sins of the Twentieth Century, *New Zealand Post College of Business, Jubilee Lecture*, (1998), The New Zealand Business Roundtable's View of Lobbying, *The 8th Annual Public Affairs and Lobbying Summit*, 18 March.
116 Murray, G. (1993–1997), Respondent 97.
117 *The New Citizen*, January/February/March (1997), p. 9.
118 NZCTU (1999), p. 5.
119 Gaynor, B. (1999), 'Analysis: Filling Foreigners' Pockets' *New Zealand Herald*, 2 October, p. C12.
120 Rosenberg, B. & Kelsey J. (1999), 'The Privatisation of New Zealand's Electricity Services', *International Seminar on the Impact of privatization of the electricity sector at the global level*, 20 September, Mexico City.
121 Rosenberg, B. & Kelsey J. (1999).
122 Clifton, S. (1999), 'A Word in Your Ear...', *Business Review Weekly*, Http:/www. *BRW.* com.au/content/130798/*BRW*06.htm.
123 Clifton, S. (1999).
124 Argy, F. (2003), 'Achieving Equality of Opportunity', [Accessed online December 2, 2006] http://evatt.labor.net.au/publications/papers/96.html.
125 Andrews, K. (2005), interviewed on *AM*, ABC Radio, 17 November.
126 For example North, D. (1691), Smith, A. (1776), & Ricardo, D. (1817).
127 O'Hara, P. (2006), *Growth and Development in the Global Political Economy*, Routledge, Oxford.

Chapter 7

Gender and the Ruling Classes

We now have evidence that the Australian and New Zealand ruling class do not represent the population at large because they have high incomes, they go to elite clubs, elite schools and universities and they enjoy exclusive and expensive social, sporting and cultural lives.[1] They also have had ways and means, through think tanks and lobby groups, of generating an ideology that legitimates and sustains their privileged world as 'the way that things are' and it shares with us that 'their interests are our interests'.[2] Now the question is 'Does the ruling class equally embrace women?' The task of this chapter is to look at the evidence to see whether this is happening; to see whether ruling class opportunities exist for all women at work, no matter what class they are; or whether mobility into ruling class work exists only for ruling class women; or whether there are no job openings for women at top levels at all.

This chapter outlines the empirical evidence of the reality of women in business and then looks at the ruling class's response to this reality. The bulk of the evidence comes from interviews by the author with female directors and with male directors in Australia and New Zealand discussing the role of their female colleagues. The others source of evidence is secondary source data from interviews by others, from texts and from surveys on women managers.

The Reality of Women in Business

According to Bagwell, Australia still has one of the most gender-segregated workforces in the OECD countries. Extrapolating from past rates of increase, Australian women can anticipate being directors in equal numbers to men by the year 2065.[3] Leonie Still, Amanda Sinclair and others suggest that big business is sexist because it has a male executive culture that is consistent with the sexism of the wider Australasian culture.[4] Anne Summers, in *The End of Equality*, provides a very pessimistic assessment of the progress that women in Australia have made in the twenty-first century. Summers, using Australian Bureau of Statistics data, shows that whilst women are now participating in the paid workforce, they are in poorly paid areas of work where jobs are often part-time and casual. In August 2005, women held 67.3 per cent of all casual, part-time positions.[5]

This unequal access to rewards at work is seen at a variety of levels:

1. Is there a segregated labour market with gender-specific low-paid and high-paid job areas?
2. Is payment being made according to gender?

3. Are there still complaints of gender harassment?
4. Does the tyranny of beauty follow women into work?
5. Is the business ideal male no matter what women do?

Finally, we look at the ruling class response to the evidence of sexism in business.

Recruitment

Although recruitment for the top jobs in business is improving it started from a low level. Speaking of her own recruitment, Margaret Jackson, the 2006 chairperson of Qantas, said:

> It is true that when I first graduated from university and applied to a number of chartered accounting firms, I received letters back that said, 'We're terribly sorry, Miss Jackson, we don't employ women.' That certainly doesn't happen these days. Back in the 1980s the way that people were chosen as directors was very much from personal networks, it was who knew somebody that knew somebody.[6]

Margaret Jackson, AC

Qualifications: Monash University — BEc 1973, Melbourne University — MBA with distinction, Fellow, Institute of Chartered Accountants, Fellow, Australian Institute of Company Directors

Current Positions: March 1994 to date Director, ANZ Banking Group, July 2000 to date Director, Billabong International, Chairperson, Qantas Airways (Director since 1992), Director, John Fairfax Holdings.

Career Summary: 1992 to date Full-time Director, 1990–1992 Partner, KPMG 1983–1990 Partner, BDO Nelson Parkhill, Chartered Accountants, 1977–1983, Manager and Supervisor, BDO Nelson Park Hill, Chartered Accountants 1973–1977 Price Waterhouse.

*Source:*Margaret Jackson, Chief Executive Women, www.cew.org.au/index.cfm?

Other women think females are still handicapped by not having the recruitment networks that men have and an acceptance of the need for diversity. Some female directors on boards are trying to change this innate conservatism and bring about a greater diversity, according to Margaret Jackson, who goes on to say:

> I think that shareholders though tend to be a little more conservative and there are some trophy names and they get excited when boards appoint a trophy name but sometimes there's some fantastic talent that the shareholders might think that that's an unusual appointment, that's a lateral appointment or it's somebody that they don't know. As a chairman of a board, what I and my board at Qantas think is that what we want is that we want as diverse a group of people as possible, we want people from diverse geographies, we want people from diverse training, experience and background.[7]

Segregated Access

In 2005, the Australian gender pay gap (GPG) was 15 per cent — that is, men on average earn 15 per cent more than women.[8] Why? Barbara Pocock and Michael Alexander show Australian evidence identifying 'between 58 and 81 per cent of the gender pay gap' comes from female location in a segmented labour market.[9] The segmented market identifies women's placement into work (for example dress making) designated as inferior, rationalising an inferior wage and an inferior status. Equal pay is not going to solve the segmented work problem as women are 'ghettoised' into 'women's work'.

Kerry Brown and Stacey Ridge, in their 2002 Australian study comparing and contrasting gender figures in management in Australian state Senior Executive Services, found that males could negotiate their way to the top in female dominated sectors in ways that women could not in male areas.[10] That is, it did not matter if the lower ranks of the agency were dominated by men or women, in the upper ranks men were still over-represented. Whilst there has been some upward movement for women 'their level of participation in management structures [and] their participation remains extremely low. In the years 1997, 1998 and 1999, there were significantly more men than women across all three tiers of management, irrespective of the gender domination of the agency'.[11]

Women in management receive less expensive cars as part of their salary packages and are less likely to have access to profit driven bonuses and commissions. Mark Gaines and Craig Endicott's 1994 survey showed:

> Women executives earned 5% to 20% less and, in advertising, men held the majority of executive positions,.. The increased movement of women into the managerial ranks is lowering pay scales.[12]

This potential for downgrading the profession and lowering male pay by large scale female entry was expressed as a fear amongst law groups in the 1980s. They need not have worried because segmentation and discrimination ensured that, in law, women's pay was less than men's, particularly at the level of partnership, where female partners earned only slightly more than male non-partner lawyers and women were in the lowest paid areas.[13]

Also the places where women hold directorships are mostly in 'female-related' areas, reflecting again the segmented gendered workplace.[14] Most women directors hold non-executives rather than CEO or Chair positions. Jan Buck, an associate member of Korn/Ferry, writes, 'The only way that we are going to get a steeper climb in the number of women on boards is to have more women staying on in their corporations and moving on to their boards as executive directors'.[15] This is currently not happening as this male director suggested in an interview when asked why are women not on top boards?[16]

> At this stage in the development of Australia there are not that many women in the higher ranks of companies. They are not there to retire on to boards. What is in question

is that most senior company boards are looking to where they can, to get quality women on their boards and not finding them with the experience, or whatever qualities they need to help them out in their business. I think now there are a number of women joining boards — good women, good people with good experience that can add to the board and I think that is to be applauded and encouraged. I think that it would be quite wrong for us to prescribe that a certain percentage of women should be placed on the board. At least until such time as there is a sufficient pool of skilled women, to enable that to be done. When that does happen I sincerely hope that the women are there as much as the men.

Still's survey in *Glass Ceilings and Sticky Floors: Barriers to the Careers to Women in the Finance Industry* showed widespread discontent amongst women employed in 75 organisations of the finance industry.[17] This attitudinal study of 3,900 bank employees found that whilst banks seemed to have the appropriate systems in place to provide fair and equitable working environments, women still perceive 'considerable disparity between policy development and implementation'. Overall, women felt disadvantaged in relation to recruitment, promotion and conditions of service, whilst men felt that women were given plenty of opportunity to make progress. Men's attitudes were 'I'm OK, Jack' whereas women were dissatisfied with their under-class management status. (Women are only 15 per cent of managers.)[18]

Remuneration

In 2003, John Mohan and Nancy Ruggiero expressed irritation at what they saw as exaggerated claims about women being held back compared to men. They used their own findings to show that there is only a small 'statistical difference between male and female ... earning capacity'.[19] However, there is little support in the Australasian literature for this position. The opposite position — that women were being held back compared to men — came from Patricia Todd and Joan Eveline's 2005 work.[20] As Gillian Whitehouse writes:

> The fate of pay equity since the 1980s has received much less attention, and indeed there has been more continuity than change over the past 20 years. The resilience of the ongoing gender pay gap is a reminder of the multiple and complex causes of gender pay inequality, and the need for a multi-faceted strategy to achieve further improvement.[21]

In the mid 1990s, an Egan Cullen survey of 500 companies showed men as ninety per cent of all senior managers, with a 20 per cent advantage in their base salary and 40 per cent advantage in their car purchase price and greater access to other variable rewards.

Interestingly, if there is a woman at the head of the company (remembering there are only five women CEOs of top Australian companies) then the size of the gender-pay gap is less likely to be so large. 'Female CEO and Board Chairs bring more top women and at higher pay than is found in non-women-led firms. Specifically, female executives in female-led firms earn between 10–20 per cent more than comparable executive women in male-led firms and are between 3 and 18 per cent more likely to be among the highest five paid executives in these firms as well'.[22]

That said, class outweighs gender. As Belinda Hickman and Michelle Gunn found, 'women at the top increased their salaries by 22 per cent, or $218 a week', over a fifteen-year period (1982–1996/7).[23] However, in this same period, the salaries of working class women fell.[24]

Harassment

Women maintain that in the business environment they are bullied,[25] discriminated against[26] and sexually harassed.[27] Their harassment is alleged to take several forms. Here are two cases:

1. In a 1996 case, legal damages were awarded to Julianne Ashton, one of only two female futures traders on the floor of Sydney Futures Exchange. Ashton complained in 1993 that she was systematically targeted with sexual innuendo and offensive language whilst working for Bankers Trust. Ms Ashton said her male colleagues taunted her with such remarks as 'How about a head job?' and talk of 'bending her over'. The only other woman who worked with her, Ms Connie Nicolopoulos, said, 'It happened to Julianne on a regular basis.' When Ms Ashton complained to her superior at Bankers Trust, her work was downgraded.[28]

2. In 2005 Fiona Landreth took Finsbury Print to the Federal Court for sexual harassment. She alleged she was forced to go to a sex shop and strip club after a work dinner after being told that her performance review the next day would depend on her going.[29] Her male bosses said 'it was she who suggested visiting the sex shop'.[30]

Margaret Thornton suggests that 'harassment of women who encroach upon and disturb masculinist workplaces is by no means confined to blue-collar work'.[31] The harassment takes innumerable forms — bullying, ignoring, sexual innuendo and insult. According to L'Estrange, bullying is acceptable corporate behaviour:

> To be charitable a lot of the bullying is unintentional. Often these men have been on the board together for a long time, they went to the same school, they've played golf, they know everything about each other and then this woman gets appointed to the board. They are not used to treating women as a peer, only as a social companion.[32]

In the male executive culture, L'Estrange claimed female board appointees are ignored:

You proffer an idea but nothing is said. Then later in the meeting, someone else puts forward the same idea and suddenly everyone thinks that the idea is brilliant. Another example is when the chairman thanks everyone by name ... Thank you Ted, Good idea Bob, Yes Indeed Bill ... but the woman is not acknowledged. You feel isolated and excluded ... when they find a woman on the board they behave as they have always behaved, not realising that it is unacceptable, discriminatory and, in some cases, illegal.[33]

Rod Wilson, a director of Human Resources, explains that 'a lot of males will feel incredibly threatened by women in the workforce ... we are seeing women who are much more determined to succeed in environments where males assumed they're going to succeed. Now there is a threat from someone in the past the men have perceived as inferior'.[34]

Another problem for working women in big business is the question of children. What can they do with small children if there is no provision for them? When should women be having them, or should they be having children at all? 'In 1979, almost one in four births was to women aged 30 years and over. By 1999, this had increased to almost one in every two births'.[35] We are having what could be described as a baby bust when the ABS writes, 'a growing proportion of Australian women and their partners are not having children'.[36]

Childlessness is the route that Theresa Gattung, CEO of Telcom New Zealand, has taken because of the high demands that her job has put on her. In an interview, Katrina Nicholas suggested to her that being a female had meant making some difficult choices along the way. She answered:

Yes, of course it was tough, I mean I personally have chosen not to have children because I wouldn't have the stamina to work as hard as you need to work to get to the top and then to stay there, and have a family and a lot of women are not prepared to make that choice, and that's entirely fair enough.[37]

Discrimination

Discrimination against women can be explicitly sexual but is often just gendered.[38] Women can systematically be made to appear as under-achievers or incompetent by cutting off their access to resources or clients, and through other means not explicitly sexual in nature. These techniques continue to be used to keep women out of the top jobs. An example in 2006 was the alleged treatment of Chanelle Hughes, a foreign exchange saleswoman made redundant after going on maternity leave from an Australian branch of a multinational bank.[39] She went on maternity leave in 2004 and she claimed that the bank replaced her with two new male employees and told her that her job was made redundant due to restructuring. But according to Hughes, no such restructuring took place. She described a male culture where in their informal time men held men only drinking sessions, and work-sanctioned golf trips from which female employees were excluded. Male employees' computer screen savers were of scantily clad women, male colleagues would openly discuss the content of 'girly magazines' which were left around the office and talk about strip clubs they had visited both with and without clients.[40]

However, discrimination is applied more broadly than just to women. In 1995, Australian businesswoman, Janet Holmes a Court said, 'I frankly see prejudice operating against all sorts of people. I see glass ceilings imposed on people because they have the wrong accent, for example, or because they have been to the wrong school or university. It is not only women who are prejudiced against'.[41]

Thornton agrees that discriminatory conduct around class is more insidious 'in regard to both its character and its effects so that it is difficult to make out a complaint',[42] but costly childcare is a central gender and class issue. Anne Summers describes the costs of child care as being sometimes as much as $60 a day, that is, a huge part of a working class woman's wage.[43] Only 38 per cent of women in paid employment have access to paid maternity leave and the loss of earnings over a woman's lifetime as a result of having a child was estimated to be $160,000 after tax for the first child and $12,000–$15,000 for each subsequent child.[44] Child care is not an economic problem for women on relatively large income packages, but they too cannot count on companies to provide child-care facilities. A female director noted that 'privately paid housekeepers are essential for a female director'.[45] In another interview, the same top female director was asked whether it was difficult having children and a career?

> Yes, but not as difficult as when I had gone down to Wagga Wagga College. There I had a full-time job but they were odd hours. There were very few classes in the daytime
>
> … it was a very small place. I had a woman on call.[46]

Relative wealth gives some women access to 'a woman on call' or privatised childcare.

Appearance

The importance of good physical appearance puts pressure on women and men to look and dress appropriately, but it is a pressure experienced very unevenly by the genders. Naomi Wolf, in *The Beauty Myth*, argues that this thing called beauty is a 'collective reactionary hallucination' that serves 'nothing more exalted than the need of today's power structure, economy, and culture to mount a counter offensive against women'.[47] The power structure 'has formulaic' images that are 'endlessly reproduced' in the media but found primarily through advertising. Women, in turn, are socialised by these images and they need to free themselves entirely from this beauty myth and create a new 'pro-woman', non-hierarchical definition of beauty, which would celebrate each different woman in her own uniqueness and individuality.[48]

Beauty in its patriarchal construction can work for those who have it, in that it gives the possessor some leverage of power in an otherwise unequal situation. A female lawyer said that being a pretty woman was actually an advantage in court because:

> Judges are basically dirty old men and they like to see a pretty female face; a definite advantage in court once you have had the once-off confrontation with senior male counsel.[49]

In Australasia, the beauty myth is pervasive. Successful women are referred to in press releases in relation to their physical appearance as 'attractive', 'gracious' and even 'funnily enough, very good looking'.[50] Businesswomen are expected to be attractive and formerly attired. According to Finklestein, women will never dress as casually as men because they cannot afford to.[51] 'Elegantly tailored suits, softened by silk scarves, jewellery, hosiery and heels, have become the basis of the female working wardrobe and a sign of vocational commitment'.[52] For many women, trading in the power suit would be tantamount to parading the white flag. 'I don't know about dressing down!' exclaimed one advertising executive. 'If anything, I think women are dressing up for self-confidence so that they're on an equal level to men. I like to look like I am worth the money I get paid'.[53] This woman admitted that she had less respect for a woman in a cheaper, non-label suit than she would have if her label read Simona or Saba.[54] However, Epaminondas believes that bosses relaxing dress codes are not going to change gender 'power relations'.[55]

The Male Business Ideal Type

Women can have haute couture with designer labels, be super rich through inherited wealth or entrepreneurial ability, but they are still being overlooked for promotion because it is supposed that the businessman's ideal-type in business is a man like himself.[56] Amanda Sinclair sees this male vision of the successful executive as a god-like Ulysses on a journey of relentless trials from which he emerges neither undiverted by weariness, nor sidelined by seducing women trying to distract him from his career goals.[57] For example, Kerry Packer was quoted as having said that 'he loved the company of women but preferred to keep them, with only one or two exceptions, well away from the boardroom'[58] where he was 'happiest simply shooting the breeze with colleagues or mates'.[59]

Women are put into either whore or Madonna roles.[60] Neither of these translates into a role as a director on the board. Tensions are therefore rising as women are now saying 'a women's place is in the boardroom'.[61] The Chief Executive Women's Network (CEW) has developed five core questions for organisational introspection:

1.   Is the diversity value of female talent appreciated and counted?

2.   Are we appointing our fair share of talented women?
3.   Are we losing women too early?
4.   Does our pay distribution by gender tell a story?
5.   Are we managing our female talent for success?[62]

How do Australia and New Zealand Compare with Others?

In North America, an article called 'Wanted: A Workplace Without a Ceiling' suggests that 'women in the workplace still face hurdles, especially when attempting to enter the top ranks; only 5.1 per cent of top corporate officers are women, despite the obvious fact that no company can afford to exclude females'.[63] In the UK in 2004, two UK government reports, *The Higgs Review* and *The Tyson Report*, drew 'attention to board independence, the lack of female directors and the potential positive contribution of female participation to UK corporate governance'. Their study examined 'the situation of female directors in the top 350 UK companies … in particular, female non-executive directors account for just over 6 per cent of the non-executive directors and receive about two-thirds the remuneration of their male counterparts'.[64]

Norway's high number of female directors can be held as a beacon of light in an otherwise dark firmament for working women. Norway's parliament passed legislation on 1 January 2006 forcing the country's largest publicly traded companies to increase to 40 per cent the number of women on boards of directors. The Norwegian parliament did this because it had passed a 2003 law inviting privately owned public companies to 'elect a board where there should be a minimum number of both sexes in the board'. But by July 2005, only 68 of 519 companies had fulfilled these requirements and only 16 per cent of the board members were women.[65] Penalties are to apply from 2007.[66] Table 7.1 compares board gender figures from Australian and New Zealand against other countries.

Table 7.1: Female Directors in Nine Countries

Country	No. of companies with women	% of companies with at least one female director	Total No. of directors	Total No. of female directors	% of female directors
1. Norway	-	74	-	-	21 (all sectors) 15 (private)
2. U.S	432	86.4	5,771	779	13.6
3. Canada	241	48.2	-	-	11.2
4. Australia	141	47	2,345	251	10.7
5. South Africa	113	37.7	3094	180	5.8
6. U.K.	84	42	2,006	109	5
7. New Zealand	66	75	575	29	5
8. Spain	72	24	2,486	115	4.6
9. Japan	72	3	43,115	81	.2

Sources: 1–9 are found in endnotes.[67]

New Zealand trails the poor performances of both the US and the UK, whereas Australia just trails the US. Table 7.1 shows that Australia comes fourth and New Zealand seventh in this list of nine countries. A 2004 Australian inaugural census surveyed 152 top companies listed on the Australian Stock Exchange and reported that women held 8.6 per cent of executive management positions and 47.1 per cent of companies had no female directors. EOWA also published figures showing that women held 8.8 per cent of executive management positions. This figure went up 0.4 per cent on 2003's figures, which equates to approximately 'five female managers joining Australia's business elite over the past 12 months'.[68]

Structurally, women were not well placed to move into key executive roles: 62.1 per cent of women occupied support positions, as opposed to line positions that ultimately lead to CEO or board appointments (compared with only 31.4 per cent of men who held support positions). Thornton, suggests that the 'metaphor of the glass ceiling captures the way that well-qualified and competent women often reach a point in organisations beyond which they are not promoted [and] whether one looks at private corporations, the professions, universities or public corporations, the same gendered pyramidal structure is clearly discernible'.[69] Her argument is that this happens because in Australia there is a masculinist culture of authority that condones the 'scapegoating and harassment of individual women who have been promoted to the higher echelons as a strategy for impugning their ability'.[70]

Ann Pomeroy reports that in New Zealand they have a 'chronic under-utilisation of women's skills and talents in governance... in the private corporate sector', with only five per cent of female board directorships of publicly listed companies.[71] Her research embracing 89 companies found 546 male and 29 female board directors and that nearly three-quarters of these companies had no female directors. Four companies had two female directors, none had more than two.[72] New Zealand women, in bright young things companies, held '16 per cent of board directorships' in twelve public companies or '35 per cent of board directorships'[73] on state boards.

Ruling Class Response to Sexism in Business

Gilding claims that the successful businessmen featured in the *BRW* rich lists are 'unashamedly sexist'.[74] Based on a modified version, Sinclair's categorisation can identify four broad responses to the existence of sexism in senior business ranks:
1. Denial that sexism is unjust ('Women should not get top jobs in business. It's not the best use of their time')
2. Recognition and dismissal ('the steel industry has not been friendly to women. They should go elsewhere')
3. Experimentation with reform ('We believe very strongly in balanced teams')
4. Commitment to partial change ('the lack of Australian or New Zealand female directors is appalling, in comparison to American women, we will have to make changes soon') or total commitment to change ('we'll target 50 per cent women on boards or not register the company').

Denial that Sexism is a Problem

Denial that sexism is a problem encompasses that collection of attitudes that believe the lack of women in big business is not a problem but an advantage for business. This is a conservative position that women's role is in the home and was expressed by a male director in this way:

> [I have] a big problem with equal opportunity. I think that humans are important in this world. More important than anything else and I happen to think that motherhood is the prime basis of humanity. I think that we are bastardising motherhood... Working mothers will say that they give their children quality time. I'll give you an example; we had a lady who was the assistant global treasurer of one of our companies. She told her immediate boss John that she gave her children quality time. He said 'Well Jean, I have to say this, if you responded to me about your employment in Atwell — 'Don't worry John I don't have many hours with you but they are quality hours when I do'. I would say go find another job. If you cannot devote time to this job like you're saying you cannot devote time to your kids then you really shouldn't have had kids in the first instance.[75]

The same denial perspective is also encapsulated in another interview from an extremely successful female director. Her response to a question about what power meant to her was:

I think that there is an obsession with power that I thoroughly dislike. This obsession is particularly evident in the women's movement. They equate power with some sort of freedom whereas the truth is the higher up the hierarchy the less power you have. Unless you are a Hitler.[76]

These quotes show hostility to female workplace success. The problem remains that there are few women at the top and a lot of women crowded at the bottom of promotional ladders: 'Glass ceilings are indeed an issue but of far greater significance is the material of the ground floor, where most women start and where the majority finish'.[77]

Recognition — There is a Problem, but is it with Women?

This perspective acknowledges that a problem exists in that there are few women in big business, but then casts the problem as belonging to individual women.[78] When this American director was interviewed, he identified a gender problem in access to board membership.[79] He also felt his company degraded women and this clearly irritated him:

> I would say that women truly at the board level are a long way off because of the dominance of the principal shareholders on boards and because of the old boy's network.

Dame Leonie Kramer, Chancellor of the University of Sydney and a director of ANZ, was reported as criticising women within an anti-feminist 'backlash'.[80] Dame Leonie was quoted as saying that women are not denied jobs like hers because of discrimination but because they lacked confidence: 'women... go a bit limp when things get tough'.[81]

In a 1995 interview, in response to the question 'Why are women not on top boards?'[82] a female director replied:

> I don't think that it crosses people's minds. It just happens to be top heavy. In fact I think that there is now a reverse bias, encouraging women to take their place. There is no explicit affirmative action programme but a general sense of encouraging women where possible. I think it's good. Our priority is performance and one is not better than another, but there is only a certain pool of people available for this performance needed at any one time. So the process is going to alternate between genders.
>
> *Interviewer*: Aren't women structurally hampered from doing well in business?
>
> *Female Director:* Women have to work out what are the important issues in life and how they are they going to handle them. So that changes that have taken place in the last twenty years have led to a different level of participation in the workforce and the effect of that on families is something that we have yet to test. I say that in another 40 years or so the outcome would be clearer.

Dame Leonie Judith Kramer

Qualifications: BA (Melbourne), MA (Sydney) and DPhil (Oxford)
Career Positions: Non executive director of the ANZ since 1983, Chancellor of Sydney University since 1991, Deputy Chancellor 1989–91, Emeritus Professor in Australian Literature, University of Sydney (Chair 1968–89), Fellow of the Senate, 1989 and 1969–74, Member of the Board of Studies, NSW since 1989, Senior Fellow of the Institute of Public Affairs, Chairperson Board of Directors of the National Institute for Dramatic Arts (NIDA), 1987–92, Chairperson of *Quadrant* Magazine since 1989, Member of International Council Asian Society since 1991, National President of Australia Britain Society, Member of the Council of NRMA since 1985, Member of Council of ANU 1984–87, Britannia Award 1986, Director of Western Mining since 1984, Chairperson of ABC 1982–83, Member of the University Council 1977–86, National Accreditation Council for Translators and Interpreters 1977–81, Secondary Schools Board 1976–82, Council of National Library 1975–81, Vice President of Australian Society of Authors, 1969–71, Associate Professor University of NSW 1963–68, Tutor and Postgraduate student of St Hugh's College Oxford 1949–52.
Biographical Details: Born 1 October 1924, the daughter of A. L. Gibson, educated at Presbyterian Ladies College (Melbourne), she married Harold Kramer in December 1952 and has two daughters.
Publications: Henry Handel Richardson and some of her sources 1954, *Australian Poetry* 1961, *Companion to Australia Felix* 1962, *Coast to Coast* 1963–64, *Myself when Laura* 1966, *A Guide to Language and Literature* (jointly) 1977, *A. D. Hope,* 1979, *The Oxford History of Australian Literature* (ed) 1981, *The Oxford Anthology of Australian Literature* jointly 1985, *My Country: Australia Poetry and Short Stories: two hundred years* (2 volumes) 1985, *James McAuley* (editor) 1988, *Collected Poems* 1989.
Recreation: Gardening and music.
Sources: Dame Leonie Kramer in *Who's Who in Business in Australia* 1994, p. 514, *Who's Who in Business in Australia* 1998, p. 591.

When interviewed, a male director gave this 'women don't come our way' response:[83]

> It's up to the women of course but I think that they would be better off in some other industry than the old Steel Industry. We have some beaut women. A woman runs one of our big factories. Robyn runs one of our bigger factories and she does a terrific job. So there is plenty of opportunity for the right women but they just don't seem to come our way.

Another way of presenting this perspective came from a New Zealand director in 1992. He believed that, 'If you want the honest truth, women aren't very good in business' because:[84]

Males are aggressive ... Look, I wake up in the morning and I say 'Who are we going to kill today?' That is what the aggression of the takeover game is. How can we find one who has fallen by the wayside that we can knock off? But women hate language like that, they hate you talking like that. I had a woman employed here, I love employing women because they are the cheapest brains that you can get. They are much better value for money. However I have found that they do not enjoy the aggression that is involved in my sort of business. All business is about aggression and women are not nearly aggressive enough. Women's instincts are good in politics where manipulation is important. The test of the market's objective is the only important thing in business. If I cannot sell more bras I go broke. But the test of manipulation is who listens to you. Women's skills are not good at the top levels of business, which is highly competitive and aggressive.[85]

The reasons women are not directors on a board slides from a constructivist explanation ('women don't fit into the culture') to a biological one ('women aren't genetically equipped').[86]

Experimentation with Reform

In Australia there is some positive evidence in the direction of reform because women have apparently opened some heavy corporate doors in recent times: Coles Myer, the National Australia Bank and David Jones have all recently welcomed a woman director for the first time into their boardrooms. An American male director said:

I have used every weapon in my arsenal to improve the conditions for women. And it is just like pulling teeth. ... I am doing things that I used to say I would never fall into the trap of doing. Things that would be regarded as tokenism; putting women forward. ... There are very capable women in Australia. I am the chairman of the American Chamber of Commerce in Victoria. We have an executive committee ... There are no women on that committee. I got to be chairman after two and a half years. When I became chairman I said that we are going to have women on this committee or I am not going to lead it. We now have two women on the committee ... We now have women on a management committee group that is very successful. They have hit a nerve in this business community that there has not been much attention paid to.[87]

The question then is whether there is likely to be any general initiative for change and where will it come from? This is how a New Zealand male director, also a partner in a law firm, responded to the question: 'Where is the push for change for women, going to come from?'

The push for change is coming from women and a few concerned men. Even though women's success may still be regarded as tokenism, women are beginning to be included in top positions in companies. Their efforts are being supported on a number of fronts — by shareholders. We get asked by shareholders [about the absence of women] ... and I think that we recognise and support these kinds of views ... In our law firm half the graduates are now women and out of fifty-three partners there are three women but they've all become partners within the last five years.[88]

So some commitment to experiment is taking place within the companies where concerned male directors implement affirmative action, re-education 'gender-sensitising' programmes and token gestures. The push for this has come from more egalitarian business cultures but they identify the final responsibility as belonging to women, that is, women directors, women shareholders speaking up at AGMs and maybe boycotting women consumers.

Commitment to Change

The last category that Sinclair identifies is the commitment to change driven from the top but marked by self-inspection.[89] When he arrived in Australia, George Trumbull, an American, fitted into this category. He said 'Australian culture is reasonably sexist and this company [AMP] is at least a good model for the country if not worse'.[90] Turnbull set about changing the male culture at AMP.[91] He recruited and promoted fifteen women into the 60-strong senior executive team where there had been none. He sacked two senior male executives for sexual harassment and in the process he won a lot of female fans amongst his staff.[92]

If organisations lack commitment to change, there are few places left for ambitious women to turn. Two are seldom raised as orthodox possibilities, because to do so exposes the fear of men 'that women are going to get some advantage because of their sex'.[93] These short cuts are inheritance of a company from a dead father or spouse or marrying the boss. Neither of these options is recommended as easy.

The option of marrying the boss can be difficult. In 1995, female director Lynette Mayne was reported to have experienced this situation and its associated problems.[94] Mayne, a well-qualified woman in her own right, married her boss, Stuart Hornery, head of a top 30 company called Lend Lease. Jackson reported that the whole perception relayed by inside sources was that Hornery 'married one of his underlings [and this would] cause problems'.[95] These fears were realised in the resignation of his CEO, John Morchel. Tension rose even though measures were in place to check decision-making between couples. For example, Mayne's pay rise was outside Hornery's sphere of influence. Jackson wrote that this incident shows 'uncomfortable truths about how corporate Australia copes, or fails to cope, with powerful women'.[96] Issues of sexuality in the workplace are thrown up 'as important when women are involved. As soon as women are in the workplace it is as though sexuality enters. It is seen as something women bring, not something that men bring'.[97] Workplace sexuality is a female, rather than a male, problem.

Sexuality, as in problematic promiscuity, is associated with a woman's presence in the workplace rather than any behaviour that she may exhibit.[98] Sinclair quotes a CEO as saying 'Promiscuity ... if it's an issue, it's a women's issue, doesn't seem to be a men's issue'.[99]

To combat these pressures, women use networks and lobby groups or, when they are excluded from these, they use their husbands' networks, as in this case when a female director and her female friend, also a director, said:

> The old boy network, as it is spoken of, is difficult to overcome. Even though now it is not the traditional old boy network in the Northern Club, the Auckland Club, whatever, it will be there amongst the new breed in their thirties who have largely shared their experiences, their failures and their business deals together.[100]

Lobby Groups

As the BCA was reported not to 'treat women's needs as a high priority',[101] businesswomen created their own lobby group, the Australian Council of Businesswomen (ACOB).[102] Now located in Sydney, ACOB aims to have 'a single mission: to ensure that the opinions, ideas and vision of Australia's businesswomen form part of the top level debate with governments, the media and business in Australia. ACOB has expertise to lobby governments, the media and business to deliver the views of businesswomen and women's organisations direct to the policy-makers, decision-makers and the media'.[103] The ACOB attempts to 'emulate the Business Council of Australia in influencing government policy and commenting on issues that affect the whole spectrum of women in business'.[104] Chief Executive Women (CEW) is another corporate Australian women's organisation including businesswomen, women from the professions, academia, public service and the not-for-profit sectors. Established in 1985, it is a small network of influential women, aiming to encourage and promote women's leadership talents by Australian business, government and the community.[105]

Katie Lahey
Chief Executive Business Council of Australia
Brief Summary: Lahey took up the position as Chief Executive of the Business Council of Australia in September 2001. The Business Council of Australia is an association of Chief Executives of the top 100 companies. Before joining the BCA, Ms Lahey served five years as the Chief Executive of the State Chamber of Commerce (NSW).
Board Member: David Jones Ltd Major Performing Arts Board (Australia Council) *Education:* Bachelor of Arts (Hons), Master of Business Administration.
Management Experience: Board member, CEO (P & L).
Source: Katie Lahey, Chief Executive Women
http://www.cew.org.au/index.cfm?apg=membership&bpg=profilemember&ai
d=46.

A male director pointed out in relation to the few females associated with the BCA: 'There is a view here in Australia that if women are capable then they will find their own way along the corporate ladder and it will happen. I think that is a crazy attitude'.[106]

Heather Ridout
Chief Executive of the Australian Industry Group, ansd has previously held the positions of Deputy Chief Executive and Executive Director — Public Policy and Communications. *Education:* Bachelor of Economics (Hons) University of Sydney*Broad Experience:* Corporate, Government, Politics, Functional Experience, Public Policy.
Management Experience: Board member- CEO (P & L), General Management Area of Expertise: Education, Government, Manufacturing, Media, Regulatory Services.
Source: Heather Ridout, www.cew.org.au/index.cfm?

Women's Relation to the State

The relationship women in business have with the state obviously will vary. However, Summers, in her disappointment about the state's lack of support of women, gives names within the Labor and Liberal Parties of people who have failed to support women; politicians who have failed women's need for social, political and economic rights and reforms.[107] She writes of her outrage regarding Prime Minister John Howard's failure to appoint a female governor-general, and then his subsequent leaking to the media that he had wanted to, leaving women with the knowledge that in John Howard's estimation there was not a single woman in the country who was adequately qualified. Summers took a copy of *Who's Who*, and in less than an hour came up with names of 45 women who were more than qualified. She also expressed her disappointment that the 60 female members and senators, who are over a quarter of the politicians on the federal benches, have allegedly failed to fight for women. She singles out Emily's List (the Labor women's organisation funding female candidates) for its alleged inability to demonstrate that they have galvanised women to act on pro-women commitments once elected.

Currently there is a Federal Sex Discrimination Commissioner, Pru Goward, described as a 'toothless tiger'.[108] A former Sex Discrimination Commissioner, Ms Sue Walpole, said that 'this government has made it clear …to…other independent bodies, that they do not like independent criticism'. [109]

Alternatives

There are examples of very negative alternatives for women everywhere outside the Western world. Mele, in an African report, writes that 'The Holy books of the two major religions most Nigerians practise state that [if] God created woman out of man, God has enunciated that man provides protection for the woman, while the woman submits totally to the headship or leadership of the man'.[110] We have, in other words, come from a very fundamentalist understanding of race and gender that still exists in some parts of the world as we speak. So we have made progress. But is this partial progress enough? Of course not, we need action to get equal opportunity to rewards at work everywhere.

On the practical front, equal opportunity for women could follow some achieved examples. The punishing choice between paid work or children should not be the only option for women. Companies and the state should provide childcare; they should provide excellent, innovative and attractive childcare that is free to all children. In Norway since 1975, there have been excellent systems of free childcare that all countries could emulate. Their childcare includes day care for under school age children with good opportunities for development and activity in close understanding and collaboration with the children's home. It is legislated that childcare should be educationally oriented with teaching staff that are 'trained preschool teachers'.[111] These childcare conditions provide a realistic basis for women to achieve the first steps toward equality at work.

Increasing the number of women on boards in Norway is also a state priority, with the Norwegian parliament bringing in new laws to enforce affirmative action if the companies themselves do not voluntarily bring more women onto their board.[112] Sanctions will be applied and they 'won't just be a slap on the wrist'.[113] By 2007, all limited liability 'companies will have to disclose satisfactorily in their annual reports details of pay levels for male and female employees, and the number of women in managerial positions and on the board'.[114]

Feminism stopped applying praxis: using a theory of rights and female inequality to form the basis of a fight back for women at work. Recent theory such as post structuralist feminism came from academics in the 1980s and it was too focused on the psychological and the subjective states of women. Problems of working-class women, their work and motherhood, were never a strong priority of the post-feminist movement, but have become even less so. Heath and Potter argue that 'the real reason the women's movement is losing momentum [is that] third wave feminism does not answer women's present or future needs because patriarchy is still firmly in control and 'post-feminists such as 'Camille Paglia, Katie Roiphe and Rene Denfield, Naomi Wolf ... are out of touch'.[115] These women 'rail against second-wave feminists who continue to portray women as unconscious victims' as being 'unwittingly indoctrinated into the phallocentric language of patriarchy'. Paglia criticises the 'infantile whining about America, men and capitalism', for what these post-feminists want is for women to have 'an ethic that stresses not collective victimisation, but personal responsibility and individual achievement'.[116] Heath and Potter's rejoinder is that 'it is hard not to be suspicious about the political motivations of a small group of white, attractive, media-friendly, well-educated women suggesting that women's oppression is a state of mind, and that the solution is to not fight but to enthusiastically join the cut-throat world of capitalist individualism'.[117]

Another facet of post-feminism is identity politics or the *politics of difference*.[118] Identity politics means that only gender is a causal factor of sexism and what happens to women in work is the result of their gender. Behind this politics of gender difference is a post-structuralist denial of what they call unifying categories because they associate these categories with 'a Marxian analysis that relies on systemic logics with "class relations" or "capital accumulation" motivating the central explanatory dynamic. Instead, post-structuralist feminists have emphasised the emancipatory possibilities of fragmentation, deconstruction, difference, and multiplicity, along with contradiction and incommensurability'.[119] One of the most familiar slogans emerging from this way of thinking is the demand that no groups should 'speak for another group'.[120] By contrast, the Marxist argument is that we only have collective power through the strike; this is the only thing that hurts capitalists, so we must act together. This means not putting female needs any higher or lower than others' exploitation in the fight against capital.

Conclusion

This chapter provides evidence to show that women and ethnic minorities are systematically being kept outside of top business partly because of historical factors limiting their participation in the paid workforce and because of their socialisation into failure, but primarily because of institutionalised sexism. Female directors, like male directors, are capitalists so it is nearly impossible to present a sympathetic case for their being exploited rather than exploiters, but they do have an interesting position of being exploited exploiters. The root of their problem is that capitalism itself is further disempowering women generally and using divisions to further restrict women's access to resources. The dynamic of this drive for competitive advantage demands divisions such as that of women against men for less pay and more perks. The logic of capitalism is to use gender exploitation, a by-product of class relations, to advance capitalist interests. A key part of this has been the segmentation of the labour force. By dividing male and female work into different occupational areas and rewarding them with differential pay rates, women experience an unequal access to power and rewards. For, though women have been making slow incursions into senior executive and directors' positions, they are most often in low paid, part-time or casual work with consequently weaker access to unions and weaker unions. Corporate profits in Australia have increased, as evidenced by the record share of profit recorded in Australian national income in

2005 and in the record low ratio of wages to profits.[121] Sexism has played some part in the maintenance and growth of these profits for the ruling class, but it is not at the core of the reproduction of capitalism and ruling class power. In the future, when women will conceivably make more advances into positions of ruling-class power, there is no guarantee that this will mean that they will turn around and contribute to the ending of the exploitation of working class women and men.

We were told that women are the cheapest, most easily exploited forms of labour, so whilst capital should be gender blind and make way for all available top talent (the feminist argument), gender is used to divide labour. Post-feminism and identity politics are not helping women in their united stance of dismissing class politics and class struggle and trying to bring back a gender-centred theory of individualism. We do not want an ideal of justice for women that focuses on the greedy individual.[122]

One final point: I would have liked to be able to extend this chapter to look at ethnic minorities' mobility in to ruling class work but was prevented by the almost complete lack of any evidence. There would seem to be no indigenous directors on top Australian boards and no evidence to support there are any Maori directors on top New Zealand boards either. There are a very gradually increasing number of Asian directors on top Australasian boards but they are usually operating from their home Asian countries, Singapore or Hong Kong. In future this will no doubt be an area of big change — and, it is to be hoped, research.

Notes

[1]   See Chapter 3.
[2]   See Chapter 6.
[3]   Bagwell, S. (1996a), 'Women make Slow Progress', *Australian Financial Review*, Friday, 26 April, p. 9.
[4]   Still, L. (1993), *Where to From Here? The Managerial Woman in Transition*, Sydney, Business and Professional Publishing; Still, L. (1997), 'Glass Ceilings and Sticky Floors: Barriers to the Careers to Women in the Finance Industry' Westpac and Human Rights Commission; Sinclair, A (1994), *Trials at the Top, Chief Executives talk about Men, Women and The Australian Executive Culture*, Parkview, University of Melbourne Press: Summers, A (1975), *Damned Whores and God's Police: the Colonisation of Women in Ringwood, Australia*, Penguin; Curtin J. & M. Sawer (1996), 'Gender Equity and the Shrinking State: Women and the Great Experiment', (ed.s) F. Castles, R. Gerristen & J. Vowles, *The Great Experiment Labour Parties and Public Policy Transformation in Australia and New Zealand*, Sydney, Allen and Unwin.
[5]   Summers, A. (2003), *The End of Equality: Work, Babies and Women's Choices in 21st Century Australia*, Sydney, Random House. ABS (2006), *Employee Earnings, Benefits and Trade Union Membership, August 2005*, Cat. No. 6310.0, Canberra, March.
[6]   Nicholls, K. (2005), 'Women in the boardroom', *Business Sunday Nine MSM* Saturday, 17 September, 2005, http://businesssunday.ninemsn.com.au/article.aspx?id=63145.
[7]   Nicholls, K. (2005).

8   The gender gap information is found in ABS [2005] 6302 Average Weekly Earnings, Australia 17/11/2005 located also in Todd, T. & Eveline, J. (2005), 'Gender Pay Equity: It's Time (Or Is It?),' [Accessed 1 January, 2006].http://www.lmsf.mq.edu.au/wmer/papers/trishtodd.pdf.

9   Pocock, B. & Alexander, M. (1999), 'The Price of Feminised Jobs: New Evidence on the Gender Pay Gap in Australia', *Labour and Industry*, 10(2), pp. 88.

10   Brown, K. & Ridge, S. (2002), 'Moving into Management: Gender Segregation and its effect on Managerial Attainment', *Women in Management Review*, v.17 n.7, pp. 318–27.

11   Brown, K. & Ridge, S. (2002), pp. 318–327.

12   Gaines, M. & Endicott, C. (1994), 'Women Stymied by Sharp Salary Gender gap', *Advertising Age*, v.65 n. 51 p. S1 (2) 5 December.

13   Rewritten in Murray, G. (2003), 'New Zealand Women Lawyers at the End of the Twentieth century in New Zealand', (eds.) G. Shaw and U. Schultz, in *A Challenge to Law and Lawyers: Women in the Legal Profession*, Hart Publishing, Oxford.

14   EOWA (2004), Australian Census of Women Board Directors Australian Government Equal Opportunity for Women in the Workplace Agency, http://www.eowa.gov.au/information_centres/media_centre/media_releases/2004_austra lian_women_in_leadership_census/factsheet_board_dir.doc.

15   Bagwell, S. (1996a). Note: Korn/Ferry International (NYSE:KFY) is an executive recruitment group conducting over 100,000 senior-level searches for clients worldwide.

16   Murray, G. (1993-1997), *Economic Power in Australia ARC Project*, Respondent 73.

17   Still, L. (1993); Still, L. (1997).

18   Still, L. (1993); Still, L. (1997).

19   Mohan, N. & Ruggiero, J. (2003), 'Compensation differences between male and female CEOs for publicly traded firms: a nonparametric analysis', *Journal of the Operational Research Society* Dec. v.54 i12 p. 1242 (7).

20   Todd, T. & Eveline, J. (2006).

21   Whitehouse, G. (2004), *Pay Equity — 20 years of change and continuity* School of Political Science and International Studies, University of Queensland, Human Rights and Equal Opportunity Commission. webfeedback@humanrights.gov.au.

22   Bell, L. (2005), 'Women-Led Firms and the Gender Gap in Top Executive Jobs', *Institute for the Study of Labour* (IZA) in its series IZA Discussion Papers, n.1689.

23   Hickman, B. & Gunn, M. (2000), 'New Class Divide': Rich and Poor Women', *The Australian*, 21 June (4), 1.

24   Masterman-Smith, H. (2006), *Hidden Seeds: a Political Economy of Working Class Women in Campbelltown (NSW)*, PHD, and University of Western Sydney.

25   Carbon, D. (1996), 'Aiming for the Board', *The Courier Mail*, Saturday, 24 August, 1996, p. 1, section 1.

26   Summers, A. (2003).

27   Thornton, M. (2002), 'Sexual Harassment Losing Sight of Sex Discrimination', *Melbourne University Law Review*, August v.26 i.2 p. 422 (23).

28   AAP (1996), p. 28.

29   Moran, S. (2006), 'Rude Awakening for Female Bankers', *The Australian Financial Review*, Friday, 10 February, p. 80.

30   Moran, S. (2006), p. 80.

31   Thornton, M. (2002), pp. 422 – 45.

32   L'Estrange, N. (1996), quoted in Carbon, D. (1996), p. 1, s. 1.

33   L'Estrange, N. (1996).

34   R. Wilson, quoted in Jackson, S. (1995), 'Witch-Hunt', *The Australian*, 1-2 April, p. 1.

35   ABS, (2001), Australian Social Trends 2001, Family — Family Formation: Older mothers, p. 1. http://www.abs.gov.au/Ausstats/abs@.nsf/0/48699b8e9bfa2629ca256bcd0082556a? Open Document.

[36]   ABS (2002), Australian Social Trends 2002 Family — Family Formation: Trends in childlessness *Australian Bureau of Statistics.*

[37]   Nicholls, K. (2005), 'Women in the boardroom', Business Sunday *Nine MSM* Saturday, 17 September, 2005 http://businesssunday.ninemsn.com.au/article.aspx?id=63145

[38]   Thornton, M. (2002,), pp. 422 – 45.

[39]   Moran, S. (2006), p. 80.

[40]   Moran, S. (2006), p. 80.

[41]   Holmes a Court, J. (1995), Janet Homes A Court Interview with Don Argus, *Australian Financial Review Magazine* pp. 8–13.

[42]   Thornton, M. (2002), pp. 422 – 45.

[43]   Summers, A. (2003).

[44]   Summers, A. (2003).

[45]   Murray, G. (1990), Respondent 44.

[46]   Murray, G. (1993–1997), Respondent 90.

[47]   Wolf, N. (1990), *The Beauty Myth,* London, Chatto & Windus, Vintage, p. 167.

[48]   Wolf, N. (1990), p. 167.

[49]   Murray, G. (1984), *Sharing in the Shingles,* MA Thesis, Auckland University.Respondent 50, p. 189.

[50]   Sinclair, A. (1994), p. 24.

[51]   Finklestein, J. (1996), *After a Fashion*, Melbourne, Melbourne University Press.

[52]   Finklestein, J. (1996).

[53]   Epaminondas, G. (1996), 'Unsuitability, Why Corporate Australia is Getting Undressed' *The Weekend Australian Review*, 13-14 April, pp. 1–2.

[54]   Epaminondas, G. (1996), pp. 1–2.

[55]   Epaminondas, G. (1996), p. 2.

[56]   Sinclair, A. (1994).

[57]   Bronson, P. (1995), *The Bombardiers*, London, Martin Secker and Warburg.

[58]   Crisp, L. (2006), 'Cranky Horse Loving Lazarus had a big heart,' *The Weekend Australian Financial Review*, 2 January, p. 19.

[59]   Walsh, R. (2006), 'The Bully and the Charmer', *The Weekend Australian Financial Review*, 2 January, p. 18.

[60]   Summers, A. (1975), Sinclair, A. (1994).

[61]   Thomson, P. & Graham, J. (2006), *A Woman's Place is in the Boardroom*, London, Palgrave Macmillan.

[62]   Quoted in Fox, C. (2006), 'Family First, not Everyone wants to Go it Alone. Many women are opting for the Companies Big enough to give them what they Want', *Financial Review, Boss*, February, p. 54.

[63]   Melymuka K. (2000), 'Wanted: A Workplace without a 'Ceiling', *Computerworld*, 24 January, p. 50 (1).

[64]   Li, C. & Wearing, B. (2004), 'Between Glass Ceilings: Female Non-executive Directors in UK quoted companies,' *International Journal of Disclosure and Governance*, October, v.1 i.4 p. 355 (17).

[65]   Ministry of Children and Family Affairs Norway (2005), 'Rules regarding gender balance within boards of Public Limited Companies', Press release n.: 05116, 8 December.

[66]   Alvarez, L. (2003), 'Norway vs. the Glass Ceiling', *New York Times*, 14 June.

[67]   Sources:
    1   Baue, W. (2004), 'Women Directors Rare Even in Developed Economies, According to First Global Study', 20 April.
        http://www.socialfunds.com/news/article.cgi/article1399.html.
    2   Based on data in the 2001 Catalyst Census 'Women Board Directors of the Fortune 500'. See Baue, W. (2004).

3   Total percentage combines figures from the Top 200 Industrial/Service companies and those from the Top 100 Financial companies. See Baue, W. (2004).

4   Information from the 1999 CWDI Report: Women Board Directors of Australian Companies, publication of Corporate Women Directors International. See Baue, W. (2004).

5   Information from the 2000 CWDI Report: Women Board Directors of South Africa's Top Publicly-listed and Government-owned Companies, publication of Corporate Women Directors International. See Baue, W. (2004).

6   Based on data in 'Women on Boards of Britain's Top 200 Companies 1997, an initiative of the Opportunity 2000 Campaign'. See Baue, W. (2004).

7   Pomeroy A. (2004), Public Affairs Report July 2004. [ann.pomeroy001@msd.govt.nz].

8   Figures based on estimate in Women on Boards of Britain's Top 200 Companies (1997).

9   Information from the 1998 CWDI Report: Women Board Directors of Japanese Companies, publication of Corporate Women Directors International. Data for 2,396 companies listed in 8 Japanese stock exchanges. The 842 OTC companies in the report were excluded from the comparison because information for the U.S., U.K., and Canada include only the equivalent of the Japanese listed companies.

68   EOWA (2004).

69   Thornton, M. (2002), pp. 422 – 45.

70   Thornton, M. (2002), pp. 422 – 45.

71   Pomeroy A. (2004).

72   Pomeroy A. (2004).

73   Pomeroy A. (2004).

74   Gilding, M. (1997) *Australian Families: A Comparative Perspective,* Addison Wesley Longman Melbourne, p. 14.

75   Murray, G. (1992–1997), Respondent 98.

76   Murray, G. (1992–1997), Respondent 90.

77   Keating quoted in Bagwell, S. (1996b), p. 13.

78   Sinclair, A. (1995), p. 9.

79   Murray, (1990), *New Zealand Corporate Capitalism,* Respondent 106, p. 214.

80   Bagwell, S. (1996c), 'Backlash in Cycle of Blame', *Australian Financial Review,* Wednesday, 19 July, p. 16.

81   Illing, D. (1996), 'Intrepid Brown takes up Gauntlet', *The Australian,* Wednesday, 3 April, p. 14.

82   Murray, G. (1992–1997), Respondent 90.

83   Murray, G. (1992–1997), Respondent 23.

84   Murray, G. (1992–1997), Respondent 91.

85   Murray, G. (1992–1997), Respondent 91.

86   Berger, P. & Luckman, T. (1996), *The Social Construction of Reality: A Treatise in the Sociology of Knowledge,* New York, The Free Press.

87   Murray, G. (1992–1996), Respondent 75.

88   Murray, G. (1992–1996), Respondent 95.

89   Sinclair, A (1994), p. 9.

90   Bagwell, S. (1997e), 'The Two Sides of George Trumball', *Australian Financial Review Net services,* Friday, 9 May, pp. 1– 6.

91   Bagwell, S. (1997e), pp. 1– 6.

92   Bagwell, S. (1997e), pp. 1– 6.

93   Dowd, M. (2006), *Are Men Necessary? When Sexes Collide,* Sydney, Hodder.

94   Jackson, S. (1995), 'Witch-Hunt', *The Australian,* 1-2 April, p. 1.

95   Jackson, S. (1995), p. 1.

96   Jackson, S. (1995), p. 1.

97   Jackson, S. (1995), p. 1.
98   Pringle, R. (1988), *Secretaries Talk: Sexuality, Power and Work*, Sydney, Allen and Unwin.
99   Sinclair, A (1994), p. 21.
100   Murray, G. (1990), p. 213.
101   Bagwell, S. (1996b), 'New Women's Group Out to Mobilise the Economy', *Australian Financial Review*, 6 January, p. 5.
102   Bagwell, S. (1996b), p. 5.
103   Australian Council Of Businesswomen contact [ACOB], acob@bigpond.com.
104   Bagwell, S. (1996a), 'Women make Slow Progress', *Australian Financial Review,* Friday, 26 April, p. 9.
105   CEW website http://www.cew.org.au/.
106   Murray, G. (1992–1997), Respondent 75.
107   Summers, A. (2003).
108   Goward, P. (2002), 'Balancing Baby and the Budget', *The Age*, 12 December, p. 1.
109   Bagwell, S. (1997d), 'Williams Accused of Move to Muzzle Rights of Commission', *Australian Financial Review Net Services,* Friday, 31 July, pp. 1–2.
110   Mele, P. (2005), 'Women Empowerment, a Catalyst', *Africa News Service*, 22 September, P. NA.
111   Ministry of Children's and Family Affairs (2006), Child Care Institutions in Norway, Act n. 19 of 5 May 1995 on Day Care Institutions with Regulations, (Day Care Institutions Act), http://odin.dep.no/bld/english/doc/legislation/acts/004005-990082/dok-bn.html#1.
112   Mørkhagen, P.L. (2005), 'The Position of Women in Norway' Ministry of Foreign Affairs http://odin.dep.no/odin/engelsk/norway/social/032091-991525/index-dok000-b-n-a.html.
113   Fouché, G. (2005), 'A Woman's place is ... on the Board', *The Guardian*, Wednesday 10 August, http://money.guardian. co.uk/work/story /0,1456,1546251, 00.html.
114   Fouché, G. (2005).
115   Heath, J. & Potter, A. (2005), 'Feminism for sale: find out the Real Reason the Women's movement is Losing Momentum, and why Political Action is the only Way to take Down the Patriarchy', *This Magazine*, May–June v.38 i.6 p. 20(8).
116   Quoted in Heath, J. & Potter, A. (2005), p. 20(8).
117   Quoted in Heath, J. & Potter, A. (2005), p. 20(8).
118   See Sinclair, A (1994), p. 9; Gibson-Graham, G. (1994), 'Beyond Patriarchy and Capitalism: Reflections on Political Subjectivity' in B. Caine and R. Pringle (eds.) *Transitions New Australian* Feminisms, Sydney, Allen and Unwin.
119   Biewener, C. (1999), 'A Postmodern Encounter: Poststructuralist Feminism and the Decentering of Marxism', *Socialist Review*, p. 3.
120   Gardiner, A. (1998), Pers com.
121   ABS [Australian Bureau of Statistics] (2005), *Australian National Accounts*, n. 5209.0 http://www.abs.gov.au/
122   Thornton, M. (2002), pp. 422 – 45.

Chapter 8

Back to the Future

This final chapter draws together the key points from the previous chapters and discusses their implications for power and policy. It reiterates the central argument that, yes, Australasia does have ruling classes in the sense that they are a disparate segment of society that holds most of the economic and political power, and this situation is sustained in various ways by the state. Then the chapter asks whether a corporate-centric organisation of society is the best way to organise our lives and is it in our interests that decisions about the common good are made by the market? Is this Liberal understanding of the market, as neutral, rational and benign, correct? Are we to trust to the social responsibility of a businessman who seeks:

> his own gain, and he is in this, as in many other cases, led by an invisible hand to promote an end which was no part of his intention ... nor is it always the worse for the society that it was no part of it. By pursuing his own interest he frequently promotes that of society more effectively than when he really intends to promote it?[1]

Adam Smith's quote translated to the present means that your greed ensures that the two-year-old boy next door has food, the widow down the road has clean sanitation, your grandmother gets to hospital in an ambulance, and the child you see from your four-wheel-drive goes to school because the money you make in your company, on the stockmarket, in the boardroom or at blackjack will somehow trickle down to them to make sure they are provided with these necessities of life.

The Arguments So Far

The book started by challenging the common assumption that Australasian societies are classless. The evidence shown indicates that this is a self-serving proposition and that it is wrong. There is a ruling class in both Australia and New Zealand; they are internally and nationally divided but they have a common interest in getting more profit from labour. They are therefore supporters of economic liberalism. Economic liberalism is an ideology that has always sustained, supported and been used to spread (through lobby groups and think tanks) capitalism and capitalist interests. The reason that the ruling class wants and needs to rule is they benefit most from the circuit of capital. This circuit is the underlying dynamic of all corporations and it is fed by competition and exploitation. Competition is intrinsic to this process and it led to the need for more markets that were found in the colonies. The convicts and the working class were capital's reluctant colonial pioneers. But, because of the high demand for their labour, workers were able to demand and receive better social, political, civil and welfare rights in the colonies than they had 'back at home'. However, company boards of directors are still monopolised by men. These male directors act as the political conduit and cadre of their class, but they do not enjoy the ultimate power and control of top companies. This belongs to the banks due to their managed investment funds. So despite the real chances for democracy in postcolonial Australia and New Zealand, the ruling classes have managed to avoid any real redistribution of their wealth and continue to sustain their own very high level of living even in a period when global economic growth is diminishing.

So let us begin this conclusion by looking at some problems associated with this corporate success for the Australasian ruling classes.

Global Growth and the Invisible Hand

Global corporate economic growth is not happening in the ways that those who advocate the unfettered market would have us believe it should. In *Growth and Development in the Global Political Economy,* O'Hara gives a global overview of the company from 1960 to 2002, using 2003 World Bank World Development indicators to show that even within the world of the company operating in the unfettered market, investment and productivity are not working out in ways they should.[2] American top 500 TNC profit rates have declined from 7.7 in the 1950s to 3.3 in the 2000s. That is, in 50 years the decline has been 4.4 per cent. Globally, the decline is slightly less: for the top 500 transnational corporations, the profit rate has gone from 5.48 per cent in the 1950s to 1.8 per cent in the 2000s. That is a decline of 3.68 per cent in 50 years. Real global investment growth rate has declined 5.6 per cent in 42 years and, after taking account of population growth, the real per capita global GDP growth rate has declined 2.19 per cent in 42 years.[3]

Why has GDP fallen globally in this way and will it hit Australasia? The easiest answer is that, within capitalism, all countries operating a capitalist system experience business cycles.[4] Marx suggests that, over the long term, the rate of profit must fall because of an imbalance between the organic composition of capital and the rate of surplus value created. To explain this, it is necessary to look at what the falling rate of profit is. When capitalists invest in constant capital (such as buildings, machinery, raw materials) in preference to investing in variable capital (that is, capital spent on wages of productive workers) maybe because of increased demands for higher wages, then less value is created. As labour creates value this causes problems. There is a tendency to spend less on labour and more on labour-saving technological processes (e.g. robotic car plants) and therefore within what is called the organic composition of capital, the ratio between constant and variable capital favours constant capital.[5] The rate of profit is a function of two variables, the organic composition of capital and the rate of surplus value. The rate of profit rises as the rate of surplus value rises, but it falls if the rate of surplus value is constant and the organic composition of capital rises. Whilst the organic composition of capital can keep expanding (through further automation), the rate of surplus value cannot for it has finite limits. Marx's hypothesis is that the rate of profit will decline over the long term, though it may fluctuate in the short or medium period and that the crises provoked by recessions and depressions lead to class struggle.

Table 8.1: Global Investment, Profits and GDP 1950s to 2002

Element	1950s %	1960s %	1970s %	1980s %	1990s %	2000–02 %
US Top 500 TNC profit rate	7.71	7.15	6.30	5.30	4.02	3.30
Global Top 500 TNC profit rate	5.48	3.68	3.38	2.66	2.46	1.80
Real global investment growth rate			7.78	3.97	3.24	2.24	2.10
Real per capita global GDP growth rate			3.19	2.11	1.27	1.05	1.00

Key: TNC = transnationals corporation.
Modified source: O'Hara, (2005) p. 77.

Long economic declines are likely to eventuate in cyclical crisis. Marx writes eloquently about the inevitability of economic crises under capitalism. 'As a matter of principle in political economy, the figures of a single year must never be taken as the basis for formulating general laws. We must always take the average of six to seven years, a period in which modern industry passes through successive phases of prosperity, over production and crisis, thus completing the inevitable cycle'.[6] His understanding was that these periodic crises of over-production were cyclical since the first identifiable crisis of over-production in the world market for industrial goods in 1825. Capitalist economic crises are crises of over-production of commodities (exchange values), as opposed to pre- and post-capitalist economic crises, which are essentially crises of under-production of use-values (the use it has to an agent or buyer).[7] Under capitalist crises, expanded reproduction (economic growth) is stopped because of excessive amounts of production forming mountains of commodities with no buyers. This leads to an accelerating movement of firms collapsing, workers being fired, fewer sales, fewer orders for raw materials and machinery, new redundancies, new contraction of sales of consumer goods etc.

Mandel writes that crisis is a process of contraction in which 'prices (gold prices) collapse, production and income is reduced, capital loses value. At the end of the declining spiral, output (and stocks) has been reduced more than purchasing power. Then production can pick up again and as the crisis has both increased the rate of surplus-value (through a decline of wages and a more 'rational' labour organisation) and decreased the value of capital, then the average rate of profit increases. This stimulates investment. Employment increases, value production and national income expand and we enter a new cycle of economic revival, prosperity, overheating and the next crisis. No amount of capitalist (essentially large combines and monopolies) 'self-regulation', no amount of government intervention, has been able to suppress this cyclical movement of capitalist production.[8]

O'Hara further comments that, globally, economic crises have frequently appeared in the period between 1945 and 1997.[9] Using a 21-nation sample, from 1945 to 1971, he shows that there have been 37 currency crises, one banking crisis and one 'twin crisis', accounting for approximately 5.2 per cent of GDP lost on average.[10] In 1973–97, the numbers accelerate, with 86 currency crises, 26 banking crises and 27 'twin crises, accounting for approximately 7.8 per cent of GDP lost on average'. Of all the banking crises between 1970 and 1999, 6 per cent were in the 1970s, 35 per cent were in the 1980s, and 59 per cent were in the 1990s (primarily in the developing nations and former planned economies).[11]

Table 8.2: Unevenness in Sections of the World Economy 1998-2000 (%)

1998 – 2000	World	Western Europe	North America	Asia & Pacific	Latin America	Sub-Saharan Africa	East & Central Europe	Mid-East & North Africa
FDI inflow (% world total)	100	37.4	34.8	10.1	5.8	2.3	0.8	0.3
Exports (% world total)	100	33.1	30.4	19.7	6.0	1.0	2.9	4.0
Home base of top 100 TNCs	100	53	25	20 (Japan = 16)	2	0	0	0

Key: FDI = Foreign Direct Investment.
Source: O'Hara, P. (2005) p. 73.

Table 8.2 shows how rich Western European and North American countries have been investing in themselves or others like themselves. They were not taking their money to either Eastern Europe or Africa. Nor were they exporting in large quantities to poorer nations. Nor were there any of the top 100 TNCs based outside Western Europe, North America, Asia and the Pacific or Latin America.

The greatest impact of the lack of global growth has been on global class relations. Classes have experienced a rising polarisation of income inequality throughout nations. O'Hara illustrates this using the Gini coefficient to measure inequality: with a figure of 1 meaning that one person has all the national income.[12] The figure 0 means that income is shared equally. The figures in the USA from 1970 to 2001 show an increase from 0.39 to 0.44. In the UK from 1975 to 1999, there was an increase in the Gini coefficient from 0.26 to 0.36. In Australia an increase in the Gini coefficient from 0.32 to 0.45 between 1968 to 2000; in Chile from 1971 to 2000 an increase in the Gini coefficient from 0.46 to 0.57; increase in the former Eastern European communist block from 1988 to 1997 an increase in the Gini coefficient from 0.28 to 0.35; and current communist China from 1987 to 2001 an increase in the Gini coefficient from 0.20 to 0.45. No country selected by O'Hara has been immune from this global trend toward a polarisation of income and class.

So globally there is evidence to show that free market capitalism is not working as well for companies as it was, it does not work so well for poor countries and in the period of entrenched economic liberalism, from the 1970s, there has been a deepening polarisation of class into rich and poor.

What about Australasian companies and the lives of the individuals within them?

The Company and the Invisible Hand

For some Australasian companies 2005 was a year of record profit share. They have gone against the world trend and made very large corporate profits. Figure 8.1 shows that Australian company profits have escalated since 2000, and although they plateaued in 2004 it was at the high level of almost 27 per cent.

We saw in chapters two, three and four that individual ruling class Australasians have benefited enormously from their corporate positions by receiving inordinately high salary packages, access to elite primary, secondary and tertiary education, to elite clubs, to important government and non government committees and to public honours. They owe all of this to the corporation and its organisational structure that allows them to acquire the profit (surplus value) from the labour of workers. Or do they? Some writers argue that the corporation, understood in its entirety, is by definition psychopathic and therefore it may follow that the individuals are its victims?[13] Who and what are responsible for the system that we have? For possible solutions, some fictional and some actual anecdotal evidence collected over seventeen years of interviewing top businessmen and women in four different countries will be critically looked at.

Figure 8.1: Profit Share of Total Factor Income

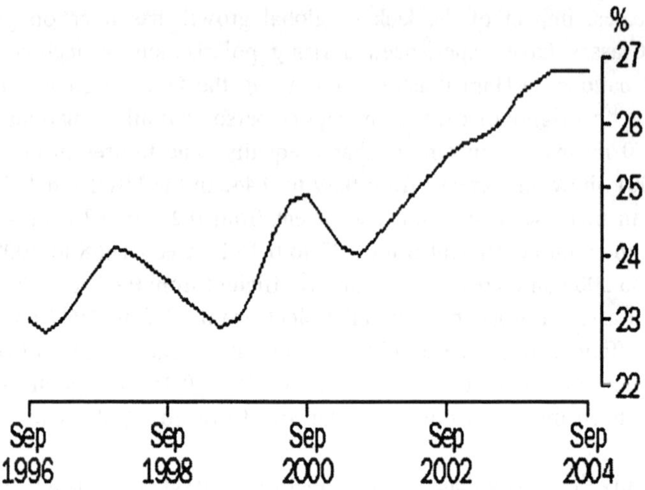

Source: *Australian National Accounts: National Income, Expenditure and Product, cat. no. 5206.0*

Fictional Man and the Man Behind the Invisible Hand

Recent controversy over the nature of corporations and the nature of corporate man or woman has arisen because of a rush of books,[14] documentaries[15] and films[16] portraying them as psychopathic. What exactly is a psychopath? A working definition is a person who has 'a personality disorder characterised by extreme callousness, who is liable to behave antisocially or violently' in getting his or her own way, and then expressing no empathy for the suffering they cause for others.[17]

Corporations, it is argued, produce these people 'because the corporation is legally-mandated to put profit above everything, even the public good, and of course it is an extraordinarily competitive environment at the same time, that frequently manifests a kind of behaviour in individuals which we wouldn't see them express to their families ... they have a different set of values within corporate culture than they do in society at large'.[18] So how can we recognise this suit-wearing psychopath? According to Jennifer Abbot and Mark Achbar, they are identifiable by their insincerity, arrogance, untrustworthiness, manipulativeness, insensitivity, remorselessness, shallowness, lack of empathy, and a tendency to blame others for things that go wrong. They have a low frustration tolerance and are therefore impatient with things, erratic, unreliable, unfocused, and selfish, parasitic and take advantage of the goodwill of people they work with.[19] Other recent writers of this literature describe corporations as psychopathic-incubators, arguing therefore that the most successful individuals within these corporations will be those most fully developed as psychopaths.[20]

Po Bronson in 1995 was amongst those at the beginning of a trend of ex-financiers doing a warts-and-all literary exposure of the manic, funny, tough, everyday reality of financiers.[21] His brilliant fictional description of the life of bond traders, or what he called bombardiers, in their blitzkrieg market battlefield gave us Sid Greeder and his trading office at Atlantic Pacific Corporation (AP). The story moves fast through their fictional world centring on profit fantasies that they help initiate. These profit fantasies are realised and lost as the reader becomes painfully aware of how deadly their own and the rest of the world's dependence on these very ordinary men and women and their extraordinary acts of self-interested lunacy, is.

Tom Wolfe, in 1987, wrote the not too dissimilar *Bonfire of the Vanities* in a corporate-critical, funny vein.[22] This is another fast meter-paced story of ambition, racism, and individualism that manifests as greed and psychopathy.

Non-Fictional Man and the Man Behind the Invisible Hand

How real are the lives of these frenetically hard-driven capitalists as drawn by Bronson and Wolfe? If we read Doug Henwood's *Wall Street*, which is a parallel piece of political economy but in an academic form, we can see how close Bronson's fictional world is, in particular, to the real world of the market.[23] Henwood, like Bronson and Wolfe, starts from his own experience of the New York money market. Henwood locates himself as beginning in:

> a small brokerage firm in downtown Manhattan ... My title was secretary to the chairman, which meant not only that I typed his letters, but also that I got his lunch and went out to buy him new socks when he'd left his old ones in a massage parlor. And I studied the place like an anthropologist, absorbing the mentality and culture of money ... One morning, riding the elevator up to work, I noticed a cop standing next to me, a gun on his hip. I realized in an instant that all the sophisticated machinations that went on upstairs and around the whole Wall Street neighborhood rested ultimately on force. Financial power, too, grows out of the barrel of a gun.[24]

And then Henwood continues in easily accessible language to deconstruct the world of finance. Among his concluding thoughts is that 'corporations should be placed increasingly under a combination of worker, customer, supplier and public control'.[25]

Another critical, non-fictional account of the corporate world is Peter Elkind and Bethany McLean's book, *The Smartest Guys in the Room: The Amazing Rise and Scandalous Fall of Enron.*[26] This retells the 2000 story of Enron, the seventh largest company in the US, and worth $60 billion. A company lauded in the 1990s stock boom by money magazines making stars out of the directors, chairperson

Ken Lay and CEO Jeff Skilling. Ken Lay, a personal friend of President George Bush, was chairperson of the highly successful energy company.[27] And it leaves us with disbelief as to how it could happen that this energy company allegedly stole close to $11 billion from the citizens of California and Washington with the support and assistance of government officials, and left twenty thousand workers jobless with no superannuation or pensions as the executive directors 'in its last days looted the retirement funds of its employees to buy a little more time'.[28]

Another non fiction work that looks into the consequences of the modern corporation, rather than the bad behaviour of corporate executives and directors, is Morgan Spurlock's *Don't Eat This Book: Fast Food and the Supersizing of America,* in which he documents his own eating of nothing but McDonalds' food for a month. He makes his stomach-expanding journey into an entertaining and lively documentary that discusses his body's experience as a starting point for a critical inquiry into the corporation's influence on national health, nutrition, trendy diets, the spread of obesity, the history of processed food and chemical additives, food marketing and branding, government regulation and the internationalisation of the American fast food lifestyle.

These fictional and non-fictional critics of the corporation lend weight to placing blame on its fundamental structural problems as creating poor individual behaviour.

The State and the Invisible Hand

Companies want — and need — to be in very close working relationships with the state. When they do not feel that the state is acting as their friend, as in periods when there is a social democratic form of government, then they are uneasy. This is how a leading BCA director describes this anxiety in one of these periods in the early 1990s:

> We need better coordination between sectors and associations in the research and development of the private sector view. We need to have the people that are in government advisory groups to network with private sector researchers so that they can get support in their advisory roles. They need to use better mechanisms to pool the experiences gained in individual firms and bi-lateral councils so that we can give this information to government and also organise current information in a more rigorous way.[29]

The top business lobby is always producing directive material for state politicians to read, but sometimes they go further with their strongly recommended statements. For example, Hugh Morgan the ex-BCA President (2003–2005), on their website congratulated and directed the Howard government after its 2004 Coalition electoral victory to use this 'unique opportunity to tackle major issues that remain outstanding or are now emerging that could act as a brake on future growth'.[30]

The agenda to remove the brakes on corporate growth included:

Ongoing tax reform to ensure that business and individual tax regimes remain an incentive, not a barrier to growth and competition; further de-regulation of workplace relations that underpins sustained productivity gains; addressing skill shortages that threaten to curtail growth in key sectors of the economy; further reforms to education and training that improve Australia's skill competitiveness; and developing a national population policy that addresses Australia's ageing and shrinking workforce, with specific emphasis on skilled immigration.[31]

Here are the issues that the BCA believes Australians must learn to accept as fundamental to achieving Australian greatness:

a regulatory system which is consistent with international trends (as determined by the WTO), the removal of the taxation disincentive to Australian headquartered firms to grow overseas ... All Australians need to understand the cost of meeting our commitments under the Kyoto Protocol may be a lower economic standard of living.[32]

On the New Zealand Business Roundtable website there is the suggestion in an article called *Does Privatisation Work?* that one of their primary needs, is still — for more privatisation. The state needs to sell more of their assets and the ruling class need to acquire them.[33] Big business does not yet have enough for its needs; its needs are a black hole of constant demand. Roger Kerr, in an open letter to deputy Labor Party leader Dr Michael Cullen, urged him to keep on moving with privatisation. When he rhetorically asked 'Hasn't it all been done in New Zealand?' he answered himself with 'Not at all', for he is afraid of:

Re-nationalisation of accident insurance, the government's purchase of an 82 percent stake in Air New Zealand, the start-up of Kiwi bank, the Auckland rail corridor buyback and the planned Wellington buyback, the pressures for the government to buy back parts of the main rail network, and the planned build up of assets in the government's New Zealand Superannuation Fund. At the same time, New Zealand (alone, it would appear, amongst the OECD countries) has had a comprehensive ban on privatising SOEs [state owned enterprises].[34]

During the last 30 years, economic liberal formulated policy and its support from economic liberal think tanks and top business lobby groups have fuelled the New Zealand and Australian states. The type of business commitment that they espouse is encapsulated in the words of this New Zealand finance director:

Government should be limited and what we want is a very minor government. It doesn't really matter in a way how you get hold of it ... I think unfortunately you need one body to cope with crime. I think most of us would rather be subject to one bully than be subject to lots of bullies and that's really how governments develop. I think personally you need one bully, but hopefully he's a very restrained bully and very limited in powers. But there's where I see the problem of government ...

Interviewer: The state is also providing an infrastructure for business ...

Well, what ever, I don't want to be protected by the state. The bloody state should get out of our lives. Fortunately, it has been a lonely old place for me to be for a long while, but the world is coming through a learning curve and people who think like I do are having a bit of fun watching the states fall over. The state is a pox on society.[35]

The 'bloody state', or the more accurately the 'bloody welfare state', is dying the death of economic liberal strangulation. Susan George quotes a major capitalist of her acquaintance saying 'for my group of companies, globalisation is being able to produce where I want, when I want and to buy and sell whatever I want without the restrictions ... coming from labour laws and social conventions'.[36] This is what is new about globalisation; it is the marketing and packaging of economic liberal policy insertions into governments, through overt and covert means. The ruling class has used economic liberal ideas powerfully knowing how to work with the state to achieve their ends.[37] We are experiencing a corporate culture that invites, indeed demands, that the rich relentlessly pursue profit, use their expensive legal firms and tax havens to avoid paying taxes that sustain welfare systems and continue demanding further privatisation so that corporations can reach the control of areas of society from which they were formerly excluded and continue to make even larger profits. On a global scale the result is an imbalance of resources that leaves the 'poorest 52 nations in the world to continue to service debt at the rate of $28,000 every minute'.[38]

Therefore the question becomes: how do we get out of this? The first thing to do is name the problem and the causes and identify who is to blame and why.

Is the Individual to Blame?

Are the individual capitalists to blame? After all, they are the ones that are reaping the benefits of high living? Their response would be 'No, we are not to blame. We are workers who just work smarter than you do — we all have to work.' We are kept in work by fear. Fear is what motivates us and keeps us in the system. We fear being unemployed; we fear losing our homes; we fear losing our old age nest eggs; we just fear not having enough money; and we also fear being seen with too much money and being known as a conspicuous consumer or worse, we fear not being seen as a conspicuous consumer (his Porsche is bigger than my Lexus). Money is everything in this corporate world that we live in, as expressed by this New Zealand director:

We are about making money. We think that business is making money. If it were a yacht race then the only place we can operate is first, and the only place in business is winning ... that's the wonder of the market economy in that inducements only need to be self interest and the outcomes are collectively useful.[39]

Are we all in danger of waking up each morning saying 'who am I going to kill today?' as the director in chapter seven said.

What motivates metaphoric corporate killers? Caulkin addresses this question, 'What exactly motivates men to strive for salaries way beyond utility, common sense, or ordinary greed?'[40] Why was the median pay of American CEOs in 1998 $3.09 million a year? He opts for an easy answer and blames the greedy individual and accuses him or her of addictive behaviour. 'We're talking about addiction here ... pay is not rational but a throwback to primal human make-up'.[41] Competition is the key here. We compete because we need to, to live and then we do not know how to stop. Like compulsive eaters, gamblers or drinkers, non-executive and executive directors keep asking for more as their fair share of income.

What is fair? Is it fair that Australian executives' income went from 22 times to 74 times the average Australian's wage (from 1992 to 2002) with no positive correlation between the amount that an executive director earns and the profitability of the company?[42] The following ABS data shows that the wage share of workers in national income has decreased since 1996. This is in inverse relation to the increase in company profits seen in Table 8.2.

Figure 8.2: Wages Share of Total Factor Income

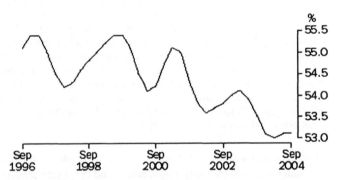

Source: Australian National Accounts: National Income, Expenditure and Product, cat. no. 5206.0

With this fall in wages earned is a corresponding fall in the social wage with the implementation of economic liberal policies that demand payment for what was previously a right paid through taxation. Workers now pay heavily for education, childcare and health care.[43]

So is the individual to blame for this growing inequity everywhere? The Nuremberg defence that I just 'accepted the boss's orders' has only a limited life. We have to question and bring about change.

Is the Business System to Blame?

Is it the nature of the business and the business environment that creates psychopathic behaviour? This is how Amanda Sinclair explains it:

> What we're in at the moment is a very high-pressure environment, when a lot of the traditional sorts of structures that contained us and protected us are being stripped away. So, a lot of us are involved in virtual interactions and high-speed interactions and a situation that one theorist has described as 'overburdening', which means giving people more tasks than they can possibly do, but under the mistaken belief that putting them under that sort of pressure is going to bring out the best in them. Bosses are routinely asking us to deliver far more than we can possibly do. So what that means is that we then see leaders as being overly-demanding, overly-pressured, controlling, unable to let go, unable to delegate, unable to see the bigger picture, and so on. Because, of course, they're in a system too. They're reacting to pressures higher up from themselves. [44]

Henwood's words about the complexity of new and changing financial instruments were echoed in an interview of an extremely experienced finance director who said: [45]

> The problem for a financier is that people are continually creating new instruments because there is an opportunity that they can see. There is an opportunity and they are playing on a market. The entrepreneurs are creating new ideas that create new values. Ten years ago in Australia there were rigid rules and regulations. The moment that you pull down the fences you create a new environment. We used to have rigid control on credit by the reserve bank. With deregulation this is no longer there. That meant an explosion of money and speculation. Ultimately, someone loses in that process and they did. It's imprudent. If there is excess money supply you have to post credit restrictions on the central bank and say to the banks we are going to take five per cent of your deposits into a special fund ... There is a penalty, which the market should pay.
>   I think my feelings on free markets have covered the gamut. I suppose I have gone from socialist to right of Genghis Khan and back again. I think that a lot of people are questioning internationalisation of a lot of things. [46]

Insiders, both for and against the market, recognise capital's anarchic nature and the roller coaster ride that this puts corporations and corporate leaders through. An extreme enthusiast for this system phrased the same sentiments differently:

> You can blame the banks ... it had nothing to do with Australia or New Zealand alone — it was worldwide. The boards were weak and they just let the entrepreneurs charge off and commit the company to God knows what without any other review from anyone else at all. Well it was just a crazy period of psychological aberration which communities go through every twenty years or so. People who spent money then started to realise that it doesn't grow on trees and needed to take a bit more care of it. The banks lose their money and the investors lose theirs and everyone goes back to fundamentals ... You cannot be a cowboy ... and go around wasting other people's money unless both shareholders and bankers are stupid enough to lend or give it to you ... the climate of 1987 was when that happened. The public are now screaming and

yelling about the entrepreneurs leading companies astray. But they would come to annual board meetings and they'd treat the entrepreneurs like Messiahs. No wonder it went to their heads — there were all these people wanting to throw money at them. You only had to float a company called X limited and preferably not say anything about it all. List its stock and people oversubscribed it ten thousand times and the shares doubled over night. We had dozens of examples of that. That's not the entrepreneurs' fault; that's the crazy stupid investors' fault.

Interviewer: Maybe there should be some structural controls?

No for Christ's sake — it's the market. People have to learn![47]

Another victor from the system, George Soros (1930–), the chairperson of Soros Fund Management, said:

Markets are amoral; the untrammeled pursuit of self-interest does not necessarily serve the common interest, and military might may not be right. This may be an unpopular thing to say ... but it is nevertheless true.[48]

Marx writes in *Capital* that the inner logic of capitalism is not only that we work for our needs, or even profit, but also that we work to accumulate capital. 'Accumulate, accumulate; that is Moses and the Prophets'.[49] Capitalists must work this way as a result of competition. Competition fuels this terrifying cascading logic: just as detailed in the circuit of production in chapter one; we start from capital — we add value to a commodity from the mix of labour and machines (creating surplus value) — we get more capital — more accretion of surplus value — more accretion of capital and so on. We have to make more money so we can buy up other businesses that are struggling and keep away competitors who may try to take over or control our business. 'Without competition, the fire of growth would burn out'.[50]

The irony is that the resources to make profit are finite. We need to reinvent the corporation in our own image.

Reinventing the Corporation

This book has provided a body of evidence to show that directors and owners of companies, and the company itself are a dominant force in our society with no social, civil or political accountability. Corporate members are making decisions that affect our daily lives with no elected mandate to do so. How do we change this situation? The first possibility is to ...

Leave it up to the Corporations to Change

Economic liberals believe that making money for themselves leads to others also profiting. More enlightened members of corporations see that this does not work and that there is a need to be more proactive. They think that corporations need to practise corporate social responsibility (CSR). They also think they will do this if companies can see that there is something obviously in it for them. The CEO of Westpac, David Morgan, is quoted as saying, 'Corporate social responsibility may be difficult to put into a financial model but it is vital for bottom line drivers such as employee commitment and retention'.[51] So CSR is possible to sell to companies if it helps gain profit. Change will also come if there is enough public pressure put on directors and executives to accept a socially responsible position as in the James Hardie Industries' case, where workers dying from work related asbestos conditions have been subject to a company behaving in a 'grossly irresponsible way'.[52] They have acted, after a very bitter public fracas with the union and the victims, sufficiently honorably to give $4.5 billion back to the people damaged.

The problem becomes whether it is possible to get agreement amongst all companies that profit increase depends on meeting CSR for all stakeholders, direct and indirect. There is a discernable low level of grudging commitment to this. CSR 'has become an industry; it has been hijacked by the consultants and government. But at the end of the day, it's a hygiene issue — it's about doing basic business properly'.[53] But the bottom line on CSR remains Milton Freidman's when he said 'the social responsibility of business is to increase its profits'.[54] In chapter one, we saw how if one company does not exploit its workers by driving down wages and conditions, then another company will, and this will undercut them and make their survival tenuous. For good economic reason, companies cannot be trusted to put their social and civic responsibilities over their mandate to make profits in this competitive business world.

So if the corporations cannot be trusted to be responsible because this has to interfere with their profits, where else can we look?

The State Must Improve the Regulatory Environment

In the existing capitalist environment, the state must take responsibility for the behavior of the corporation. This does not mean setting up a community–business partnership to advance corporate social responsibility with the aim that businesses 'meet or exceed the ethical, legal, commercial and public expectations that society has of business' and then having the government representative (like Robert Gerard) fail to attend any of the meetings for the first eighteen months.[55] That is to kill the partnership with intentional neglect. This would mean, in the words of Bakan, that 'government regulation should be reconceived and relegitimated as the principal means for bringing corporations under democratic control and ensuring that they respect the interests of citizens, communities and environments'.[56]

If the community and the environment are to survive, corporations, that is, all companies from every part of the world, must be licensed to operate in Australia and New Zealand. The community should be able to determine the content of the corporate licence democratically. There should be options that are agreed to and voted on as to who will be awarded licences to operate. Deciding criteria should be based on what the company does for the public good. Controversial companies should be subject to public debate as to whether their services are necessary for the community. Other possible criteria could be the company's willingness to give at least 10 per cent of its profit to a fund available for public projects. A licence could also be conditional on having corporate board leadership that is taken from both genders, mixed races and the unions.

Recreate a Healthy Public Sphere

Privatisation has been used to greatly enhance the wealth of corporations. We need to reclaim public spaces and utilities now in the hands of private business. The logic of economic liberals and public choice theorists that only business can organise public utilities is wrong — indeed, not only wrong, but it has proved to be dangerous. The privatisation of essential services has led to endangering life. There is the example of the Victorian Ambulance Service.[57] Premier Jeff Kennett's economic liberal government outsourced the essential ambulance service 'to generate cost savings in response to concerns of the Government over the level of government contributions to the Service and its ongoing financial viability'.[58] What Victorians received in return was increased length of response times (threatening human life), the introduction of inadequate technologies (computers that broke down and gave inaccurate information), corruption and debt. This is the part of the summary finding made by the official judicial review of the ambulance service in its report to parliament:

> The breadth and consistency of these deficiencies were such that it would be an oversimplification to suggest that they all could be solely attributed to managerial incompetence. A continual hands-off approach by the management of the Service showed a total disregard for the Government's outsourcing guidelines and repeated concerns raised in the Parliament regarding the Service's operations. In effect, management created an environment that enabled the consultancy firms to reap significant financial benefits without challenge ... Total payments to the firm eventually amounted to over $1.5 million.[59]

Privatisation in the form of the corporatisation of government departments and their functions, contracting out state work, selling state assets and enforcing user pay regimes on the physically and mental ill have compounded the daily burdens of low paid workers.

We need to take initiatives like the Swedes did with their wage earner funds. Swedish funds obliged firms to put part of their profits back into the community in the form of capital for labour-managed investment funds. According to Phillip Whyman, this 'legitimised collective investment funds as a potential instrument of economic democratisation, while demonstrating that pursuit of social goals need not undermine allocative efficiency'.[60]

Confront International Economic Liberalism

Commitment to economic liberal policy regimes, bringing about more intrusive capitalism, has taken us to the brink of social, political, civil and ecological disaster. Sweezy argues that although scientists globally are aware of the seriousness of the ecological threat facing the planet, they still are not at the point of acknowledging that the cause of the threat is capitalism itself.[61] The ecologists and the public at large do not yet see that capitalism must be replaced by a social system that puts the life giving capacity of the earth as its first and highest priority, not the ad hoc decision-making that is done on the basis of private profit for a few individuals.

Fred Argy suggests that if we want to change the degree of inequity that currently exists in economic liberal saturated Australasian society, we need to urgently implement an egalitarian reform agenda that includes:

1. equal opportunity as its central goal;
2. a gradual implementation over a five year period (no Whitlam-like revolution);
3. the sacrifice to be seen as equitably borne;
4. effective marketing. [62]

Politically, this means economic liberalism has to be replaced as the rationale for state policy. We could license corporations, particularly media corporations, by putting the onus on them to prove their public utility.[63] Most of all we want to be freed from the dictatorship of the corporation and learn to make the important decisions ourselves, imaginatively, in ways that will energise democracy.

Vitalise Democracy

We need to start by accepting that the corporation is people making a profit for themselves. This is not democratic. This is what a finance capitalist said about democracy:

> It's a strange system. I mean, after all, why should a kid of eighteen have the same value of vote as I do for example…I don't think you need a democracy…because the trouble with democracy is that democracy is arrogant. There is no country in the western world that's had even fifty per cent of its people equal. In Australia and New Zealand they're all minority governments. Well they're normally minority governments, so the arrogance of democracy is that 30 or 40 per cent of the people vote for a whole pastiche of conflicting things. With one vote every three years creating a government that's allowed, that's got some divine right, to do any bloody thing it likes. That's effectively the myth of democracy and it creates very arrogant governments because they say, 'We're elected by the people, we're allowed to do anything we like to the bloody people.[64]

Once we reject rule by the corporate leaders and rule of the corporation — that is, rule for the corporation, by the corporation, and of the unelected and unaccountable corporate members — then we can move on. We can move back to the source and ask what did Perikles, for example, mean by democracy?[65] What does real rule for the people, by the people and of the people mean? We have to look for new democratic solutions. We have to think imaginatively about sustainable economic systems that are not capitalist.

Robinson, a science fiction writer, commented in a what-is-in-the-future speculative interview that 'it will be tough if the egalitarian movement fails in this next 30 years to control the runaway train of global capitalism'.[66] Ours is a system wedded to competitive acquisition at the individual and corporate level, motivated by the idea of leaving something material, particularly money, for your son or daughter. There is a 'hierarchy in which a small percentage of the people on earth benefit enormously more than they need to benefit from the work of all, and that the majority of those living today, as well as the biosphere itself, is suffering as a result'.[67] We should look at the living systems outlined by Marge Piercy in *Women in the Edge of Time*[68] and Ursula LeGuin in *The Dispossessed*. Both writers try in different ways to work out what LeGuin calls 'ambiguous utopia', whereby society is flawed but evolving laterally into new unexplored humane dimensions.[69] These are attempts to visualise how pacificist, socialist and anarchist society would function in reality. We also have to be aware of the dystopias that warn us like Aldous Huxley's *Brave New World* and George Orwell's *1984*. Much of what they said is prescient and still very relevant to our lives today.

In our pursuit of democracy, public opinion needs to be made aware of the 'ridiculous hierarchy that rules us now and the institutionalisation of greed, hatred, and delusion' that they practise.[70] Susan George at the Social Forum in Porto Alegre, Brazil, in 2005 said to 15,000 people gathered there, 'Dear friends and comrades look around you ... What we have accomplished in this brief moment is breath taking. So we should see our presence here and the very existence of this movement and the World Social Forum as a great victory'.[71]

David Peetz argues in his book, *Brave New Workplace* that cooperation has been a key feature of our social and evolutionary advance, and collectivism and the will to form unions is a natural outcome of this impulse. 'Organising workers is really part of the broader task of organising and empowering people in all situations to confront, rather than acquiesce to, those who have power'.[72]

Conclusion

Class offends our feelings of belonging and egalitarianism, which is why it is largely denied in Australian and New Zealand. We believe class is dead because we have been told so often. If we experience class, we deny it — not just because it is hurtful but because we know that it cannot exist in a democratic society like our own. So this is the first and last thing that this book challenges. This book says that class in Australia and New Zealand is alive and well and has been since the colonies started. Class, and its pernicious complexities and limiting of possibilities, has to be brought back squarely on to the agenda. Given the evidence compiled in this book — excessive income packages to corporate bosses that have no relationship to positive corporate performance, glass ceilings, sticky gumboots for all except white, upper middle class men, networking in clubs that have monetary and clothing prohibitions that seem excessive — we can now say definitively that class privilege exists in Australia and New Zealand. We can say that inter-generational privilege in business is backed up by structural systems such as elite educational institutions, clubs and government bureaucracy. Now we have to think about ways that we can change it. Rising class inequality, not just between nation states but also within nation states, ensures that class struggle is maintained. Whilst there is the necessity for class struggle, capitalism is never safe.

Notes

[1]   Smith, A. (1776), B.IV, Ch.2, Of Restraints upon the Importation from Foreign Countries in paragraph IV.2.9, *An Inquiry into the Nature and Causes of the Wealth of Nations*, [originally published London, J. Dent].

[2]   O'Hara, P. (2005), *Growth and Development in the Global Political Economy*, Routledge, Oxford.

[3]   O'Hara, P. (2005), p. 84.

[4]   There is a large business cycle literature. Some of the more creditable work includes Mandel, E, (1972), *Late Capitalism*, London, New Left Books; Kondratieff, N. (1928), *The Long Wave*, New York, Richardson and Synder; Schumpeter, J. (1934), *Business Cycles: a theoretical, Historical and Statistical Analysis of Capitalist Process*, New York, McGraw Hill; Freeman, C. (1984), *Long Waves in the World Economy*, London, Frances Pinter; Keynes, M. (1936), *The General Theory of Employment, Interest and Money*, London, McMillan; Marx who wrote of 'spirals of capital', Marx, K. (1983), *Capital*, vol. 1, Moscow, Progress Publishers.

[5]   Marx, K. (1983), pp. 181–93.

[6]   Marx, K. (1975), *Free Trade*, Collected Works, London, Lawrence and Wishart, 6.458.

[7]   'A quantitative relation is the proportion in which values in use of one sort are exchanged for those of another sort, a relation constantly changing with time and place. Hence exchange-value appears to be something accidental and purely relative'. Marx, K. (1977), p. 139.

[8]   Mandel, E. *Karl Marx*, 'Chapter VIII. The Laws of Motion of the Capitalist Mode of Production', [Accessed 3 January, 2006]. http://www.marxists.org/archive/mandel/19xx/marx/ch08.htm.

[9]   O'Hara, P. (2005), p. 56.

[10]   O'Hara, P. (2005), p. 56.

[11]   O'Hara, P. (2005), p. 56.

[12]   O'Hara, P. (2005), p. 58.

[13]   See Bakan, J. (2004), *The Corporation: The Pathological Pursuit of Profit and Power* New York, Free Press, Korten, D. (2001), *When Corporations Rule the world*, Bloomfield, Kummarian Press, CT, Moore, M. (2001), *Stupid White Men*, New York, Harper Collins; Stiglitz, J. (2002), *Globalisation and its Discontents*, New York, W.W. Norton.

[14]   See Bakan, J. (2004), Korten, D. (2001), Moore, M. (2001); Stiglitz, J. (2002).

15 Walker, I. (2004), 'Psychopaths in Suits', *Australian Broadcasting Association, Background Briefing Sundays* at 9.10am, repeated Tuesdays at 7.10pm, Sunday 18 July.

16 Abbot, J. & Achbar, M. (2004), *The Corporation*, a documentary based on Bakan's book op cit, with a cast including R. Anderson, M. Barlow, C. Barrett, N. Chomsky, N. Klein, L. McCabe, M. J. Mikael, R. Monks, M. Moore, V. Shiva.

17 Online dictionary http://www.allwords.com/query.php?SearchType=0&Keyword =psychopath&Language=ENG&NLD=1&FRA=1&DEU=1&ITA=1&ESP=1&v=97962 753.

18 Abbot, J. & Achbar, M. (2004).

19 Abbot, J. & Achbar, M. (2004).

20 See Bakan, J. (2004), quoting interview with Mark Kingwell, p. 135.

21 Bronson, P. (1995), *The Bombardiers*, London, Martin Secker & Warburg.

22 Wolfe, T. (1987), *Bonfires of the Vanities*, New York, Farrar, Straus & Giroux.

23 Henwood, D. (2005), *Wall Street*, http://www.leftbusinessobserver.com/WSDownload .html [Accessed 23 January, 2006].

24 Henwood, D. (1997), p. 1.

25 Henwood, D. (1997), p. 320.

26 Elkind, P. & McLean, B. (2003), *Smartest Guys in the Room: The Amazing Rise and Scandalous Fall of Enron* New York, Portfolio Trade.

27 St Clair, J. (2004), 'Teresa Heinz Kerry Gets Lay' *Counterpunch'*, 4 October, [Accessed 20 January, 2006] http://www.counterpunch.org/stclair10272004.html.

28 Ebert, R. (2005), Enron: Smartest Guys in the Room, Review, *Chicago Sunday Times*, http://rogerebert.suntimes.com/apps/pbcs.d11/article?AID=/20050428/Reviews/5041300 4/1025.

29 Murray, G. (1993–1996), *Australian Economic Power* ARC Research, Respondent 93.

30 Morgan, H. (2004), 'BCA President, Press release 'Statement on the Federal Election', 10 October, http://www.bca.com.au/content.asp?newsID=96793.

31 Hugh Morgan, (2004).

32 Schubert, J. (2005), 'Let's make Australia great: Business Council of Australia' *Business Council of Australia* http://www.bca.com.au/content.asp?staticID=search.

33 Berry, P. (2004), 'Does Privatisation Work?' *New Zealand Business Roundtable*, n.5.http://www.nzbr.org.nz/documents/speeches/speeches-2002/speech_collection_2002.pdf p. 79.

34 Kerr, R. (1997b), *Seven Deadly Sins of the Twentieth Century*, New Zealand Post College of Business, Jubilee Lecture, Palmerston North, Massey University, 6 August.

35 Murray, G. (1993–1997), Respondent 91.

36 George, S. (2005), Interview, TNI Home Page, p. 2. [Accessed 12 January, 2006], http://www.tni.org/interviews/booktalk.htm.

37 Harvey, D. (2003), *The New Imperialism*, Oxford, Oxford University.

38 George, S. (2005).

39 Murray, G. (1990), Respondent 14, p. 157.

40 Caulkin, S. (1998), 'Rise Six Million Dollar Man' *Electronic Mail and Guardian*, 29 September, pp. 1–3).

41 Caulkin, S. (1998), pp. 1–3.

42 See Chapter Three.

43 Peetz, D. (2005), 'Coming soon to a Workplace near you—the new Industrial Relations Revolution,' *Australian Bulletin of Labour* June v.31 i.2 p. 90 (22).

44 Sinclair, A (1994), *Trials at the Top, Chief Executives talk about Men, Women and The Australian Executive Culture*, Parkview, University of Melbourne Press, p. 9.

45 Henwood, D. (2005).

46 Murray, G. (1993–1996), Respondent 93.

47 Murray, G. (1993–1996), Respondent 91.

48 Soros, G. (2002), *On Globalisation*, New York, Public Affairs, p. 165.

49   Marx, K. (1983), p. xxiv–853.
50   Mandel, E. *Karl Marx*, [Accessed 4 January, 2006]
     http://www.marxists.org/archive/mandel/19xx/ marx/ch08.htm.
51   David Morgan (2006), quoted by Cornell, A. 'The Business and Politics of People
     behaving Badly', *The Australian Financial Review*, Monday, 16 January, p. 45.
52   Simpson, D. (2005), 'Why tougher laws won't make Corporates more responsible' Dell,
     http://www.onlineopinion.com.au/view.asp?article=2903.
53   David Morgan quoted by Cornell, A. (2006), p. 45.
54   Friedman, M. (1970), The Social Responsibility of Business is to Increase it Profits",
     New York Times Magazine, 13 September.
55   Cornell, A. (2006), p. 45.
56   Bakan, J. (2004), p. 161.
57   Pha, A. (2001), 'Hands off Ambulance Services' *The Guardian*, 22 August,
     http://www.cpa.org.au/garchve4/1059amb.html
58   Victorian Government [Accessed 2006] 'Audit by the Attorney general of the Victorian
     Ambulance service',http://www.audit.vic.gov.au/old/sr49/ags4901.htm.
59   Victorian Government [Accessed 3 January, 2006].
60   Whyman, P. (2004), *An Analysis of Wage-Earner Funds in Sweden: Distinguishing
     Myth from Reality Economic and Industrial Democracy*, v. 25, n. 3, pp. 411–45
61   Sweezy, P. (1998), 'The Communist Manifesto' today', *Monthly Review*, May, v.50 n.1,
     p. 8.
62   Argy, F. (2003), 'Achieving Equality of Opportunity', online 29 December, 2005
     http://evatt.labor.net.au/publications/papers/96.html
63   Katz-Fishman, W. & Scott, J. (2005), 'Comments on Burawoy: a view from the Bottom
     Up', *Critical Sociology*, v. 31, pp. 371–374.
64   Murray, G. (1993–1996), Respondent 91.
65   See J. Coleman on Perikles, Coleman, J. (2000), *Political Thought from Ancient Greece
     to Early Christianity*, Oxford, Blackwell, pp. 19, 27–30, 32, 38, 40, 44.
66   Robinson, K. (2002), 'Kim Stanley Robinson, Science Fiction Socialist', *Monthly
     Review*, July–August, v.54 i.3, p. 87.
67   Robinson, K. (2002), p. 87.
68   Piercy, M. (1979), *Woman on the Edge of Time*, London, Women's Press Ltd.
69   LeGuin, U. (1974), *The Dispossessed: an Ambiguous Utopia*, New York, Harper.
70   Robinson, K. (2002), p. 87.
71   George, S. (2005).
72   Peetz, D. (2006), *Brave New Workplace*, Sydney, Allen & Unwin, p. 181.

Bibliography

Abbot, J. & M. Achbar (2004), *The Corporation*, based on Bakan's book op cit, with a cast including Ray Anderson, Maude Barlow, Chris Barrett, Noam Chomsky, Naomi Klein, Luke McCabe, Mikela J. Mikael, Robert Monks, Michael Moore, Vandana Shiva.

Abbott, T. (2003), *The Left the New Elites* according to David Flint, transcript from PM ABC, Friday, 1 August, 6.39pm.

ABS [Australian Bureau of Statistics] (1991), *Year Book Australia*, Canberra, Commonwealth Government Printer.

ABS [Australian Bureau of Statistics] (1992), *Feature Article — Leading Indicators of the Australian Business Cycle: Performance over the Last Two Decades*, n. 1350.

ABS [Australian Bureau of Statistics] (1993), Australian and New Zealand Standard Industrial Classification (ANZSIC), Government ABS Catalogue n. 1292.0.

ABS [Australian Bureau of Statistics] (1994), 'Australian Social Trends', n. 4102.0.

ABS [Australian Bureau of Statistics] (1997), Australian Standard Classification of Occupations, (ASCO), ABS Catalogue No. 1220.

ABS [Australian Bureau of Statistics] (2001) Australian Social Trends 2001 Family — Family Formation: Older mothers, p. 1.
http://www.abs.gov.au/Ausstats/abs@.nsf/0/48699b8e9bfa2629ca256bcd0082556a?OpenDocument

ABS [Australian Bureau of Statistics] (2002), Children, Australia: A Social Report, n. 4119.0

ABS [Australian Bureau of Statistics] (2003), Australian System of National Accounts, ABS Catalogue n. 5204.

ABS [Australian Bureau of Statistics] (2005), Industry gross value added, chain volume measures ($m)(a), 5204.0 Australian System of National Accounts, Table 9. (Canberra Time), 16 November.

ABS [Australian Bureau of Statistics] (2004), *Measuring Australia's Economy Section 1. Measuring Economic Activity*, n. 1360,
http://www.abs.gov.au/Ausstats/abs@.nsf/94713ad445ff1425ca25682000192af2/70ef43745fa5445eca256cbf0017216f!OpenDocument.

ABS [Australian Bureau of Statistics] (2005), *Average Weekly Earnings Survey*, n. 6302.0 http://www.abs.gov.au/.

ABS [Australian Bureau of Statistics] (2005), *Australian National Accounts*, n. 5209.0 http://www.abs.gov.au/.

Australian Council of Business women [ACOB], acob@bigpond.com

Adcock, G. & Dennis, E., Eastal, S., Huttley, G., Jermiin, L., Peacock, J. Thorne, A. (2001), 'Mitochondiral DNA sequence in Ancient Australians: Implications for Modern human Origins', *Proceeding of the National Academy of Sciences of the United States*, 16 January.

Adele L.H. & Whyte; S. J. Marshall; G. K. Chambers (2005), 'Human Evolution in Polynesia' *Human Biology*, April, v.77, i.2, p. 157(21).

Aglietta, M. (1979), *A Theory of Capitalist Regulation: the US Experience*, London, Verso.

Allen, L. (2006), 'Hats Off a Master Tactician' *The Weekend Financial Review*, 2 January, p.4.

Alvarez, L (2003), 'Norway vs. the Glass Ceiling', *New York Times*, 14 June.

Annual Report Alliance (2004), [Accessed 18 February, 2006], http://www.alliance.co.nz/PDF/Alliance%202004% 20Report.pdf

Annual Report Fletcher Building, (2005), [Accessed 6 February, 2006], http://www.fletcherbuilding.co.nz/ 2_investing_ in_us/downloads /2005%20FBL%20 Annual%20Report.pdf

Annual Report Foodstuffs (2005), [Accessed 8 February, 2006], http://www.foodstuffs.co.nz/OurCompany/AnnualReports/.

Annual Report Fonterra (2005), [Accessed 23 February, 2006], http://www. Fonterra.com/content/shareholderfinancial/resultsreports/default.jsphttp://www.fonterra.

Annual Report J. P. Morgan (2005), [Accessed 14 February, 2005], http://www. jpmorgan.com/cm/cs?pagename=Templates/Page/JPMorgan_CacheHome&cid=801036 9.

Annual Report PPCS (2005), [Accessed 2 February, 2005], http://www. ppcs.co.nz/default.asp?p=about-us/ownership/].

Annual Reports (2004, 1999, 1992), Top 30 Australian Companies [Accessed online July-August 2005] http://www.connect4.com.au/cgi-bin/subs/login.cgi

Argy, F. (2003), 'Achieving Equality of Opportunity', [Accessed online 29 December, 2005] http://evatt.labor.net.au/publications/papers/96.html

Armstrong, W. & Bradbury, J. (1983), 'Industrialisation and Class Structure in Australia, New Zealand and Canada 1870–1980', in Wheelwright and Buckley, *Essay in Political Economy of Australian Capitalism,* Frenchs forest, NSW, Australia, Australian and New Zealand Book Company.

Australia Stock Exchange [ASX] (2003), *Principles of Good Corporate Governance and Best Practice Recommendations,* March http://www.asx.com.au/about/pdf/ASX Recommendations.pdf

Australian Dictionary of Biography [Accessed 4 July, 2005] http:/Gutenberg.net.au/.

Australia Stock Exchange [ASX] (2000), 'ASX 2000 Survey', 8 February, http:www. asx. com.au.

Australian Election Study [AES] (2004), computer file, *Australian Social Science Data Archives*, Australian National University, Canberra

Australian Financial Review (2004), Economic Thermometer, 4 June, p. 57

Australian Government (2006), Culture and Recreation Portal website [Accessed 21 January] http:/www.cultureandrecreation.gov.au/articles/australianhistory/

Australian Historical Statistics (1987), http://www.library.usyd.edu.au/subjects/government/ austhist.html#WPTOHTML11.

Bagwell, S. (1996a), 'Women Make Slow Progress', *Australian Financial Review,* Friday, 26 April, p. 9.

Bagwell, S. (1996b), 'New Women's Group Out to Mobilise the Economy', *Australian Financial Review*, 6 January, p. 5.

Bagwell, S. (1996c), 'Backlash in Cycle of Blame', *Australian Financial Review,* Wednesday, 19 July, p. 16.

Bagwell, S. (1997a), 'Westpac Backs off the Survey that it Backed', *Australian Financial Review, Net Services,* Wednesday, 26 February, p. 19.

Bagwell, S. (1997b), 'Fair Go' Keeps Executives Pay in Check', *Australian Financial Review Net Services,* Monday, 19 May, pp. 1–3.

Bagwell, S. (1997c), 'What Keeps Chief Executives Awake at Night', *Australian Financial Review Net Services,* Thursday, 24 July, pp. 1–3.

Bagwell, S. (1997d), 'Williams Accused of Move to Muzzle Rights of Commission', *Australian Financial Review Net Services,* Friday, 31 July, pp. 1–2.

Bagwell, S. (1997e), 'The Two Sides of George Trumball', *Australian Financial Review Net Services,* Friday, 9 May, pp. 1–6.

Bakan, J. (2004), *The Corporation: The Pathological Pursuit of Profit and Power,* New York, Free Press.

Baran, P. & Sweezy, P. (1968), *Monopoly capital: an essay on the American Economic and Social Order,* New York, Monthly Review Press.

Barnes, R. & Ritter, E. (2001), 'Networks of Corporate Interlocking 1962–1995,' *Critical Sociology,* 1 July, v.27, n. 2, pp. 192–220.

Barry, P. (1993), *The Rise and Rise of Kerry Packer,* Sydney, Bantam Books.

Bateman, D. (2002), *New Zealand Official Yearbook,* Wellington, Government Printer.

Baue, W. (2004), 'Women Directors Rare Even in Developed Economies, According to First Global Study', 20 April, [Accessed 25 July, 2005] http://www. Social funds. Com /news/article.cgi/article1399.html.

BCA website http://www.bca.com.au/content.asp?staticID=about.

Bean, C., & McAllister, I., Gibson, R., Gow, D. (2004), *Australian Election Study,* The Australian National University au.edu.anu.assda.ddi.01079.

Beder, S. (1999), 'Fronting the Environment, the Intellectual Sorcery of Think Tanks,' *Arena Magazine,* June, p. 30.

Bedggood, D. (1980), *Rich and Poor in New Zealand,* Wellington, Allen and Unwin.

Bell, L. (2005), 'Women-Led Firms and the Gender Gap in Top Executive Jobs', *Institute for the Study of Labour* (IZA), series IZA Discussion Papers, no. 1689.

Berger, P. & Luckman, T. (1996), *The Social Construction of Reality: A Treatise in the Sociology of Knowledge,* New York, The Free Press.

Bergmann, V. (2004), 'Active Citizenship against Marketisation: Community Resistance to Neo Liberalism' in G. Patmore (ed.) *The Vocal Citizen: Labor Essays 2004,* Melbourne, Australian Scholarly Publishing, pp. 116–31.

Berle, A. & Means, G. (1932), *The Modern Corporation and Private Property,* New York, Macmillan.

Berry, P. (2004), 'Does Privatisation Work?' *New Zealand Business Roundtable,* no.5.http://www.nzbr.org.nz/documents/speeches/speeches-

Biewener, C. (1999), 'A Postmodern Encounter: Poststructuralist Feminism and the Decentering of Marxism', *Socialist Review,* p. 3.

Block, F. (1987), 'Revising State Theory' in *Essays in Politics and Postindustrialism,* Temple University Press, Utah.

Booth, D. (2001), *Australian Beach Cultures: The History of Sun, Sand, and Surf,* London, Frank Cass.

Borch, M. (2001), 'Rethinking the Origins of Terra Nullius', *Australian Historical Studies,* v. 32, n.117, pp. 222–39.

Bourdieu, P. (1973), 'Cultural Reproduction and Social Reproduction' in R. Brown (ed.) *Knowledge, Education and Social Change,* London, Tavistock, pp. 71–112.

Bourdieu, P. (1979), *Distinction: A Social critique of the Judgement of Taste,* Harvard, Harvard University Press.

Bourdieu, P. & Wacquant, L. (1992), *An Invitation to Reflexive Sociology,* Cambridge, Polity Press.

Boyd, M. (1997), 'Feminising Paid Work', in Murray, G & Tulloch, G. Feminism: The Big Challenge for the 90s, *Current Sociology,* Trend Report, v.46, n.1, pp. 1–9.

Bramble, T. & Kuhn, R. (1999), 'Social Democracy after the long boom: economic restructuring under Australian labor 1983–1996', in M. Upchurch (ed.) *The State and Globalisation: Comparative Studies of labour and capital in National Economics,* London, Mansell, pp. 20–55.

Brawley, S. (1996), *Beach Beyond: A History of the Palm Beach Surf Club 1921–1996,* Sydney, University of New South Wales Press.

Bronson, P. (1995), *The Bombardiers,* London, Martin Secker and Warburg.

Broomhill, R. (2001), 'Neoliberalism Globalism and the Local State: a Regulation Approach', *Journal of Political Economy,* December, n. 48, pp. 115–40.

Brown, K. & Ridge, S. (2002), 'Moving into management: gender segregation and its effect on managerial attainment', *Women in Management Review,* v.17, n.7, pp. 318–27.

Bryan, D. (1995a), 'The Internationalization of Capital and Marxian Value Theory, *Cambridge Journal of Economics,* 19, pp. 421–40.

Bryan, D. (1995b), 'International Competitiveness: National and Class Agencies, *Journal of Political Economy,* v.35, pp. 1–23.

Bryan, D. (1996), *The Chase Across the Globe: International Accumulation and the Contradictions for Nation States,* Boulder, Westview Press.

Byan, D. (2000), 'The Rush to Regulate: The Shift in Australia from the Rule of Markets to the Rule of Capital', *Australian Journal of Social Issues,* November, v.35, i.4 p. 333.

Bryan, D. & Rafferty, M. (1999), *The Global Economy in Australia: Global Integration and National Economic Policy,* St Leonards, Allen and Unwin.

Buffini, F. & Kitney, D. (2005), 'Plenty of Extras in CEOs Pay packet', *Financial Review,* Wednesday 16, November, s2.

Burch, P. (1972), *The Managerial Revolution Reassessed,* Massachussetts, Lexington Books.

Burnham, J. (1943), *The Managerial Revolution,* D.C. Heath, Lexington.

Burt, R. (1992), *Structural Holes: The Social Structure of Competition*, Cambridge, Harvard University Press.

Business Council of Australia Homepage [BCA] website http://www. bca. com.au/content. asp?staticID=about.

Business Review Weekly [BRW] (1992), 'Top 1000 Companies', *Business Review Weekly*, 23 October, p. 76.

Business Review Weekly [BRW] (1998), 'Rich 200' *Business Review Weekly*, 27 May, p. 120.

Business Review Weekly [BRW] (1998), 'Top 1000 Companies', *Business Review Weekly*, 16 November, p. 120.

Business Review Weekly [BRW] (2004), 'Top 1000 Companies', *Business Review Weekly*, 11–17 November, p. 88.

Business Review Weekly [BRW] (2004), 'Rich 200' *Business Review Weekly*, 30 May, p.120.

Butlin, N. (1987), 'Australian National Accounts', in *Australian Historical Statistics*, W. Vamplew (ed), Fairfax, Syme & Weldan Associates, Broadway, NSW, v. 10.

Butterworths Law Books [Accessed online 5 July 2005] http://www. butterworthsonline. com/lpBin20/lpext.dll/bw/L8/15/corps/1?f=templates&fn=bwaltmain-j.htm&contents =yes&szPath=/bw/L8/15/corps/1.

Buttle & Wilson (1986), *Buttle and Wilson Share Registry*, December, Auckland.

Cahill, D. (2004), 'Contesting hegemony: the radical neo liberal movement and the ruling class in Australia', in N. Hollier *Ruling Australia: the Power, Privilege and Politics of the New Ruling Class*, Melbourne, Australian Scholarly Publishers, pp. 87–105.

Campbell, E.W. (1963), *Sixty Rich Families: Who Owns Australia*, Sydney, Current Book Distributors.

Carbon, D. (1996), 'Aiming for the Board', *The Courier Mail*, Saturday, 24 August, s.1, p.1.

Carmichael, G. (1992), 'So Many Children: Colonial and Post Colonial Demographic Patterns', in Saunders, K, & Evans, R. (ed.s) *Gender relations in Australia: Domination and Negotiation*, Harcourt, Brace & Jovanovich, Sydney.

Carroll, W. (2004), *Corporate Power in a Globalizing World*. Toronto, Oxford University Press.

Carroll, W. (2006), 'Mapping Global Corporate Power: a Longitudinal Network Analysis of Elite Social Organization', Durban, ISA Congress.

Carroll, B. & Alexander, M. (1999), 'Finance Capital and Capitalist Class integration in the 1990s: Networks of Interlocking Directorships in the Canada and Australia,' *The Canadian Review of Sociology and Anthropology*, August, v.36, i.3, pp. 331–50.

Carroll, W. & Carson, C. (2003), 'The Network of Global Corporations and Elite Policy Groups: a Structure for Transnational Capitalist Class Formation', *Global Networks*, v.3, n.1, pp. 29–57.

Carroll, W. & Fennema, M. (2002), Is There a Transnational Business Community? *International Sociology*, Sept 2002 v17, i.3, p. 393 (27).

Carew, E. (2006), 'Strongarm Tactics Backfire Badly in Tilt at Westpac', *The Weekend Australian Financial Review*, 2 January, p. 19.

Catalyst Census (2001), 'Women Board Directors of the Fortune 500' http://www.catalystwomen.org/ Figures based on estimate in Women on Boards of Britain's Top 200 Companies 1997.

Cathcart, M., & Burgmann, V. Connell, R. W., Mayne, S., McGregor, C. (2004), 'Class in Contemporary Australia', pp. 154-81 reprinted in Hollier, N. (2004), *Ruling Australia*, Melbourne, Victoria, Australian Scholarly Publishing.

Caughey, A.M. (1988), *An Auckland Network*, Auckland, Little Shoal Press, in Hunt, G. (2003), *The Rich List, wealth and Enterprise in New Zealand 1820–2003*, Auckland, Reed Publishers, Birkenhead Auckland.

Caulkin, S. (1998), 'Rise Six Million Dollar Man' Electronic Mail and Guardian, September v.29, pp. 1–3.

Centre for Independent Studies [CIS] website [Accessed 2 January, 2005] http://www.cis. org.au/.

Chanticleer (2006), 'Demerger Issue Looms Large', *The Australian Financial Review*, 3. January, p. 48.

Chartists [Accessed on 20 January2006] http://www.chartists.net/Transported-to-Australia

Chenoweth, N. & Maley, K. (1997), 'Australia's New Establishment' *AFR Net Services*, Saturday, 13 September, pp. 1–10.

Chief Executive Women [CEW] website http://www.cew.org.au/.

Clark, A. (2006), 'Media Giant who used Politics as an Arm of Business', *The Weekend Australian Financial Review*, 2 January, p. 3.

Clark, M. (1961), *A Short History of Australia*, New York, Mentor Books.

Clifton, S. (1999), 'A Word in Your Ear...' *Business Review Weekly*, Http:/www.*BRW*.com.au/content/130798/*BRW*06.htm.

Clune, F. (1969), 'The Scottish Martyrs', HRNSW v2 p. 826.

Cockett, R. (1995), *Thinking the Unthinkable: Think Tanks and the Economic Counter Revolution, 1931–1983*, London, Harper Collins.

Coleman, J. (2000), *Political Thought from Ancient Greece to Early Christianity*, Oxford, Blackwell.

Communications Update (1999), 'Annual Media Ownership Update', i.151, February, pp. 7–9.

Connell, R.W. (2002), 'Moloch Mutates: Global Capitalism and the Evolution of the Australian Ruling Class 1977-2002', *Overland*, n. 167, pp. 4–14.

Connell, R.W. (2004), 'Moloch mutates: global capitalism and the evolution of the Australian Ruling Class', in Hollier, N. (2004), *Ruling Australia*, Melbourne, Victoria, Australian Scholarly Publishing.

Connell, R. W. & Irving T. H. (1992), 'Yes Virginia, there is a Ruling Class', in T. Jagtenberg & P. Dalton (ed.s) *Four Dimensional Space*, Artarnon Harper Educational pp. 39–44.

Cornell, A. (2005), 'In the Belly of the Beast' *The Australian Financial Review Magazine*, p. 59.

Cornell, A. (2006), 'The Business and Politics of People Behaving Badly', *The Australian Financial Review*, Monday, 16 January, p. 45.

Coser, L. (1977), *Masters of Sociological Thought: Ideas in Historical and Social Context,* New York, Harcourt Brace Jovanovich.

Costlow, T. (2000), 'Design Automation Suffers a Gender Gap', *Electronic Engineering Times,* 19 June, p. 183.

Courier Mail (2005), 'Powerful Man Packs a Political Punch', 28 December, p. 4.

Courier Mail (2005), 'The Many Faces of an Empire Builder', 28 December, p. 4.

Crisp, F. (1970), *Australasian National Government,* Longman Cheshire, Melbourne.

Crisp, L. (2006), 'Cranky Horse Loving Lazarus had a Big Heart,' *The Weekend Australian Financial Review,* 2 January, p. 19.

Cronin, B. (2001), *The Politics of New Zealand Business Internationalisation 1972–1996,* v. 1 & v. 2. Auckland University, PhD thesis.

Cullinane, T. (1995), *The Business Roundtable in 1995,* The Spectrum Club, Rotorua, New Zealand, 12 June.

Curtin, J. & Sawer, M. (1996), 'Gender Equity and the Shrinking State: Women and the Great Experiment', (ed.s), F. Castles & R. Gerristen, J. Vowles, *The Great Experiment Labour Parties and Public Policy Transformation in Australia and New Zealand,* Sydney, Allen and Unwin.

CWDI Report (1998), *Women Board Directors of Japanese Companies,* Publication of Corporate Women Directors International.

CWDI Report (1999), *Women Board Directors of Australian Companies,* Publication of Corporate Women Directors International.

CWDI Report (2000), *Women Board Directors of South Africa's Top Publicly-listed and Government-owned Companies,* Publication of Corporate Women Directors International.

Cyert, R. & March, J. (1963), *A Behavioural Theory of the Firm,* Englewood Cliffs, N. J, Prentice Hall.

Da Silva, W. (1996), 'The New Social Focus', *The Australian Financial Review Magazine,* June, pp. 18–28.

David, A. & Wheelwright, T. (1989), *The Third Wave: Australia and Asian Capitalism,* Sutherland, N.S.W, Left Book Club Co-operative.

Davis, G. (1991), 'Agents without Principles? The Spread of the Poison Pill through the Intercorporate Network', *Administrative Science Quarterly,* n. 36, pp. 583–613.

Davis, W. (1982), *The Rich a Study of the Species,* London, Sidgwick & Jackson.

Davison, G. & Hirst, J, Macintyre, S. (2001). 'Aboriginal Resistance', *The Oxford Companion to Australian History,* revised edition, pp. 11–12.

Deans, A. (2006), 'Kerry Frances Bullmore Packer', *Bulletin,* 4 January, p. 24.

Delahunty, J. (1986), 'Pat the Knife', *Public Eyes,* n.4 October, p. 4.

Denham, J. (1993), 'The Ideas Brokers: the Impact of Think Tanks on British Government', *Public Administrator,* v. 71, Winter, pp. 491–506.

Department of Foreign Affairs Canberra (1995), No. 2 New Zealand ANCERTA — trade [Accessed 12 January, 2005] http://www.dfat.gov.au/ geo/newzealand/ anzcer/ anzcerta1 .pdf.

Devine, H. (2000), Email from Westpac, 16 June.

Dictionary of New Zealand Biography (2005), [Accessed 10 January, 2005] http://www.dnzb.govt.nz/.

Dierickx, I. & Cool. K. (1989), Asset stock and Accumulation and Sustainability, *Management Science*, n. 35, pp. 1504–11.

Dilnot, A. (1990), 'From Most to Least: new Figures on Wealth Distribution', *Australian Society*, July, pp. 14-17.

Donaldson, M. & Poynting, S. (2004), 'The Time of Their Lives: Time, Work and Leisure in the Daily Lives of Ruling Class Men', in Hollier, N. (ed.) *Ruling Australia: Power, Privilege and Politics of the New Ruling Class*, Melbourne, Victoria, Australian Scholarly Publishing.

Dowd, M. (2006), *Are Men Necessary? When Sexes Collide*, Sydney, Hodder.

Dyer, A. (2003), The 'Haves' Have More, *Business Review Weekly*, 22 May–18 June, pp. 30–1.

Easton, B. (1996), 'Philosophers, Kings and Public Intellectuals', *Auckland University Winter Lectures*, Auckland, Auckland University, Tuesday 20 August.

Easton, B. (2000), 'Sutch, William Ball 1907 – 1975' *Dictionary of New Zealand Biography*, v.5. (1941-1960), pp. 504-6.

Easton, B. (2004), 'Who's Hugh?' *Listener*, 17 November, p. 24.

Economic Terms [Accessed 20 January, 2006], http://www. louisville .edu /bmhzwo)1/econpage/ meanings. html

Elder, B. (1988), *Blood On the Wattle — Massacres and Maltreatment of Australian Aborigines since 1788*, Sydney, National Book Distributors.

Eldred-Grigg, S. (1997), *The Rich: A New Zealand History*, Auckland, Penguin Books.

Elkind, P. & McLean, B. (2003), *Smartest Guys in the Room: The Amazing Rise and Scandalous Fall of Enron*, New York, Portfolio Trade.

Emmison, M. & Baxter, J, Western, J. (1991), *Class Analysis and Contemporary Australia*, Melbourne, Macmillan.

EOWA (2004), Australian Census of Women Board Directors Australian Government Equal Opportunity for Women in the Workplace Agency, http://www.eowa.gov.au/information_centres/media_centre/media_releases/2004_austra lian_women_in_leadership_census/factsheet_board_dir.doc.

Epaminondas, G. (1996), 'Unsuitability, Why Corporate Australia is Getting Undressed', *The Weekend Australian Review*, 13-14 April, pp. 1–2.

Equity Investments (1966–7), Wellington, Berle Publications.

Erakovic, L. & Goel, S. (2004), 'Building Effective Board-Management Relations: Evidence and Prescriptions from New Zealand', *University of Auckland Business Review*, v.6, i.1, pp. 20–37.

Evans, R. (2006), pers com.

Evans, R. & Thorpe, W. (1992), 'Power Punishment and Convict Labour: Convict Workers and Moreton Bay, *Australian Historical Studies*, v. 25, n.98, April, pp. 91–103.

Evans, R. & Thorpe, W. (1998), 'Commanding Men: masculinities and the convict system', *Journal of Australian Studies*, n.56, p. 17.

Fennema, M. & Schijf, H. (1979), 'Analysing Interlocking Directorates: Theory and Method', *Social Networks*, v. 1. n. 1, pp. 297–332.

Fennema, M. (1982), *International Networks of Banks and Industry*. Boston, MA, Martinus Nijhoff.

Festinger, L. & S. Schachter, K. Back (1948), *Social Pressures in informal Groups*, Cambridge, Mass. MIT Press.

Finklestein, J. (1996), *After a Fashion*, Melbourne, Melbourne University Press.

Fligstein, N. & Brantley, P. (1992), 'Bank Control, Owner Control or Organizational Dynamics: Who Controls the Large Modern Corporation?' *American Journal of Sociology*, n. 98, pp. 280–307.

Foster, J. B (2004), 'The Commitment of an Intellectual: Paul M. Sweezy (1910–2004)', *Monthly Review*, Oct v.56, i.5, p. 4 (36).

Fouché, G. (2005), 'A Woman's place is ... on the Board', *The Guardian*, Wednesday 10 August, http://money.guardian.co.uk/work/story/0,1456,1546251,00.html

Fox, C. (2006), 'Family first, not every one wants to go it Alone. Many Women are Opting for the Companies Big enough to give them what they Want', *Financial Review Boss*, February, p. 54.

Fox, L. (1940), *Monopoly*, Sydney, Left Book Club.

Frances, R. (1994), 'The History of Female Prostitution in Australia', in Perkins, R. Prestage, G. Sharp, R. & Lovejoy, F. (ed.s) *Sex Workers and Sex Work in Australia*, Sydney, University of New South Wales Press.

Frankel, B. (1998), 'Elites', *Arena Magazine*, October, pp. 29–42, (1).

Freeman, C. (1984), *Long Waves in the World Economy*, London, Frances Pinter.

French, J. (2005), 'The Convict Death Fleet, Australia's second fleet — 1790', IFHAA *shipping Pages*, IFHAA', [Accessed 12 January, 2006], http://freepages.genealogy .rootsweb.co/~ifhaa/ifhaa/ships/2ndfleet.htm).

Friedman M. (1970), 'The Social Responsibility of Business is to Increase it Profits', *New York Times Magazine*, 13 September, 1970, reprinted in Donaldson T. and Werhane, P. (1983), *Ethical Issues in Business: A Philosophical Approach*, 2nd Edition, Englewood Cliffs, NJ, Prentice Hall.

Friedman, R. & Friedman, M. (1980), *Free to Choose: A Personal Statement*, New York, Harcourt Brace Jovanovich.

Friedman, R. & Friedman, M. (2005), *Free to Choose: Why I did it*, [Accessed 23 August, 2005] http://www.freetochoose.com/.

Gaines, M. & Endicott, C. (1994), 'Women Stymied by Sharp Salary Gender Gap', *Advertising Age*, v.65, n.51, p. S1 (2) December 5.

Galbraith. J. (1967), *The New Industrial State*, Boston, Houghton Mifflin.

Gardiner, A. (1998), Pers com.

Gaynor, B. (1999), 'Analysis: Filling foreigners' pockets', *New Zealand Herald* 2 October, p. C12.

George, S. (2005), *Another World is possible if....* New York, Verso.

George, S. (2005), *Interview*, TNI Home Page, p. 2. [Accessed 12 January, 2006] http://www.tni.org/interviews/booktalk.htm.

Gibson-Graham, G. (1994), 'Beyond Patriarchy and Capitalism: Reflections on Political *Subjectivity'* in B. *Caine and R. Pringle (eds.) Transitions New Australian* Feminisms, Sydney, Allen and Unwin.

Giddens, A. (2001), S*ociology*, Polity Press Cambridge.

Gilding, M. (1997), *Australian Families: A Comparative Perspective,* Melbourne, Addison Wesley Longman.

Gilding, M. (1999), 'Superwealth in Australia: Entrepreneurs Accumulation and the Capitalist Class', *Journal of Sociology*, v. 35, n. 2, pp. 169–71.

Gilding, M. (2002), *Secrets of the Super Rich, Pymble*, NSW, Harper Collins.

Glasberg, D. (1987), 'The Ties that Bind? Case Studies in the Significance of Corporate Board Interlocks with Financial Institutions', *Sociological Perspectives*, v. 30, n.1.

Goshal, S. & Bartlett, C. (1990), 'The Multinational Corporation as an Inter Organisational Network', *Academy of Management Review, v.*15, i.3, pp. 603–25.

Goward, P. (2002), 'Balancing Baby and the Budget', *The Age*, 12 December, p. 1.

Gramsci, A. (1971), *Selections from the Prison Notebooks*; International Publishers, New York, [Also Accessed on line 2 January] http://www. marxist. org archive/gramsci/editions/spn/state_civil/index.htm.

Granovetter, M. (1973), 'The Strength of Weak Ties', *American Journal of Sociology*, 78 (6), pp. 1360-80.

Granovetter, M. (1985), 'Economic Action and Social Structure: the Problem of Embeddedness', *American Journal of Sociology*, n. 91, pp. 481–510.

Granovetter, M. (2005), 'The Impact of Social Structure on Economic Outcomes', *Journal of Economic Perspectives*, 19, p. 33 (18).

Grattan, M. (1997), 'The Dirty Trail of a Think Tank Grant', *Australian Financial Review*, 21 April, pp. 25–31.

Grenfell, D. (2004), 'Getting the Government off our Backs? The Ruling Class and New Trends in the State's Management of Dissent', in N. Hollier *Ruling Australia: the Power, Privilege and Politics of the New Ruling Class,* Melbourne, Australian Scholarly Publishers, pp. 70–86.

Griffiths, P. (1999), 'Labor's Tortured Path to Protectionism*',* Labour History Conference, Wollongong, Department of Political Science, ANU.

Griffiths, P. (2005), *Understanding Australian history*, PHD Thesis, ANU, [Accessed online 25 July, 2005] http:/members.optsnet.com.au/~griff52/crisis-ah.html.

Grønmo, S. (1995a), 'Structural Change during Deregulation and Crisis; the Position of Banks in the Norwegian Intercorporate Network', *International Social Networks Conference* London, July.

Grønmo, S. (1995b), 'Assessing the Centrality of Banks in Intercorporate Networks, Research on Banking, Capital and Society', Report n. 63 Oslo: *Research Council of Norway.*

Hannan, E & Carney, S. (2005), 'Thinkers of Influence', *The Age,* 10 December [Accessed on line 15 March 2006] http:www.theage.com.au.

Harding, A. (2002), 'Towards Opportunity and Prosperity, Trends in Income and Wealth Inequality in Australia', *NATSEM,* Canberra, University of Canberra, p. 11.

Harvey, D. (2003), *The New Imperialism,* Oxford, Oxford University.

Heath, J. & Potter, A. (2005), 'Feminism for sale: find out the real reason the women's movement is losing momentum, and why political action is the only way to take down the patriarchy', *This Magazine,* May–June v.38, i.6, p.20 (8).

Henwood, D. (1997), *Wall Street,* London, Verso. Also in electronic form found at, http://www.leftbusinessobserver.com/WSDownload.html.

Herd, B. (1999), 'The Left's Failure to Counter Economic Rationalism in Australia: Classical Economists Legacy to Government, Bureaucracy, Think Tank and the Union Movement', to be submitted PHD, Griffith University.

Hickman, B. & Gunn, M. (2000), 'New Class Divide': Rich and Poor Women', *The Australian,* 21 June (4), 1.

Higley, J. & Deacon, D., Smart, D. (1979), *Elites in Australia,* Boston, Routledge.

Hilferding, R. (1981), *Finance Capital,* London, Routledge Keagan & Paul, [Originally published 1910].

Hollier, N. (2004), *Ruling Australia*: Power, *Privilege and Politics of the New Ruling Class,* Melbourne, Australian Scholarly Publishing.

Holmes a Court, J. (1995), Janet Homes A Court Interview with Don Argus, *Australian Financial Review Magazine* pp. 8–13.

Hooper, N. (2005), 'Money Makers at Full Throttle', *The Weekend Australian Financial Review,* 23-37 December, p. 17.

Hooper, N. (2006), 'Schubert's Restrained Melody', *The Weekend Financial Review,* 11-12 February, p. 22.

Howard, John (2002), MP, Prime Minister of Australia, November [Accessed 12 June, 2004] http://www.ceda.com.au/New/Flash/html/about_ceda.htm H.R. Nicholls Society Website, (2004), http://www.hrnicholls.com.au/work.html.

HR Nicholls Society (2004), website, http://www.hrnicholls.com.au/work.html.

Hughes, R. (1987), *The Fatal Shore: the History of the Transportation of Convicts to Australia, 1787–1868,* London, Vintage.

Hunt, G. (2003), *The Rich List, Wealth and Enterprise in New Zealand 1820–2003,* Birkenhead Auckland, Reed Publishers.

Hywood, G. (1997), 'BCA Needs New Energy', Editorial, *Australian Financial Review,* 13 February.

Illing, D. (1996), 'Intrepid Brown takes up Gauntlet', *The Australian,* Wednesday, 3 April, p. 14.

Jackson, S. (1995), 'Witch-Hunt', *The Australian,* 1-2 April, p. 1.

James, S. (1993), 'The Ideas Brokers: the Impact of Think Tanks on British Government', *Public Administrator,* v. 71, Winter, pp. 491–506.

Jesson, B. (1980), *The Fletcher Challenge, Wealth and Power in New Zealand*, Published by the author, South Auckland, P. O. Box 8.

Jesson, B. (1989), *Fragments of Labour, The Story Behind the Labour Government*, Auckland, Penguin.

Jesson, B. (1999), *Only their Purpose is Mad, Money Men take over New Zealand* Palmerston North, Dunmore Press.

Katz-Fishman, W. & Scott, J. (2005), 'Comments on Burawoy: a View from the Bottom Up', *Critical Sociology*, v. 31. pp. 371–74.

Kerr, R. (1990), 'The New Zealand Roundtable Roles and Goals', Auckland Rotary Club Speech', Auckland, 12 November.

Kerr, R. (1997a), 'Producer Board Acts Reform Brierley, Submission by the New Zealand Roundtable, April, [Accessed 20 December, 2005]. http://ww.nzbr. org.nz/ documents/ speeche...es-97/producer-boards-act.doc.htm.

Kerr, R. (1997b), *Seven Deadly Sins of the Twentieth Century*, New Zealand Post College of Business, Jubilee Lecture, Palmerston North, Massey University, 6 August.

Kerr, R. (1998), *The New Zealand Business Roundtable's View of Lobbying*, The 8th Annual Public Affairs and Lobbying Summit, Wellington, BCA, 18 March.

Kerr, R. (1999), *Cooperatives versus Corporates New Zealand Agribusiness and Food congress*, Christchurch.

Keynes, J. M. (1967), *The General Theory of Employment, Interest and Money*, [Originally pub. 1936], London, Macmillan.

Kirch, P. (2000), *On the Road of the Winds: An Archaeological History of the Pacific Islands before European Contact*, Los Angeles University of California Press, quoted in Adele L.H. Whyte; SJ. Marshall; G.K. Chambers (2005), 'Human Evolution in Polynesia' *Human Biology*, April v.77, i.2, p. 157(21).

Kontratieff, N. (1984), *The Long Wave*, New York, Richardson & Synder.

Korn Ferry International (1993), *Decade of the Executive Woman*, New York, Korn Ferry International.

Korten, D. (2001), *When Corporations Rule the World*, Bloomfield, Kummarian Press.

Kuhn, R. (1996), 'Class Analysis and the Left in Australian History', in R. Kuhn & T. O'Lincoln (ed.s) *Class and Class conflict in Australia*, Melbourne, Longman, pp. 145–62.

Lahey, K. (2005), *Chief Executive Women* [Accessed 26 December, 2005] http://www.cew. org.au/ index.cfm?apg=membership&bpg=profilemember&aid=46.

Langmore, D. (1949), The *Dictionary of Australian Biography* [Accessed 5 October, 2005] Angus and Robertson, Online http://gutenberg.net.au/dictbiog/0-dict-biogMc.html.

Larner, R. (1970), *Management Control and Large Corporations*, New York, Dunellen.

Latham, M. (2004), *Great Australian Schools*, Campaign, ALP Policy Paper.

Lavelle, A. (2001), Who Rules Australia? *Socialist Workers Review*, n. 4, May.

L'Estrange, N. (1996), in Carbon, D. (1996), 'Aiming for the Board', *The Courier Mail*, Saturday, 24 August, 1996, p. 1, s.1.

Le Guin, U. (1974), *The Dispossessed, an Ambiguous Utopia*, New York, Harper.

Lenin, V. (1964), *Imperialism the Highest Stage of Capitalism*, [Original pub. 1916], Collected Works, n. 22, v.45 Moscow, Progressive Publishers.

Li, C. & Wearing, B. (2004), 'Between Glass Ceilings: Female Non-executive Directors in UK quoted companies,' *International Journal of Disclosure and Governance*, October, v.1, i.4, p. 355(17).

Lind, M. (1996), *Up from Conservatism: why the Right is Wrong for America*, New York, Free Press.

Lineham, P. (2005), Department of Statistics Census of Population and Dwelling 1186, in *The Religious History of New Zealand*, [Accessed 5 July, 2005]. http://www. massey.ac .nz/.

Lindsay, G. (1996), 'Greg Lindsay Speaks Out about the Early CIS', interviewed by Andrew Norton, *Policy*, Winter & on the internet, http://www.cis.org.au/glint.htm.

Littler, D. (1998), 'Competitive Advantage' (ed.s) C. Cooper & C. Argyris et al, *The Concise Blackwell's Encyclopaedia of Management*, Oxford, Blackwells.

Lum, R. & Murray, G. (1988), *Centralisation in top New Zealand Business 1966–1986*, Department of Sociology, Auckland University.

Lynch, H. (2005), Chief Executive Women [Accessed 15 July, 2005]. http://www.cew.org. au/index.cfm?apg= membership&bpg=profilemember&aid=46.

Magdoff, H. (2003), *Capitalism as a World Economy* (Review of The Month) (Interview) by Huck Gutman. *Monthly Review*, September, v.55, i.4, p. 1 (13).

Maloney, S. (2005), Address to Scotch College, [Accessed 26 July, 2004] http://archives. econ.utah.edu/ archives/marxism/2004w35/msg00251.htm.

Malthus, T. (1798), *An Essay on the Principle of Population, as it affects the Future Improvement of Society, with Remarks on the Speculations of Mr Godwin, M. Condorcet and Other Writers*, London, J. Johnson.

Malthus, T. (1803), An Essay on the Principle of Population; or a View of its past and present Effects on Human Happiness; with an Inquiry into our Prospects respecting the Removal or Mitigation of the Evils which it occasions, 2 v.s, London, J. Johnson.

Managh, C (1989), 'Knights' driver Sticks to Issue', *Sunday Star*, 12 February, s. A, p. 11.

Management, (1998), 'Top 200 NZ Companies', December p. 76.

Management, (2004), 'Top 200 NZ Companies', December p. 62.

Mandel, E. (2005), *Karl Marx*, [Accessed online 15 July, 2005]. http://www.marxists. org/archive/mandel/ 19xx/marx/ch08.htm.

Mandel, E. (1972), *Late Capitalism*, London, New Left, Books.

Mandeville, B. (1988), *The Fable of the Bees; or, Private Vices, Publick Benefits*, 1714 reprinted Indianapolis, Liberty Fund.

Marsden, S. (1932), *The Letters and Journals of Samuel Marsden 1766–1838*, (ed) John Rawson Elder, Dunedin, Coulls Somerville Wilkie, AH Reed for the University of Otago University Council, pp. 325–26.

Marsh, I. (1994), The Development and Impact of Australia's 'Think Tanks', *Australian Journal of Management*, December, pp. 177–200.

Marshall, M. (1987), *Long Waves of Regional Development*, Houndsmile, Macmillan.

Marx, K. (1956), *Capital*, v.2 [1880] Moscow, Progress publishers.

Marx, K. (1959), *Capital,* v.3 [1863–1883], Moscow, Progress publishers.

Marx, K. (1969), *Theories of Surplus Value,* London, Lawrence and Wishardt.

Marx, K. & Engels, F. (1977), *The Communist Manifesto,* in the Collected works of Karl Marx and Fredrich Engels, Moscow, Progress Publishers.

Marx, K. (1971), *Contributions to the Critique of Political Economy,* London, Lawrence Wishart.

Marx, K. (1974), *Capital,* v 1–3, London, Penguin/New Left Review.

Marx, K. (1975), *Free Trade,* Karl Marx and Fredrick Engels, Collected Works, London, Lawrence and Wishart.

Marx, K. (1977), *German Ideology,* in *The Selected Works,* Moscow, Progress Publishers.

Marx, K. (1983), *Capital,* [1867] v. 1, Moscow, Progress Publishers.

Masterman-Smith, H. (2006), *Hidden Seeds: a Political Economy of Working Class Women in Campbelltown (NSW),* PHD, University of Western Sydney.

Mayne, S. (2004) 'Nick Greiner's Record number of Board Seats' *Crikey dot com,* 28 April [Accessed 1 January, 2006] http://www.crikey.com.au/articles/2004/04/28-0003.html.

McGregor, C. (1997), *Classes in Australia,* Ringwood, Victoria, Penguin.

Mele, P. (2005), 'Women Empowerment, a Catalyst', *Africa News Service,* 22 September, p. NA.

Melymuka K. (2000), 'Wanted: A workplace without a 'Ceiling', *Computerworld,* 24 January, p. 50 (1).

Michels, R. (1911), *Political Parties: a Sociological Study of the OligarchicalTendencies of Modern Democracy,* New York, Free Press.

Miliband, R. (1969), *The State in Capitalist Society,* London, Weidenfield & Nicholson.

Milne, G. (2006), 'Key Staff at AWB on Public Payroll', *Sunday Telegraph,* 5 February, p. 15.

Ministry of Children and Family Affairs Norway (2005), 'Rules Regarding Gender Balance within Boards of Public Limited Companies', Press release n. 05116, 8 December.

Ministry of Children's and Family Affairs (2005), 'Child Care institutions in Norway, Act no. 19 of 5 May, 1995 on Day Care Institutions with Regulations', (Day Care Institutions Act) [Accessed 4 July, 2005] http://odin.dep.no/bld/english/doc/ legislation /acts/004005-990082/dok-bn.html#1.

Mintz, B. & Schwartz, M. (1985), *The Power Structure of American Business,* Chicago, University of Chicago Press.

Mizruchi, M. (1982), *The American Corporate Network,* Beverly Hills, Sage.

Mizruchi, M. (1996), 'What Do Interlocks Do? An analysis, Critique and Assessment of Research on Interlocking Directorates', *Annual Review of Sociology,* v.22, pp. 271–302.

Mohan, N. & Ruggiero, J. (2003), 'Compensation differences between Male and Female CEOs for Publicly Traded Firms: A nonparametric analysis', *Journal of the Operational Research Society* December, v.54, i.12, pp. 1242 (7).

Moore, M. (2001), *Stupid White Men,* New York, Harper Collins.

Moran, A. (1990), 'Writing non-fiction: An interview with E.L. Wheelwright', *The Australia Journal of Media and Culture,* v. 4, n. 1, p.1.

Moran, S. (2006), 'Rude Awakening for Female Bankers', *The Australian Financial Review*, Friday, 10 February, p. 80.

Morgan, H. (2004), 'BCA President, Statement on the Federal Election', 10 October, http://www.bca.com.au/content.asp?newsID=96793.

Mørkhagen, P.L. (2005), 'The Position of Women in Norway' Ministry of Foreign Affairs http://odin.dep.no/odin/engelsk/norway/social/032091-991525/index-dok000-b-n-a.html.

Mosca, G. (1896), *The Ruling Class*, New York, McGraw Hill.

Mourell, M. (2005), pers com 10 May.

Mun, T. (1929), *England's Treasure by Forraign Trade,* [Original pub. 1630] in Rubin, I. *A History of Economic Thought*, New York, Pluto Press.

Murray, G. (1990), *New Zealand Corporate Capitalism*, PhD, Thesis, University of Auckland.

Murray, G. (1993–1996), *Economic Power in Australia*, ARC Funded Interviews.

Murray, G. (2001), 'Interlocking Directorates: What do they tell us about Corporate Power in Australia?' *Journal of Australian Political Economy*, June, n. 47, pp. 5–27.

Murray, G. (2003), 'New Zealand Women Lawyers at the End of the Twentieth century in New Zealand', (ed.s) Grisela Shaw and Ulrike Schultz, in *A Challenge to Law and Lawyers: Women in the Legal Profession*, Oxford, Hart Publishing.

Natapoff. S. (2004), 'Rogue Whale: Seventy Years after FDR, JP Morgan finally got its revenge against banking regulations with its Chase Merger. But a new FDR is watching', *The American Prospect,* March v.15, i.3, p. 16 (2).

National Archives http://www.catalogue.nationalarchives.gov.uk/RdLeaflet.asp?sLeaflet ID=347&j=1.

National Business Review Rich List (1996), www:/nbr.co.nz/.

National Business Review Rich List (1997), www:/nbr.co.nz/.

National Business Review Rich List (1998), www:/nbr.co.nz/.

National Business Review Rich List (2002), www:/nbr.co.nz/.

National Business Review Rich List (2004), www:/nbr.co.nz/.

New Zealand Business Who's Who (1987), Christ Church, Printpac, Fourth estate.

New Zealand Census (2001), Statistics New Zealand.

New Zealand Council of Trade Unions [NZCTU] (1999), *A Trade Unionists Guide to the New Zealand Business Roundtable*, ISBN 0-09011-17-6, June.

New Zealand Official Yearbook (2002), Auckland, Statistics New Zealand.

New Zealand Official Yearbook (2004), Auckland, Statistics New Zealand.

New Zealand Herald (2005), 'Executives are Raking in the Cash', *New Zealand Herald*, 9 January, C1.

New Zealand Herald (2005), 'PPCS posts $17.46m half-year profit' 28 March [Accessed online 12 December, 2005] http://www.nzherald.co.nz/organisation/story.cfm?o_id=176&objectid=10122756.

Nicholls, K. (2005), 'Women in the boardroom', *Business Sunday Nine MSM* Saturday, 17 September, 2005 http://businesssunday.ninemsn.com.au/article.aspx?id=63145.

Ninness, G. (1992), 'Round the Table: the New Zealand Business Roundtable and Who are They?' *Sunday Star*, 1 March, pp. D. 1/3.

Nira World Directory of Think Tanks (1996), http://www.nira.go.jp/ice/tt-info/nwdtt96/1050.html.

North, D. (1691), *Discourses upon Trade,* quoted in Rubin, I. (1929), *A History of Economic Thought,* New York, Pluto Press.

Northy, J. (1981), *Introduction to Law,* 9th Edition, Wellington, Butterworths.

Nursing Standard (2005), 'Privatisation would impede learning (character for change)' n.20.v.8, 2 November.

O'Hara, P. (2005), *Growth and Development in the Global Political Economy: Social Structures of Accumulation and Modes of Regulation,* New York, Routledge.

O'Lincoln, T. (2005), 'The Most Outrageous Conduct, Convict Rebellions', *Marxist Interventions,* http://www.anu.edu.au/polsci/marx/interventions/convicts.htm.

O'Lincoln, T. (1996), 'Wealth, Ownership and Power, the Ruling Class', (ed.s) R. Kuhn & O'Lincoln, T. *Class and Class Conflict in Australia,* Melbourne, Longmans.

Oliver, D. (2005), *Australia's Finest Golf Courses,* http://www.ausgolf.com.au/ellerston.htm

Oxley, D. (1996), *Convict Maids: The forced migration of women to Australia,* Sydney, Cambridge University Press.

Oxley, D. (2004) 'Data from Convict Maids', *International Centre for Convict Studies,* [Accessed 12 July, 2005] http://iccs.arts.utas.edu.au/data/convictmaids.html#9.

Page, B. (2003), *The Murdoch Archipeligo*, London, Simon & Schuster.

Pareto, V. (1973), *Mind and Society*, London, Dover.

Paul, A. & Southgate, D. McCrane, D, Widdowssons, S. (1987), 'The Compensation of Food', *MRC Special Report* 297.

Peetz, D. (2005a), 'Coming soon to a Workplace near you — the New Industrial Relations Revolution', *Australian Bulletin of Labour* June, v.31, i.2, p. 90 (22).

Peetz, D. (2006), *Brave New Workplace*, Sydney, Allen and Unwin.

Penberthy, J. (1996), 'Absent Friends Knock Nervously on Howard's door', *Australian Financial Review,* 18 March, pp. 1/14.

Pha, A. (2001), 'Hands off ambulance services', *The Guardian,* 22 August, 2001, http://www.cpa.org.au/garchve4/1059amb.html.

Piercy, M. (1979), *Woman on the Edge of Time*, London, Women's Press Ltd.

Pilger, J. (2004), *Tell me no Lies Investigative Journalism and its Triumphs*, Jonathan Cape, London.

Pilger, J. (2002), 'Journalism in Australia has a courageous history, but Murdochism has turned it into a disgrace' 21 February, http://pilger.carlton.com/print/97358.

Plowman, D. (2005), 'Protection and Labour regulation' [Accessed 28 December, 2005] http://www.hrnicholls.com.au/nicholls/nichvo13/vol134pr.htm.

Pocock, B. (1988), *Demanding Skill: Women and Technical Education in Australia,* Allen & Sydney.

Pocock, B. & Alexander, M. (1999), 'The Gender Pay Gap in Australia: An overview of Literature and new Evidence.' *Labour & Industry,* v. 10, n. 2, pp. 75–100.

Pomeroy, A. (2004), Public Affairs Report July 2004 [ann.pomeroy001@msd.govt.nz]

Polwhele, R. (1798), *The Unsexed Females*, London, Cadwell and Davis.

Porter, M. (1985), *Competitive Advantage: Creating and Sustaining Superior Performance*, New York, The Free Press.

Porter, M. (1986), *Competition in Global Industries*, Boston, Harvard Business School Press.

Porter, M. (1990), *The Competitive Advantage of Nations*, London, Mcmillan.

Poulantzas, N. (1972), 'The Problems of the Capitalist State' (in) R. Blackburn (ed.) *Ideology and Social Science*, New York, Random Press.

Pringle, R. (1988), *Secretaries Talk: Sexuality, Power and Work*, Sydney, Allen and Unwin.

Probert, B. (2001), 'Class in the year 2001', *Australian Rationalist*, n. 56, pp. 1–14,

Pusey, M. (1991), *Economic Rationalism in Australia*, Cambridge University Press, London.

Quesnay, F. (1929), *Analyse du Tableau Economique*, [Original published 1766], in Rubin, I. *A History of Economic Thought*, New York, Pluto Press.

Ralph, J. (2004), *CBA Annual Report*, http://shareholders.commbank.com.au/GAC_File_Metafile/0,1687,2378%255Fcba%255 Ffullar%255F2002,00.pdf.

Ratcliffe, R. (1980), 'Banks and Corporate Lending: An Analysis of the Impact of the Capitalist Class Lending Behaviour of Banks', *American Sociological Review*, v. 45, pp. 553–70.

Rawling, J.N (1937), *Who Owns Australia?* Sydney, Modern Publishers.

Reich, R. (1991), *The Work of Nations, Preparing Ourselves for the 21st Century Capitalism*, New York, Alfred Knopf.

Reid, I. quoted in Kerr, R. (1999a), Cooperatives versus Corporates New Zealand agribusiness and food congress, Christchurch, p. 3.

Reynolds, H. (1987), *The Law of the Land*, Ringwood, Victoria, Penguin.

Reynolds, H. (1982), *The Other side of the Frontier*, Victoria, Penguin.

Ricardo, D. (1957), *On the Principles of Political Economy and Taxation*, [Original published 1817] London, Dent.

Robinson, K. (2002), 'Kim Stanley Robinson, Science Fiction Socialist', *Monthly Review*, July–August, v.54, i.3, p. 87(4).

Robinson, S. (1998),'Calling Home: As Globalization erases National Borders, Control of the New Zealand Economy is Shifting Across the Tasman', *Time International*, 9 November, pp. 58–60.

Root Quality Pty Ltd v Root Control Technologies Pty Ltd (2000) 177 ALR 231, 49 IPR 225, AIPC 37,826 (91–594), [2000] FCA 980.

Rosenberg, B. & Kelsey, J. (1999), 'The Privatisation of New Zealand's Electricity Services', prepared for *International Seminar on the Impact of privatization of the electricity sector at the global level*, 20 September, Mexico City.

Royal Melbourne Golf Club Website [Accessed 2 January, 2006] http://www. Royal melbourne.com.au/.

Rubin, I. (1929), *A History of Economic Thought*, New York, Pluto Press.

Rubinstein, W. (2004), *The All-time Australian 200 Rich list from Samuel Terry 'the Convict Rothchild' to Kerry Packer*, in Association with *BRW*, Crows Nest, Allen and Unwin.

Samuelson, P. (1969), 'The Way of the Economist' in P. Samuelson, (ed.) *International Economic Relations: Proceedings of the Third Congress of the International Economic Association*, pp. 1–11, Macmillan, London.

Saunders, K. & Evans, R. (1992), *Gender Reflections in Australia, Domination and Negotiations*, Sydney, Harcourt Brace.

SBS Australian Almanac 2000, (2000), South Yarra, Hardie Grant Books.

Schubert, J. (2005), 'Let's make Australia great: Business Council of Australia' *Business Council of Australia* http://www.bca.com.au/content.asp?staticID=search.

Schumpeter, J. (1934), *Theory of Economic Development*, Cambridge, Harvard University Press.

Scott, J. (1985), 'Theoretical Frameworks and Research Design', (in) Scott *et al Networks of Corporate Power*, pp. 1–19, Cambridge, Polity Press.

Scott, J. (1991), *Who Rules Britain?* Oxford, Polity Press.

Scott, J. (1996), *Corporate Business and Capitalist Classes*, Oxford, Oxford University Press.

Scott, J. & Hughes, P. (1976), 'Ownership and Control in a Satellite Economy', A discussion from Scottish Data, *Sociology* v.10.

Scott, J. & Griff, C. (1983), *Directors of Industry: The British Corporate Network, 1904–1976,* Cambridge, Polity Press.

Sharkey, L. (1957), S*ocialism in Australia: A Communist view on Democratic Socialism*, Sydney, Current Book Distributors.

Shields, J. & O'Donnell, M., O'Brien, J. (2003), *The Buck Stops Here: Private sector Executive Remuneration in Australia*, A Report prepared for the Labor Council of New South Wales, pp. 1–57.

Shirley Trust Company Limited, [Accessed at 4 July, 2005] http://www.shirleytrust.com/Resources/ trust.ap.article.htm.

Simpson, D. (2005), 'Why Tougher Laws won't make Corporates more Responsible' Dell, http://www.onlineopinion.com.au/view.asp?article=2903.

Sinclair, A. (1994), *Trials at the Top, Chief Executives talk about Men, Women and The Australian Executive Culture*, Parkview, University of Melbourne Press.

Smith, A. (1910), *An Inquiry into the Nature and Causes of the Wealth of Nations*, [original pub. London, J. Dent, 1776].

Smith, J.A. (1991), *The Idea Brokers: Think Tanks and the Rise of the New Policy Elite,* New York, Free Press.

Soros, G. (2002), *On Globalisation*, New York, Public Affairs.

Statistics New Zealand, (1999), *Income,* [Accessed 25 November, 2005]. http://www.stats.govt.nz/products-and-services/Articles/income-distrib May99.htm?print=Y.

St Clair, J. (2004), 'Teresa Heinz Kerry Gets Lay' *Counterpunch*', 4 October. [Accessed 20 January, 2006] http://www.counterpunch.org/stclair10272004.html.

Stevens, L. (1988), *New Zealand Herald*, 4 August, section 3, p. 3.

Stiglitz, J. (2002), *Globalisation and its Discontents*, New York, W. W. Norton.

Still, L. (1993), *Where to From Here? The Managerial Woman in Transition*, Sydney, Business & Professional Publishing.

Still, L. (1997), 'Glass Ceilings and Sticky Floors: Barriers to the Careers to Women in the Finance Industry' Westpac and Human Rights Commission Report.

Stilwell, F. (2002), *Political Economy, the Contest of Economic Ideas*, Melbourne, Oxford Press.

Stilwell, F. & Ansari, M. (2003), 'Wealthy Australians, Economic Notes', *Journal of Australian Political Economy*, December, Issue 52.

Stokman, F. & Zeigler, R, Scott, J. (1985), *Networks of Corporate Power*, Cambridge, Polity Press.

Stone, D. (1996a), From the Margins of Politics, *Western European Politics*, v. 19, n. 4, October, pp. 676–92.

Stone, D. (1996b), Capturing the Political Imagination: Think tanks and the Policy Process, London, Frank Cass.

Summers, A. (1975), *Damned Whores and God's police: the colonisation of women in Ringwood*, Australia, Penguin.

Summers, A. (2003), *The End of Equality: Work, Babies and Women's Choices in 21st Century* Australia, Sydney, Random House.

Sutch, W. B. (1966), *Poverty and Progress: A Re-assessment*, Wellington, A.H. & A.W. Reed.

Sutch, W. B. (1973), *Takeover New Zealand*, Wellington, A.H. & A.W Reed.

Sweezy, P. (1998), 'The Communist Manifesto' Today', *Monthly Review*, May, v.50, n.1, p. 8.

Tapp, E. (1990) 'John Jones' *Dictionary of New Zealand Biography*, [up dated 7 July 2005] URL http/www.dnzb.govt.nz/.

Tasman Institute Homepage [Accessed 29 December, 2005] http://www.tasman.com.au/about.htm#amy.

Te Ara Encyclopædia of New Zealand [Accessed 23 January, 2006], http://www.teara.govt.nz/.

The Age (2005), 'Thinkers of Influence', 10 December, [Accessed 29 December, 2005] http:// www.theage.com.au/news/national/thinkers-of-influence/2005/ 12/09/ 1134086 810518 .html.

The New Citizen (1997), January/February/March, p. 9.

Thomsen-Moore, L. (2005), 'Katie Lahey's Passion for Business', *Management Today*, July, p. 3.

Thomson, P. & Graham, J. (2006), *A Woman's Place is in the Boardroom*, London, Palgrave Macmillan.

Thornton, M. (2002), 'Sexual Harassment Losing Sight of Sex Discrimination', *Melbourne University Law Review*, August v 26, i.2, p. 422 (23).

Todd, T. & Eveline, J. (2006), 'Gender Pay Equity: It's Time (Or Is It?)' [Accessed 1 January, 2006), http://www.lmsf.mq.edu.au/wmer/papers/trishtodd.pdf.

Toohey, B. (2006), 'Licence to Print Money; *The Weekend Australian Financial Review*, 2 January, p. 16.

Topp, A. & James, T., Nichols, p. (2004), 'To Whom do Directors' Duties Apply?' [Accessed 1 December, 2005), http://www.findlaw.com.au/articles/default.asp? task= read &id=11714&site=LE.

Useem, M. (1984), *The Inner Circle: Large corporations and the rise of business political activity in the US and the UK,* New York, Oxford University Press.

van der Pijl, K. (1998), *Transnational Classes and International Relations,* London & New York, Routledge.

Vaughan, G. (2005), 'One man 97 jobs no problem: governance the busiest directors oppose any limits', Monday 27 December, C1.

Victorian Government, (2006), *Metropolitan Ambulance Service: Contractual and Outsourcing Practices* [Accessed 16 January] http://www.audit.vic.gov.au/ old/ sr49/ ags4901.htm.

Ville, S. & Fleming, G. (1999), 'Locating Australian Corporate Memory', *Business History Review,* Summer, v.73, i.2, p. 256 (9).

Von Hayek, F. (1944), *The Road to Serfdom,* Chicago, The University of Chicago Press.

Walker, I. (2004), *Psychopaths in Suits,* Background Briefing Sundays at 9.10am, repeated Tuesdays at 7.10pm Sunday, 18 July.

Walsh, R. (2006), 'The Bully and the Charmer', *The Weekend Australian Financial Review,* 2 January, p. 18.

Warder M. (1994), 'The role of think-tanks in shaping public policy; our society is well served by thinkers,' *Vital Speeches of the Day,* 1 May, v.60, n.14, p. 434(4).

Weber, M. (1968), *Economy and Society,* (ed.s) G. Roth & C. Wittich, 1922 New York, Free Press.

Wheelwright, E.L. & Miskelly, J. (1967), *Anatomy of Australian Manufacturing Industry,* Sydney, Sydney Law Book Company.

Wheen, F. (2005), 'Why Marx is Man of the Moment: He had Globalization Sussed 150 years ago', *Observer,* London: Fourth Estate, Sunday, 17 July, p. 5.

Whitehouse, G. (2004), *Pay Equity — 20 years of change and continuity* School of Political Science and International Studies, University of Queensland, Human Rights and Equal Opportunity Commission. webfeedback@humanrights.gov.au.

Who's Who in Business in Australia, (2006), Information Australia, Melbourne http://www. cserver.com.au/wholive/.

Whyman, P. (2004), 'An analysis of Wage-Earner Funds in Sweden: Distinguishing Myth from Reality' *Economic and Industrial Democracy,* v. 25, n. 3, pp. 411–45.

Williams, P. & Ellis, S. (1994), 'Dawkins Kisses and Tells all on the BCA', *Australian Financial Review,* 15 July, Friday, pp. 1/18.

Wishart, I. (1995), *The Paradise Conspiracy,* Wellington, Kowhai Gold Books.

Wolf, N. (1990), *The Beauty Myth,* London, Chatto & Windus, Vintage.

Wolfe, T. (1987), *Bonfires of the Vanities,* New York, Farrar, Straus & Giroux.

Women on Boards of Britain's Top 200 Companies (1997), Publication of the Opportunity 2000 Campaign.

Worpole, K. (1998), 'Think-Tanks, Consultancies and Urban Policy in the UK', *International Journal of Urban and Regional Research*, v. 22, n. 1, pp. 147–55.

Wright, E. O. (1997), 'Exploitation' [Accessed 18 January, 2006] http://www.The globalsite.ac.uk/press/105wright.htm.

Wright Mills. C. (1956), *The Power Elite*, New York, Oxford University Press.

Zysman, J. & Tyson, L. (1983), *American Industry in International Competition: Government Policies and Corporate Strategies*, (ed.s) Ithaca, Cornell University Press.

Index